Anxiety Disorders

The Go-To Guide for Clients and Therapists

Anxiety Disorders

The Go-To Guide for Clients and Therapists

CAROLYN DAITCH

W.W. NORTON & COMPANY

NEW YORK • LONDON

Copyright © 2011 by Carolyn Daitch

All rights reserved
Printed in the United States of America
First Edition

For information about permission to reproduce selections from this book, write to:
Permissions, W. W. Norton & Company, Inc.
500 Fifth Avenue, New York, NY 10110

For information about special discounts for bulk purchases, please contact
W. W. Norton Special Sales at specialsales@wwnorton.com or 800-233-4830

Manufacturing by Sterling Pierce
Book design by Gilda Hannah
Production manager: Leeann Graham

Library of Congress Cataloging-in-Publication Data

Daitch, Carolyn.
Anxiety disorders : the go-to guide for clients and therapists /
Carolyn Daitch. — 1st ed.
      p. cm. — (A Norton professional book)
Includes bibliographical references and index.
ISBN 978-0-393-70628-4 (pbk.)
1. Anxiety disorders—Treatment. I. Title.
RC531.D353 2011
616.85'22—dc22   2010044308

ISBN: 978-0-393-70628-4 (pbk.)

W. W. Norton & Company, Inc, 500 Fifth Avenue, New York, N.Y. 10110
                        www.wwnorton.com

W. W. Norton & Company Ltd., Castle House, 75/76 Wells Street, London W1T 3QT

2 3 4 5 6 7 8 9 0

This book is dedicated to my clients,
whose courage and perseverance have
taught me so much.

Contents

Acknowledgments

I am deeply grateful to Lissah Lorberbaum, my graduate assistant, for her tireless efforts, invaluable support, outstanding research skills, collaboration, and unwavering goodwill. The psychology profession will be enriched with a recruit as gifted as Lissah. This project benefited tremendously from Cindy Barrilleaux's astute editorial judgment, feedback, suggestions, and encouragement. Working with her was a pure delight. I want to thank my editor at W. W. Norton, Deborah Malmud, for her invaluable input and her confidence in my work. I am indeed fortunate to have had these three extraordinarily talented women on my writing team.

I also want to acknowledge, for their generosity and speedy responses, the colleagues I called on to check the accuracy of certain sections of this book: Dr. Seema Kumar and Patrick Dennis, RPh for their feedback on medications; Dr. Richard Dombrowski, Dr. D. Corydon Hammond, and Mary St. Clair, MSW on neurofeedback; Dr. Zona Scheiner on EMDR; Dr. Assen Alladin on cognitive therapy; Julie Lusk, MSW, on yoga; Dr. Arreed Barabasz on hypnosis; Julie Hamilton, MSW, on ACT; and Toby Steinberger, JD, for her insights on courtroom stressors. Likewise, I would like to express my appreciation to: Drs. Catherine Herzog, Gail Berkove, and Jonathan Falk as well as Barbara Bokram, APRN, BC, and Judith Schmidt, JD for their support and feedback. Also, special thanks to David Frost for his help compiling the references, and to Vani Kannan and Marisa Dobson at W. W. Norton for making sure no detail was overlooked.

As always, my trusted assistant, Cathy Hirsch, my unconditionally patient husband, Russ Graham, and my cheerleading son, Daniel Rubin create my solid support circle. Without them catching the balls that almost drop in the juggling act of my life, this project would have been nearly impossible.

Anxiety Disorders

The Go-To Guide for
Clients and Therapists

Introduction

"**W**ould you mind telling them I'll be right back if they call my name?" the tall blonde woman in her mid-forties said in a hushed voice to a fellow client in the waiting room. Just moments later, when I came out to the waiting room to greet her, Mary Beth was nowhere to be seen. After waiting about 10 minutes I went to check the women's restroom. No Mary Beth. Then I checked the parking lot. Not a single person was sitting in a car. I went back into my office and called the cell phone number she had written on her intake form.

I was relieved when after only a few rings Mary Beth picked up my call. "I'm sorry," a timid voice on the other end of the line began. "I just got so nervous sitting there in the waiting room. Something came over me and I just had to get out of there. There was no way I could stay," Mary Beth continued. "Thanks so much for your time, though, and sorry for any inconvenience I might have caused you." It sounded like she was about to hang up the phone.

"Where are you now?" I asked.

"I'm in my car. I'm just a few minutes away from getting back to my home."

From the sound of it, Mary Beth had no intention of coming back to my office to begin therapy. She had managed to make the initial phone call to me and to come in for a first appointment, but the fear of beginning therapy was too great: Mary Beth left my office before we had even had a chance to talk.

While the majority of the clients I see come to me because they are struggling with some type of anxiety, the thought of entering into therapy can be anxiety provoking in its own right. First of all, as you enter into therapy you are encountering a new situation. You are beginning a working relationship with someone (the therapist) you most likely have never met before. Especially if you've never tried therapy before, you have no road map that will tell you in advance the direction this new relationship will take and how your therapy will eventually work out.

Second, by its very nature, in therapy you are sitting in the "hot seat." All the attention is focused on you. And the attention is not just focused on your strengths (although identifying and enhancing your strengths is a vital component of your treatment). If you come into therapy because you are overwhelmed by the anxiety you experience and want help, you will need to admit and convey some of your greatest struggles to your therapist. For many of my clients, this process can be accompanied by feelings of shame, embarrassment, and even a sense of defeat. All these factors can coalesce to make entering into therapy seem like an intimidating and daunting task. This was initially the case for Mary Beth. Yet as the British statesman and philosopher Edmund Burke once said, "Nobody made a greater mistake than he who did nothing because he could do only a little." It takes courage to begin therapy. With a little coaxing, that's exactly what Mary Beth agreed to do.

In a firm but caring voice I said to her over the phone: "You need to turn the car around and come back *now*. I can't see you this hour, but I have a break at 2:00. How far away are you now from my office?"

"Umm . . . about 30 minutes," Mary Beth replied.

"You'll probably get here about 20 minutes early, so you can go browse in the book store that's down the street if you'd rather not sit that whole time in the waiting room."

"You want me to turn around *now*? I'm almost home."

"Yes. Just take the next U-turn and reverse your direction. You were so close to walking in the door of my office. Don't stop now, when you're so close to getting the help that you need."

Mary Beth did turn the car around, and this time when she came to my office, she made it past the waiting room. She also made it through our hour-long session, during which we discovered that she was indeed suffering from an anxiety disorder. Mary Beth had been suffering from panic disorder since she was in college. She agreed to begin seeing me for weekly sessions.

The next week at Mary Beth's appointment time, I opened my office door to find her situated calmly. I smiled at her, yet as her glance met mine, she appeared a little surprised. As soon as we were both in my office I inquired as to the thoughts that lay behind her expression.

"It's funny," she said with a slight chuckle. "Last week I was so nervous to be here—even the second time around. My heart was pounding. My hands were shaking. And when you opened the door, I thought you were really tall. I kept thinking that during the whole session. You seemed huge. It definitely felt like you were taller than me. This week, well . . . I'll just say I don't think that's the case."

At this point I should say that even when I wear platform heels, I'm not quite five feet tall. Mary Beth was almost a foot taller than me, yet during our first meeting she felt that I literally loomed over her. This is the nature of anxiety disorders: our fears can distort our perceptions, making our challenges seem larger and more intimidating than they really are. In later sessions, Mary Beth would refer to this first session with a chuckle, recalling that she initially made a giant out of a woman who shops in the petite department of clothing stores. The fears that fuel anxiety disorders subside when we learn to face and challenge them. You will find the ingredients necessary to do just that within this book.

The Intended Audience for This Book

I wrote this book for both the people who suffer from anxiety disorders and the therapists who treat them. My philosophy of therapy influenced this decision. Fundamental to my treatment approach is the principle that clients benefit most when they are active participants in their therapy. That means that not only do their therapists need to be knowledgeable about anxiety disorders, the clients do too. Both clients and therapists need to possess an understanding of the tools and techniques that, together, they plan to use. While it is up to the therapist to bring a knowledge of intervention techniques and treatment options, the client's voice is an immeasurably important component in creating an integrative treatment plan. It is important that both participate actively in this process.

So my challenge was to create a book that would interest and inform both of you: client and therapist. Trying to address the needs of both groups was daunting, in part because I didn't have any models. Psychotherapy books tend to be written either for clients (as self-help manuals) or for clinicians. But there are limitations to that approach. While books for therapists might present comprehensive lists of symptom clusters and delineate treatment protocols, they don't necessarily provide a vivid understanding of what it *feels* like for the client to live with an anxiety disorder, or what it feels like to progress through treatment. On the other hand, self-help books for clients may give some techniques and encouragement, but they usually don't explain the psychology behind their symptoms or the techniques for recovery. In *The Go-To Guide,* both therapists and clients will learn about various treatment modalities and therapeutic interventions. It is my hope that in this way, both the anxiety disorders and the treatments that we learn about will have a pulse.

My next challenge was to decide who—therapist or client—would be the primary audience. In my first book, *Affect Regulation Toolbox,* I addressed the psychotherapist as the primary audience. But many of my colleagues told me that after they read it, they recommended it to their clients because they found that the tools were also useful guides for their clients' at-home practice. Given this feedback, I decided that my primary audience for this book would be the client. So typically the "you" in the book refers to you, the client. Material that is of particular interest to the therapist is set apart in boxes within each chapter. This includes more technical information, such as references to research studies and recommendations to facilitate therapeutic protocols. However, my belief is that the entire book could benefit both clients and therapists.

How the Book Is Arranged

The material in the book is presented through a wide-angle lens at first; with each chapter, the focus gets more finely tuned. Chapter 1 provides an overview of anxiety disorders, discussing the prevalence of anxiety and introducing you to the anxiety disorders that we will be covering. Chapter 2 explains the causes of anxiety disorders, looking at the impact of genetics, perinatal and early childhood experience, and issues of attachment. Chapter 3 provides an overview of the different interventions commonly used to treat anxiety disorders, ranging from cognitive therapy to hypnosis and mindfulness-based modalities. Chapter 4 presents relaxation techniques that can be used by anyone, with or without a therapist, to reduce stress and promote well-being. Chapters 5–9 explore in depth each of the anxiety disorders: generalized anxiety disorder, panic disorder, specific phobias, social anxiety disorder, and obsessive–compulsive disorder. Clearcut explanations of each disorder are presented, along with vivid stories of clients with the disorder as they go through treatment. The chapters include detailed instructions for a range of treatment interventions, and end with the recovery stories of the clients described earlier.

The next section of the *Go-To-Guide* focuses on adjunctive approaches that can enhance your recovery process. Chapter 10 gives you a storehouse of information about medications and herbal or *neutraceutical* approaches. Chapter 11 highlights the benefits of incorporating a healthy lifestyle into your recovery program and provides cutting-edge information on diet and exercise. In Chapter 12, I discuss the critical importance of consistent at-home practice, outside the therapy room, to maintain the benefits of therapy. A large section of this chapter is addressed to therapists and provides specific strategies to help clients engage in homework assignments. One category of anxiety disorders is not addressed in this book: post-traumatic stress disorder (PTSD). PTSD is an anxiety disorder that can develop after exposure to a traumatic event. I decided that a thorough examination of such a complex disorder as PTSD would merit a whole book of its own. (Please see the Appendix for some suggested resources.) However, many of the techniques suggested in this guide are applicable and helpful to clients with PTSD and therapists treating them. Regardless of the particular anxiety disorder, *The Go-To Guide* demonstrates that recovery is possible and it doesn't take years!

How to Use the Book

If you suffer from an anxiety disorder, it might be tempting to jump immediately to the chapter that pertains to your disorder, and then close the book. I encourage you to first read about anxiety disorders, their causes, and the range of treatment approaches available. Next I recommend that everyone who reads this book, therapist and client alike, try out the relaxation exercises in Chapter 4. *Then* read the chapter about your disorder. However, don't stop there. Some of the treatments described in the other chapters might be easily adapted, by you and your therapist, to your particular situation.

If you are a clinician working with clients who have anxiety disorders, my advice is similar. One or two chapters on specific anxiety disorders may be of particular interest to you. However, other chapters included have treatment ideas that may expand your repertoire or be exactly what's needed for a particular client. One of the most important suggestions I can make to you as you read through this book is to keep an open mind. Some of the modalities included might be new, or relatively new to you. I hope that this book will serve as a launching pad that might prompt you to explore other modalities.

With *The Go-To Guide* in hand, you will have a basis for understanding both your particular anxiety disorder and the reasons that anxiety disorders develop in the first place. With this foundation set, you can then get an idea of what treatment options are available and you and your therapist can collaborate in the creation of a treatment plan that best fits your needs. The strength of many of the treatments for the disorders addressed in this book lies not in one modality's singular approach or quick fix, but rather in the combination of interventions pulling from an array of different types of therapies.

My experience with my fellow therapists is that they are steadfastly interested in learning the best treatment approaches out there, and are tirelessly looking for new strategies to help their clients. If you are a clinician, as you read this book I hope you find a compendium of effective treatment approaches and healing opportunities that will facilitate your work with the many people who sit before you who suffer from anxiety. If you are someone with an anxiety disorder who has picked up this book, I'm guessing that you are searching for a change. It is my hope that you are ready to embark upon a journey of recovery and transformation. The seeds for this change are contained within the pages of this book, and there is no time like the present to begin this journey. As Mother Theresa says, "Yesterday is gone. Tomorrow has not yet come. We have only today. Let us begin."

CHAPTER 1

Getting Started

I could see tomorrow's headline: "Anxiety Expert Bolts from Newsroom, Too Stressed to Give Interview." It almost came true. Nearly 20 years ago, I was contacted by a local news network. The winter holidays were approaching, and the network was hoping to do a segment on stress and the holiday season for their 12 P.M. news hour. Since I specialized in treating stress- and anxiety-related conditions, the station gave me a call. At first I was intrigued and flattered by the prospect of participating in a live newscast. Sharing tips for managing stress and anxiety with the general public seemed not only meaningful, but exciting. I've never been stage shy—on the contrary, I have always enjoyed public speaking. I didn't give the possibility of stage fright or performance jitters a moment's thought when I eagerly accepted the invitation.

Fast-forward one month. I was sitting just to the left of the anchorman, my hair, makeup, and stress-management tips ready to go for the live broadcast. Just three minutes remained until the anchorman would segue to the holiday stress segment, and the camera would pan over to me. I was energized and collected. In only a matter of seconds that drastically changed.

When I shifted my glance from the anchorman to the camera, a spotlight caught my eye. It was as if the heat from the light flooded directly into my face. Startled, I glanced at my watch. Not enough time to step out of the light and cool down before it would be my turn to talk. I would have to stay in my spot. I started to take a deep breath, but it was interrupted by a swift thud from deep within my chest. And then another. And another. After what seemed like an eternity (in reality probably only 10 seconds), I understood that the pounding in my chest was my heart racing. Panic flooded every bit of my awareness. A debate raged in my mind:

"I have to get out of here!"

"You can't just leave—you're about to go on live television."

The heat in my face and the pounding in my chest were too intense. The urge to flee seemed to take over my mind and body. I *had* to bolt. I could feel my feet itching to burst into motion to carry me anywhere but here. Desperately, my eyes scanned the studio for the nearest exit. *"He's a professional anchorman,"* I rationalized. *"He can cover for me. There are still two minutes to go before I go on; he can improvise."*

"But I'm a psychologist—a psychologist who helps people with anxiety! I teach *anxiety management! Hold on, what do I tell my clients to do?"*

I knew I had time to tense and relax the muscles in my upper body, a shortened version of a technique I often teach, so I began with this. Then I initiated a sequence of deep breaths with long, steady exhalations. This calmed my system enough for me to engage in some rational self-talk.

"What's the worst thing that could happen in this interview?" I asked myself.

"Well, some people in the Detroit metro area might see me as an anxious psychologist on TV."

"Could I live with that?"

"Of course I can," I told myself. The pounding in my chest muted ever so slightly. *"And I don't even* know *anyone who watches the 12 o'clock news!"* I smiled to myself as I thought about the absurdity of worrying so intensely about a performance that no one I knew would even be watching. My heart rate slowed even more.

"I can do this," I thought. *"I* will *do this."* Just then the anchorman introduced me, and I turned to the camera and spoke.

About a week later, the studio sent me a tape of my interview. I appeared calm and collected, and I spoke at a clear, steady pace. I had to laugh: in the interview, I outlined some of the stress-busting techniques that just minutes before I had been using on myself.

Anxiety and panic are universal experiences. In fact, anxiety, fear, and even panic have helped us to survive by mobilizing us to respond to and defend ourselves against threats. When seen in this light, anxiety is a gift, the presence of which can enhance our ability to not only survive, but thrive on this planet. But anxiety, when it crops up at inopportune times or when its intensity is too great relative to the current circumstance, can also be a hindrance. This was the case for me as I sat perched behind the anchor's desk 20 years ago, anticipating my turn to speak. I was experiencing what you will learn in Chapter 5 is called a panic attack. Were I being attacked by a lion, that level of nervous activation would have been quite appropriate and would have helped me to escape from danger. But I was under no such threat as I sat in the newsroom. Luckily, I had many therapeutic tools available to me—tools that made the difference in allowing me to successfully cope with my anxiety rather than succumb to it. These are the very tools that I offer to you in this book.

Overview of Anxiety Disorders

Approximately 18% of adults (18 and older) in the United States suffer from an anxiety disorder in any given year (Kessler, Chiu, Delmer, & Walters, 2005). That's more than 40 million people in the United States alone whose excessive anxiety interferes with their ability to function on a daily basis. Not to mention the countless others who, like me, have the occasional panic attack or are overly burdened by the stress of upcoming deadlines or commitments. Anxiety, and particularly anxiety-based disorders, are now recognized as some of the most common psychological disorders in this country. If you are one of the many who suffer from anxiety, this book contains information that can give you relief. I will describe the symptoms of and treatments for five of the anxiety disorders: generalized anxiety disorder, panic disorder, specific phobias, social anxiety disorder, and obsessive–compulsive disorder. Below are brief overviews of each disorder. Later in the book you'll find a chapter devoted to each of them.

Generalized Anxiety Disorder (GAD)

If you have GAD, worrying may be your main pastime. Everyday occurrences give you more cause for concern than they do for those around you. A barrage of "what ifs" can ruin a simple activity like going to the grocery store, having a health check-up, or sending your daughter off on her first day of school. "What if the car gets a flat? What if the doctor finds something wrong? What if my daughter doesn't like her new teacher, forgets her lunch, falls and scrapes her knee at recess . . . and then the kids laugh at her . . . and then her knee gets infected . . . ?" The list can go on and on. Along with this chronic worry can come the chronic physical discomfort of stomach aches or other gastrointestinal upsets, tension headaches, and the fatigue that comes from constantly being on edge.

If you have GAD, therapy or self-help techniques can help you regain the sense of emotional well-being that comes with relinquishing your constant worries and the physical well-being that comes when your body is no longer operating in a state of chronic stress. Life needn't be simply a progression from one worry to the next. Therapy can help reintroduce you to the richness and fullness of a life free of chronic worry.

Panic Disorder (PD)

If you have PD, you have had at least one panic attack. Like my attack described above, this consists of an episode in which you experience intense fear accompanied by physical sensations such as a racing heartbeat, shortness of breath, and hot or cold sweats, just to name a few. People who experience such attacks often fear they are having a heart attack or other medical emergency. You also might fear you are losing your grip on reality and think you are going "crazy."

Many people occasionally have panic attacks but do not develop panic *disorder*. This was the case for me, when I had a panic attack in the newsroom. Unlike people who have a diagnosis of panic disorder, once my panic attack was over, I never worried about the possibility that another panic attack would occur, nor did I go out of my way to avoid the environment in which my panic attack occurred; I did not begin to avoid newsrooms or interviews or media presentations. If you have PD, however, you probably frequently worry about when and where you might have another panic attack. You play possible scenarios of your next attack in your mind and begin to avoid the places where you fear another attack is likely to occur. Some people become so fearful of having a panic attack in a public place that they rarely venture from their house.

This anticipatory worry about panic attacks and avoidance is what distinguishes people with PD from those who, like me, have an occasional panic attack. With treatment, the fear of having a panic attack will no longer rule your life. You can learn that, as counterintuitive as it may seem, even a panic attack provides no reason to panic. As panic loses its power, you can regain the sense of agency and competency that you lost to your fear of panic, and more.

Specific Phobias (SP)

Phobias are an extreme fear of and aversion to a particular thing or situation. Common specific phobias include fear of dogs, snakes, spiders, heights, or the sight of blood or needles. If you have a phobia, you most likely recognize that your fear is not rational. There's no logical reason you can think of for the sight of your phobic object or situation to inspire such extreme terror. But reason with yourself as you might, your extreme fear does not abate. Like people with panic disorder, you are likely to avoid that which you fear. But unlike people with PD, you probably don't spend much time worrying about encountering your phobic object or situation. Thus phobias generally do not affect people's lives as pervasively as do the other anxiety disorders covered in this book. For that reason, people are less likely to enter into therapy for the treatment of a phobia. If you do have a phobia, however, treatment is well worth your while. There are many simple and effective treatments for phobias. Rather than attempting to steer clear of your phobia for the rest of your life, I strongly recommend giving treatment a try.

Social Anxiety Disorder (SAD)
If you have social anxiety disorder, you most likely have an intense fear of being seen, criticized, or judged by others. This probably leads you to limit your social activities and curtail your professional or academic life. You might be afraid to go to parties, participate in class, or attend staff meetings; public speaking might be unbearable to you. You might feel dread for days or weeks in anticipation of the situations or events you fear or avoid them entirely. Likewise, your choice of job and decision to pursue or forego higher education might be dictated by your fears and avoidances due to social anxiety. In some cases, people with severe SAD are afraid of answering the phone, eating or writing in front of others, or using public toilets. Physical symptoms associated with this disorder include heart palpitations, faintness, blushing, and profuse sweating when confronted with the social situations that you fear, giving you yet another reason to avoid them.

With treatment, social situations will no longer trigger this hotbed of physical discomfort and emotional unrest. You can learn to experience a sense of ease and even pleasure in the situations that you once feared and avoided, and enjoy a life no longer constrained by social anxiety.

Obsessive–Compulsive Disorder (OCD)
Recently there have been many portrayals of characters with obsessive–compulsive disorder in movies and television shows. They show people who are so afraid of being contaminated by germs that they wash their hands compulsively, wear gloves in public, and always have hand sanitizer nearby. Or you might have seen a character who needs to flip each light switch on and off three times when entering or exiting a room, or perform other repetitive checking and counting rituals throughout the day. All of these behaviors fit some of the many symptoms of OCD. If you have OCD you experience persistent, recurring thoughts (obsessions) that center around a given theme, such as fear of germ contamination. In order to quell these fears, you usually develop a ritual or routine (compulsion) that calms the anxiety spurred by the recurring obsession. Other compulsive rituals can include repeating phrases or tasks, hoarding items, and needing phys-

ical objects in your surroundings to be perfectly symmetrical or aligned. Regardless of the particular obsession or response behavior, if you have OCD you feel as if you *must* engage in your particular ritual (or in some cases, an avoidance) whenever your obsessive thoughts occur. Treatment can help you to move beyond your obsessions to a way of life in which your obsessions and compulsions don't hold you hostage any longer.

You can see that common to all of the anxiety disorders is a pervasive sense of fear and uneasiness that interferes with your ability to feel that you are OK and that takes a toll on your body as well as your mind. People with anxiety disorders are more likely to experience heightened levels of anxiety-related physical discomfort and to notice these sensations more acutely than someone without an anxiety disorder. They are also more likely to misinterpret and overreact to these symptoms, often creating a vicious cycle. In response, people often seek help from physicians to fix physical symptoms that are actually brought about by an anxiety disorder. In fact, in 1999, a study commissioned by the Anxiety Disorder Association of America found that Americans spent more than $22.84 billion in repeated visits to healthcare facilities due to physical symptoms of anxiety disorders (Greenberg et al., 1999).

Luckily, there is a solution. With effective therapy, relief from this self-perpetuating cycle is within reach.

The Mixed Blessings of Anxiety

It's natural, but not helpful, to focus only on the negatives of anxiety. Sure, you suffer more than you need to, and you definitely miss some of today's pleasures because you are worrying about tomorrow. However, being anxious is not all bad. Because of your anxiety, you are careful, alert, and cautious. You rarely make careless mistakes. You are prepared for every eventuality.

I always learn from my clients who are anxious. They are generally careful about what they put in their bodies and they read the inserts about side effects of their prescriptions. They think carefully about risks and decisions. They look ahead for the potholes on the streets and manage to avoid every one. They anticipate what can go wrong in their lives and try their best to circumvent these possibilities. Sometimes, in a session, my clients mention actions they have taken to address something in their lives: hiring an estate attorney to update their will, going to the doctor to get a stress test, investigating the side effects of a medication and the need to look for alternatives. Listening to them, for a moment I think to myself, "Goodness, I should really be investigating these things myself!" But then I inevitably forget, or else remember but fail to allocate the time to do them. My clients, on the other hand, do make the time.

Of course, you don't want to suffer intense anxiety, and you don't have to. But you can allow yourself to enjoy and appreciate the positive side of anxiety while you have it. Caution, carefulness, and even vigilance are valuable qualities. If I ever needed a lawyer, I'd want my lawyer to anticipate contingencies that I would never think of. And I'd prefer that my airline pilot and the air-traffic controller display the attention to detail that is often second nature to those with OCD. Likewise, if I needed surgery I'd want my surgeon to have just enough anxiety to make absolutely certain that he or she was precise and doing everything possible to ensure my operation went off without a hitch.

A certain amount of vigilance and alertness is ideal. Although I don't have an anxiety disorder, I know I've performed best in my life, whether leading workshops, writing, teaching, or seeing clients, when anxious enough to prepare thoroughly and—yes—sometimes to over-prepare. I can certainly relate to film director Mike Nichols, who said, "Nerves provide me with energy. They work for me. It's when I don't have them, when I feel at ease, that I get worried." When I don't assume that everything will go well, my anxiety fuels my drive to prepare and work hard.

My wish for all of you is that you retain the positive qualities inherent to your type of personality; that you remain careful, alert, conscientious, and thoughtful. The goal of treatment is not to change who you fundamentally are. It is to rein in your anxiety and allow you to truly embrace the unique gift that you have, rather than being hindered by it.

On the flip side, it is an absolute fact that no matter how anxiety disorders affect you, they create suffering. Anxiety disorders rob you of the pleasure of the now as you focus intently on fears of the future. It's sort of like borrowing trouble, suffering in advance. Your anxiety can overburden your relationships, restrict your activities, deplete your self-confidence, and compromise the ease with which you navigate your life. But despite all these challenges, I assure you that, like most people who are plagued with anxiety, you are stronger than you think. Missionary Sister Busche noted, "We are like tea bags—we don't know our own strength until we're in hot water." As you face the challenges of overcoming an anxiety disorder, I hope you will delight in the discovery of the inner resources within yourself that you are just beginning to tap.

Getting the Right Treatment

Life can be incredibly difficult for anyone with an anxiety disorder. Basic activities that most of us enjoy without thought, such as driving a car, attending a wedding reception, or eating dinner in a restaurant, can be intensely painful if not impossible for sufferers of anxiety. Worse even than the limitations on their activities is the profound shame most people with anxiety disorders feel every day of their lives. They may cover it with cheerfulness or nonchalance, but shame eats away at them. I am awed by the courage it takes to cope with what is often crippling anxiety.

Imagine, then, my frustration in knowing that some people who seek therapy end up in treatments that are not effective for an anxiety disorder. Without the right match of treatment to symptoms, therapy can take years longer than needed to produce substantial results. In worst-case scenarios, such mismatched treatments can fail to work at all. Take Sandra, for example, who had been seeing a therapist twice weekly for more than seven years in order to help her get over her fear of driving. If Sandra had lived in Manhattan, where public transit is available, her inability to drive a car might not have been much of an inconvenience. But she lived in Detroit, "The Motor City," where public transportation is very limited. She wanted to get over her fear, but after seven years of therapy she was understandably getting impatient.

Her psychotherapy had focused on the dynamics of Sandra's family of origin, and identified her feelings of abandonment by her father. After years of work, she and her therapist discovered that these deep-seated feelings were at the root of her fear of driving. However, this knowledge alone did not help Sandra get over her phobia. She decided to find another type of treatment and consulted me.

Although establishing a possible root cause of a phobia can be helpful, this type of uncovering work is often better suited *after* treatment has gotten acute anxiety under control, not before. In some cases, such understanding is not even necessary to successfully treat the phobia. Thus, I began treating Sandra's anxiety by using techniques that diffuse anxiety in the here and now. (These are the types of treatments covered in this book.) With a combination of techniques and approaches, Sandra was on the road to recovery in only two months. At that point, she chose to continue therapy with me to work on other issues. Sandra was particularly interested in exploring how the dynamics of her family of origin were affecting her marriage. But now she was able to drive herself to her therapy appointments. She even bought her first car: a sporty red convertible.

Two years after Sandra completed her treatment with me, she called to tell me that her husband, Jack, had become legally blind. She wanted me to know how grateful she was that she now could drive. "You can't even imagine how difficult it would be getting Jack to all of his appointments if I were still too afraid to get behind the wheel of a car. I'm so glad I found out there were other kinds of therapies out there! You have no idea how much working with you has helped me."

Sandra's experience is like that of many clients who come into my office having spent too much time and expense on treatments that don't incorporate state-of-the-art interventions for specific anxiety disorders. One purpose of this book is to make sure that people with anxiety find a therapist who knows how to treat anxiety disorders, and that they know the questions they need to ask of a therapist to ensure this.

Even more than most clients, those with anxiety disorders are in a hurry to experience symptom relief. It is important that at the outset of treatment, you convey your firm belief that people with anxiety disorders do recover and explain that there are concrete interventions and techniques that you will teach to immediately start the client on this path to recovery. It is likewise important to assure your clients that they will experience some improvement early in treatment. However, you also need to emphasize the importance of patience and perseverance. You should communicate that treatment is a process that will require sustained effort and practice. Some clients enter therapy with the belief that they will only need to try an intervention once for their symptoms to recede completely. It is important that you let your clients know that some interventions require repeated trials over time, and while some symptom relief may thankfully seem instant, this is not always the case. Change takes time, but with continuous effort and practice, recovery is attainable.

Finding a Therapist and Getting Started

A number of the techniques in this book can be done independently, without the help of a clinician. However, if your anxiety disorder is not getting better with self-help alone and is affecting your functioning, it is time to seek professional help. As explained above, it is important to find a clinician who is a good fit for you and well-versed in treatment options for your particular anxiety disorder. Selecting a therapist may be one of the most important decisions you make in your life. Unfortunately, some people spend more time selecting their winter boots than they do selecting a therapist. It is important that you take your time in this process and make your decision in an informed and discriminating way.

Of course, you want to select someone whom you like, with whom you feel safe and comfortable, who seems to understand and care about you. Research has shown that a good relationship is essential to positive outcomes in psychotherapy. But as they say in parenting, "love is not enough."

If your kind, caring therapist doesn't have training in your specific anxiety disorder, you are unlikely to get better. I have had too many clients who, like Sandra, tell me they were in supportive psychotherapy that they found nurturing and sometimes even illuminating for years, but their anxiety did not abate. Just as you would go to a pulmonologist if you had asthma, you need to seek a therapist who has expertise in treating anxiety disorders in order to receive state-of-the-art care.

Once you decide to seek help through therapy, get recommendations from people you respect. Ask questions about their experience with the therapist. After you have several names, you might Google them to find out more about their credentials and specialties, or go straight to the next step: call them up and ask to interview them, either in person or on the telephone. Plan the questions you want to ask in advance, and be prepared to explain the problems you want help with. If you like what you hear, you can make a first appointment without making a commitment. Remember that it's OK to interview several therapists before you make a commitment to start treatment.

Once you start working with a therapist, it is advisable that you ask for a clear treatment plan. Discuss the approach that your therapist employs and don't hesitate to ask questions if something doesn't make sense. Although your therapist should take the lead role in establishing a treatment plan, it is important that you and your therapist work as a team, together constructing a treatment that you both feel works best for you. If you are also working with any adjunctive treatment professionals (e.g., a psychiatrist, integrative medical physician, homeopath, or herbalist), it is important that all of you work as a collaborative team. Some therapists and clients like to map out a very detailed course of action for treatment. Others start with an initial, broad plan and revise it as therapy progresses. The priority is simply to have some plan of action from which you can begin.

The effectiveness of many of the treatments in this book lies in the *combination* of treatments from an array of different types of therapies. If one technique is either ineffective or simply not a good fit for you, a vast array of other techniques are available. Your clinician will select a treatment approach that incorporates your specific problems, goals, and objectives from an array of treatment models and methods.

I practice technical eclecticism insofar as I do not adhere strictly to a single theoretical perspective or school of therapy. Rather, I craft individualized treatment plans that pull from a variety of psychotherapeutic techniques and interventions based on the specific needs of each client. While my work is heavily informed by hypnosis, it is individualized and flexible. Likewise, the methods in this book are compatible with almost any psychotherapeutic modality.

As I wrote in *Affect Regulation Toolbox,* there is great deal of flexibility with regard to the order in which you can try out the interventions:

> . . . although there are some suggested guidelines as to which tools to use for which conditions, it is best to think of the tools as items on a menu. Although it is quite possible to eat anything on the menu in any order one chooses, there is a generally accepted sequence: appetizer, main course, dessert. Within each of these categories, however, there are a number of choices. And certainly, some days one might choose to order an appetizer as a main course or to eat dessert before dinner. Adaptability and flexibility are the keystones to successful use of these tools. (p. 47)

The strength of this approach is that techniques from different types of therapy can be pulled in to complement each other and fill the gaps that any one modality might not target. Thus the integration of various therapeutic interventions can combine to make a treatment plan more comprehensive and effective. There may not be much research to support these patchwork treatment approaches because they are geared to the individual client, and hence are harder to scientifically test and broadly prescribe. However, this does not mean that they are ineffective. On the contrary, I often find these eclectic treatments more effective.

Hope for Recovery

If you suffer from anxiety, you are likely to be a pessimist. I challenge you to have positive expectancy about recovering from your anxiety disorder. Indeed, in having positive expectancy, you are in actuality a realist, because *people with anxiety do get better.* I tell you what I tell my clients: if you are persistent, open, hardworking, have just a little bit of trust, and commit to your recovery, you will get better. In your hands right now, you hold an arsenal of guidance, interventions, and treatment possibilities. I have complete confidence that there is a combination of treatment options within these pages that you and your therapist can adapt to work for you. With these interventions in hand, you can move out of the anxiety trap into a more empowered, successful, and joyful life. Let's begin!

CHAPTER 2

What Causes Anxiety

Debby leaned forward in her chair. It was her first session with me, and I was interviewing her to get a history of her struggles with anxiety.

"I'm sorry to interrupt you, Dr. Daitch, but I can't stop thinking, why am I like this? I mean this constant worry about my health, for one thing, makes no sense. My doctor says there's nothing wrong with me and that I should live 'til I'm a hundred." Debby caught her breath and continued. "My grandmother was always nervous. Did I get it from her? She was afraid of driving. Then again, my sister is more than a bit obsessive. Of course, she calls it being careful and having a good work ethic. But sometimes I think she's over the top with her 60-hour work week. She gets anxious if she leaves one piece of paper on her desk at the end of the day. And Mom has panic attacks, and sometimes doesn't want to go out alone.

"Are we all just crazy? Or self-indulgent? Maybe I was just born this way. But then again this economy doesn't help, with both me and John worrying about getting laid off." She looked at me expectantly.

I assured Debby that it was perfectly reasonable to inquire about the causes of her symptoms and that I would do my best to explain what I knew about the reasons people develop anxiety. Indeed, becoming informed about the nature of your anxiety is an important part of recovery. Just finding out that many people share the constellation of symptoms you experience can be a relief. Furthermore, the knowledge that some of the symptoms you experience have biological components is likely to reduce the shame that often goes hand in hand with your anxiety. Regardless of the medical or psychological disorder you have, it is essential that you learn as much as you can about your condition.

Nature or nurture? The debate rages on: are we primarily determined by our genes, or does our environment play a significant role? A simple answer to this very complex question is *both*. An intricate interplay of environmental and genetic factors coalesce to make us who we are. As we will see, an interaction between genetic and environmental factors influences how we think, develop, and experience life.

This chapter will give an overview of the many factors that contribute to the manifestation of anxiety. We'll begin by examining the role of genetics. We will then look at developmental factors, including ineffectual parenting and traumatic stress. The role of innate temperament and how it affects resilience to stress will also be addressed. Finally, we will discuss situational factors that can exacerbate anxiety, including time urgency, chronic stress, medical conditions, and substance abuse.

Genetics

Did Debby inherit her worrying nature from her grandmother? How genetically similar were Debby and her sister? Did her mother pass on an anxious gene?

The role that genetics plays in the development of anxiety disorders is intricately intertwined with other environmental variables, which will be discussed later in this chapter. Yet it is clear that our genetic material significantly affects our personality styles and emotional vulnerabilities. Studies examining families with fraternal and identical twins have demonstrated that anxiety disorders can be influenced by genetic factors (Barlow, 2002). Current research also indicates that inherited genetic tendencies play a role in establishing each individual's baseline levels of tension or anxiety (Eysenck, 1967; Gray & McNaughton, 1996; Leonardo & Hen, 2006; Middeldorp, Cath, Van Dyck, & Boomsma, 2005). David Barlow, clinical psychologist and recognized expert in anxiety disorders, noted, "Strong biological contributions conveyed to us as part of our genetic endowment seem to create at least one set of vulnerabilities that set the stage for the subsequent appearance of anxiety" (2002, p. 63). This means that due to genetic makeup, some individuals are more predisposed to experience heightened anxiety or have a more emotionally reactive temperament than others. Likewise, some individuals are more genetically susceptible to the development of anxiety disorders than others.

At this stage of the game, scientists are discovering that it is overly simplistic and inaccurate to link one single gene with the development of anxiety or anxiety disorders. Rather, research supports the theory that contributions from many genes converge to enhance an individual's genetic susceptibility (Barlow, 2002). This is termed *polygenic transmission*, which means that many genes contribute to the expression of a singular trait. An example of a polygenic trait is skin color. Many different genes from each parent combine to create the subtleties and nuances that make each child's skin color unique, like the mixing and blending of many different shades of paint in unique ratios. And as with the expression of anxiety, skin tone can change over time, manifesting periods of darker or lighter complexion in response to life experiences.

In Debby's case, it is possible that genetic links in her family manifested differently in different members of the family. Her grandmother's anxiety was manifested in a phobia or fear of driving, her sister was obsessive and seemingly compulsive, her mother had panic attacks, probably with agoraphobia (a fear of going out alone), and Debby was a worrier with hypochondriacal tendencies (see Chapters 5, 6, 7, and 9 for a description of these disorders).

Just as the types and symptoms of anxiety disorders vary, it is likely that differing clusters of genes contribute to the development of different types of anxiety disorders. This theory is supported by research demonstrating that some anxiety disorders, such as panic disorder (see Chapter 6), have stronger genetic determinants than others (National Institute of Health, 2009). The only constant regarding genetics and its role in the development of anxiety is complexity. The dynamic interaction between experience and genes is key to understanding susceptibility to anxiety.

The Interplay of Genetics and Environment

The complexity of polygenic transmission is easier to understand in light of an example of more clear-cut genetic influence, the *monogenic* transmission of height. At first glance, the expression of height appears genetically precise. If both of your parents are tall, you will most likely grow to an above-average height. If you have siblings, they will most likely attain a tall stature too. We can't predict the exact height an individual will reach, and the height of you and a same-gendered sibling will surely not be the same. But thanks to our understanding of genetics, you can survey your parents' stature and get a ballpark estimate of how tall you will be.

However, in some cases, environmental interactions exert enough force to alter genetic predisposition. For example, let's look at an environmental influence that might occur over a long period of time: if throughout your childhood you were fed only candy bars, your growth would be impeded. You would not reach your genetically intended height due to malnourishment. This is an example of *developmental influence* on genetic expression.

Sometimes, however, a single incident can significantly alter genetic expression. Consider the case of Ellen, who fell while roller-skating when she was 10 years old. Her brain concussed at a spot that caused her to stop growing right then and there. Because of this acute, intense, and singular incident, she too failed to attain the full stature she would have otherwise reached. Unlike developmental influence, which must occur consistently over a long period of time in order to significantly alter genetic expression, a single acute incident can be powerful enough to alter genetic expression due to its intensity. As the above scenarios illustrate, even with a straight-forward example of monogenetic predetermination such as height, there is wiggle room: environment can and will intervene. This is also the case regarding the development of anxiety disorders. Anxiety disorders are not only polygenically based; they can also be influenced by environmental factors. To complicate matters further, there is increasing evidence that there are critical periods during our lifespan when we are more vulnerable to the development of anxiety disorders (Leonardo & Hen, 2006; Leonardo & Hen, 2008). It is believed that during these critical windows, the brain is particularly susceptible to environmental stressors—both acute stressors and those that are less severe, but prolonged. For the remainder of this chapter we will examine some of the many environmental stressors that can contribute to the development of an anxiety disorder. We will begin with a look at a time period in which many of the above-mentioned "critical windows" are present: the time when an individual is in utero, in infancy, and in early childhood.

Prenatal Environment

Right from the womb, we can be affected by our mother's stress. The mother and developing fetus share the same blood, and stress hormones produced by the mother cross the placental blood barrier. Thus a pregnant mother's stress can have a cascading effect: stress the mother experiences can literally be transmitted into the body of the developing child via an increase in stress hormones (Wadhwa, 2005). Of course, pregnant women, just like anyone else, experience the ups and downs of life, and the resulting stress is reflected physiologically. Moderate levels of stress are common and have not been shown to harm a baby's in-utero development. However, heightened stress over a long period of time will cause the mother's system to maintain an excessive amount of stress hormones, which flood the baby's newly developing nervous system, propelling the baby into a state of chronic stress (Wadhwa, 2005).

Researchers have theorized that such an overabundance of stress hormones actually impedes the ability of the baby's nervous system to modulate in response to stress, causing it to become overly sensitive to environmental stimuli: neural pathways are created that facilitate the release of too great a quantity of stress hormones for too long a period of time in response to a stressor. According to some researchers, mothers who experience a significant amount of anxiety during pregnancy have been shown to have infants who display many markers of an overly charged nervous system. From temperament to motor development, in-utero stress levels appear to make a difference (Huizink, Robles de Medina, Mulder, Visser, & Buitelaar, 2002). Highly anxious pregnancies tend to produce anxious babies. Thus, a pregnant mother's emotions and the resulting in-utero environment correlate with an infant's physiological and emotional reactivity.

Early Childhood Experience

The infant brain can be thought of as a vast network of possibilities. By the time a child reaches eight months of age, she is estimated to possess one thousand trillion synaptic connections—twice that of the average adult (Kotulak, 1996). If the brain were an information highway, neurons would be the pavement that makes up the roads. Neurons connect to one another at junctions called synapses, like the tracks of a vast train set, too intricate to thoroughly map, with pathways exponentially more interconnected than the roads on any city map. It is from this overabundance of possible pathways that roads are either reinforced and strengthened by use or discarded by lack of use.

The experiences during an individual's life determine which pathways are reinforced and which are discarded. This process, known as pruning, occurs primarily during the first twelve years of life, but the first three years of life are the most critical period of pruning (Kotulak, 1996). For instance, as a baby practices grasping a rubber ball, neural connections that facilitate grasping are reinforced. In the same way, if a baby cries and consistently receives comfort in response, neural pathways will be paved. If a baby's cries bring harsh treatment, or bring no one at all, the brain will pave a different road entirely. Hence, an adult has only half the synapses of an eight-month-old child, and they were sturdily and *selectively* paved.

The pruning process is highly influenced by the relationship between the infant and her parents. The baby's information about the world comes largely from those who are holding, feeding, changing, and otherwise caring for the child. Thus infant–caregiver relationships strongly impact the first paving of the network of neuronal roadways. The infant is dependent on relationships in order to have her most basic needs met. Hence when there is some rift in relational support, it can have far-reaching effects on the laying and trafficking of neuronal roadwork. Unfortunately, babies who experience a lot of stress or trauma adapt in such a way that they maintain or produce excessive levels of stress hormones even in routine situations that other babies would not find threatening.

Again, experience colors genetic expression. But what of characteristics that appear more innate, more consistent over time and resistant to the coloring of experience? Temperament is such a construct.

Temperament

Two young mothers are having lunch at a café. "Jimmy's always been outgoing, right from the start," one tells her friend. "Crawling all over the place, picking up every new object in sight. He's always on the go."

Her friend shakes her head. "Not my Danny. He always wanted to stay right near me. He's anxious about new things. Now we're practically having to force him to go to sleep-away camp, even though he knows his brother loves it there."

It is clear that children are born with different temperaments. Many parents, often reporting marked differences in the personalities of their children, corroborate the idea of innate temperament.

Research from the field of developmental psychology supports these informal observations of parents. Temperament is a component of personality style, and as such remains stable over time. Aaron Beck (2005), a psychiatrist well known for his treatment of anxiety and depression, found that differences in temperament contribute to different reactions to stress and ways of coping with stress. Jeffrey Young, psychologist and author of *Schema Therapy*, identified such innate temperamental traits in infants as *anxious v. calm* and *irritable v. stable* (2003, p. 12).

Jerome Kagan, a researcher in developmental psychology, found that 15% to 20% of American and European children were born with a "behaviorally inhibited temperamental style" (Kagan & Brim, 1980). In other words, certain infants with the inhibited style were unusually anxious in new situations and displayed physiological responses such as rapid heartbeat and higher levels of stress hormones. He also found that inhibited baby boys became shy toddlers, while inhibited baby girls became restless little girls (Kagan & Brim, 1980). It is not a far leap to hypothesize that a toddler who displays increased heartbeat and cortisol levels in novel situations might be prone to developing an anxiety disorder in adulthood. However, it is important to note that an anxious temperament early in life sets nothing in stone about later life.

Although adults with anxiety disorders often displayed inhibited responses as children, not all children with anxious temperaments become anxious adults. This fact suggests that other variables affect the outcome. We have seen how in-utero environment and infant–caregiver relationships can color the polygenic expression of anxiety. We know that soothing, nurturing family environments can mitigate innate personality styles. In childhood, modeling and learned attachment styles are key to the laying of neuronal roadways and the maps that result. This can work to the child's benefit when a child with an anxious temperament learns adaptive means of coping from caregivers. Unfortunately, the importance of modeling can work to the child's detriment when caregivers model less adaptive, more anxiety-fueling behaviors.

Modeling

Recall our example of the effect on a child's height caused by long-term physical malnourishment. The lack of growth would be the result of a deficiency of the nutrients the child's body needed to function optimally and thrive. In the same way, parents' consistent emotional nurturance predicates optimum, healthy cognitive and emotional development on the part of the child. Parenting styles that create emotional malnourishment have consequences for a child's emotional and cognitive growth.

It is not surprising that a child's perception of his parents' attitudes and expressions of anxiety influences and nourishes his emotional development. Our actions, words, body language, the risks we take, the risks we avoid, communicate to our children whether the world is a place where we can thrive, or where we should remain on edge, fearful and reticent at every turn.

Indeed, a relatively new discovery in the world of neuroscience is the existence of what are called mirror neurons. Giacomo Rizzolatti (2005), a renowned neurophysiologist, found that many of the same neurons that are activated when an individual performs an activity are activated in the individual who simply *watches* that person perform the activity. For example, Jill's husband calls to say he's bringing the boss home for dinner. Jill becomes nervous and paces back and forth as she thinks about what to cook. While her two-year-old daughter Amanda watches her mother pace in nervous agitation, many of the same neurons that are firing in her mother are firing in Amanda's brain, as if she herself were actually pacing nervously. In light of the activity of mirror neurons, "seeing is believing" can be restated as "seeing is *being*." This has radical implications for the role of modeling.

Parents who model anxiety are typically overprotective and believe that unless they hover over their children, disaster will result. Take, for example, the case of Melissa. When she was 19, she was referred for therapy due to her chronic stomach pain. It became clear that Melissa suffered from a number of symptoms of anxiety, including chronic and excessive worrying. She was rigid and uncomfortable with changes in her routine. Like many young adults with anxiety disorders, Melissa had an overprotective parent.

For any little outing, Melissa was expected to call her mother when she arrived at her destination. She described a routine get together with friends. "I was just heading to the mall, two miles away. But if my mother doesn't hear from me, she calls me constantly until I pick up or call her back. So it saves me grief just to call her every time I go somewhere." It is not uncommon for parents to ask their children to call when they go out, but Melissa's mother carried this expectation to the extreme.

Melissa responded to her mother's over-controlling nature and intrusiveness with resentment, yet she shared her mother's view that the world is a dangerous place. Most damaging to Melissa was her belief that she would not be able to function independently if she moved away from home. Everyday tasks, such as grocery shopping or putting gas in her car, took on monumental proportions and were accompanied by heightened anxiety. Like Melissa, people with anxiety disorders underestimate their own coping skills, while overestimating danger.

Overprotective parents inadvertently injure their children via the implication that the world is unsafe and that the children lack the resources to handle challenges. They often explain in great detail the dire consequences that can befall their children when they venture into the world. Unaware of the injury that she was inflicting, Melissa's mother was schooling her in this distorted belief.

Anxious parenting also harms children by engendering a lack of *self-agency,* the sense that they, not someone else, are the agents that produce a desired outcome. In other words, an *A* student whose parents excessively edit his school papers likely would not gain a sense of self-agency regarding his school work and ultimately would doubt his own ability to succeed academically.

Similarly, overprotective parents impede the development of *self-efficacy,* the sense that one has the capacity to take effective actions. Individuals with diminished self-efficacy are less resilient to stress and underestimate their own resources.

Research suggests that a high percentage of anxious individuals have overprotective parents. Some have difficulty separating from their parents in adolescence and young adulthood. College counselors report increasing numbers of students who are afraid to be on their own. They are accustomed to their parents' help with all decisions, responsibilities, even homework. When they have to adapt to college life, these young adults are adrift.

Both Amanda, the two-year-old watching her mother pace anxiously, and Melissa, tethered to her mother by her cell phone, learned anxiety through their parents' modeling. Other children develop anxiety because of weak emotional attachment to their parents.

Attachment

Nancy lies in her crib in the dark, crying. She's hungry. Her mother doesn't come. Nancy's crying grows louder, to no avail. She can't know that her mother is so depressed that she barely hears Nancy. For months Nancy's mother has been withdrawn, in a world of her own. All Nancy knows is that help doesn't come.

Liam crawls across the living room floor and reaches up for the table edge. Last time he stood up, his parents cheered for him. This time, the table tilts and falls. Liam's father shouts, jerks him off the floor, and slaps his leg. His mother turns away from him. He's put in his crib and left alone.

Infants learn to trust others and to soothe themselves through the responsive love and nurturance they receive from their parents. Their experience of the world and strategies for how to survive and thrive derive first from their early attachment to their parents. If Nancy and Liam's experiences of neglect and harshness become consistent, their ability to attach to others will be weak and their response to the world will be anxious.

When there is lack of support and emotional attunement in infant–parent and childhood relationships, less-than-optimal attachment styles arise. Marsha Kaitz and Hilla Maytal (2005), Israeli psychologists and experts in trauma, noted that some anxious mothers had a diminished capacity to respond sensitively to the needs of their children, either under- or overreacting to their children's needs. The result was that when the children became distressed, rather than seek their parents for comfort, they distanced themselves from their parents. This makes sense, given that the children did not experience their mothers as being responsive to their needs. Not only did they develop a pattern of seeking isolation rather than interaction, they didn't receive the nurturance needed to eventually learn self-soothing techniques, a skill essential to managing their own emotions throughout their lives.

Another group of children at risk for anxiety are those who assume the role of caretaker for their parents. In her memoir of her childhood, *1185 Park Avenue*, Anne Roiphe wrote about her fragile, self-absorbed mother, who abdicates mothering to nannies, viewing herself as too incompetent to parent.

> Suddenly, there is a flash of lightening and a clap of thunder . . . My mother rushes to her bed and pulls the cover over her body. She picks up a flashlight and turning it on sees me on the threshold and motions me to join her in bed. I feel her arms shaking and her legs trembling . . . I see tears in her eyes and the mascara on her face runs down her cheeks. "Don't worry," I say to her, "it's just a thunderstorm and it will be over soon. (Roiphe, 1999, p. 38–39)

Eager to be close to her parent, Roiphe seized this opportunity for connection by comforting her frightened mother. In doing so, she took on a classic role: the "parentified" child taking care of the anxious parent.

Children of alcoholics, of single parents, and of parents whose needs were unmet in their own childhoods often assume this role. Because they view their parents as vulnerable, these children often believe they must be perfect, and are afraid of making mistakes. They lack the secure, emotional infrastructure that creates a solid sense of self. Although the parentified child often grows up looking quite functional, indeed over-responsible, their psychic injuries often "leak out" in expressions of anxiety. The parentified child exemplifies just one of many patterns of attachment and attunement that are born of and foster anxiety.

Trauma

It is widely recognized that childhood trauma resulting from abuse, neglect, or illness or injuries requiring invasive medical interventions affects the development of the brain and thereby shapes future behaviors and reactions (Daitch, 2007). By age one, the infant's brain has encoded implicit memories (Siegel, 1999). Implicit memories are memories recorded without conscious awareness of the experiences behind them. Whether the memories of trauma are implicit or explicit, the trauma itself has a drastic pruning effect on neural networks of the brain, closing off pathways of security and reinforcing pathways of anxiety. Allan Schore, neuroscience writer and psychiatry researcher, wrote, "the dysregulating events of both abuse and neglect create chaotic biochemical alterations in the infant brain" (2003, p. 133). Trauma also significantly alters the neurochemicals that travel along the networks, which can increase the risk of developing anxiety and of diminished resilience to stress. The message encoded in the brain as the result of childhood trauma is that the world is unsafe. Danger lurks.

These damaging effects of trauma can result from prolonged or acute events and even from events later in life. Just think of Ellen, whose height was stunted due to one severe blow to the head. While the developing brain is especially susceptible to such traumas, shock trauma can alter the neuronal roadways at any point in life.

Medical and Substance-Related Considerations

In exploring what's behind symptoms of anxiety, it's important to remember the intricate connection between the physical body and emotions. Not all individuals who have physical symptoms of panic or anxiety have an anxiety disorder. Some medical conditions are real and treatable causes of the physiological and psychological distress associated with anxiety disorders. Shortness of breath that snowballs into hyperventilation may arise from undiagnosed or improperly treated asthma. Palpitations of the heart associated with panic may be caused by hyperthyroidism or cardiac arrhythmias or certain medications. Tremors and cold sweats can be symptoms of hypoglycemia. Hormone imbalances, including those some women experience during menopause, can dramatically affect the intensity of anxiety.

What we take into our bodies can also be the source of heightened anxiety. Psychoactive street drugs, such as speed or cocaine, are often the first example that comes to mind. Less obvious are the secondary side effects of some prescription medications, such as the steroids in some asthma inhalers, or the overuse of over-the-counter medications, such as headache or non-drowsy cold medications containing acetaminophen and caffeine. It is easy to underestimate the effects of seemingly mild stimulants such as caffeine or nicotine that can build up gradually on a day-to-day basis. Mild, undiagnosed food allergies can also be the source of anxiety. When considering the causes of anxiety, it is erroneous to jump to psychophysiological explanations before ruling out medical or substance-related causes. A trip to the physician can be just as crucial as a trip to the psychotherapist.

The Rest of the Story

Up until this point we've discussed developmental characteristics that can lead to anxiety, such as genetics, early childhood factors, temperament, and trauma. That's not the whole story, however. Many anxious people had happy, secure childhoods. So why did they become anxious? For many adults, lifestyle or environmental stressors become catalysts to anxiety.

Time Urgency and Chronic Stress

"You're all done. Hope it wasn't too stressful," said the technician as he assisted the patient off the narrow table of the MRI machine.

"Actually, I enjoyed it," the patient reported with a smile. "It was the first time I can remember that I had an entire half-hour where I did *nothing*! I don't even know if in the last 30 minutes I received a text or voicemail. How refreshing!"

It says quite a lot that for some people, the only relief from a rushed lifestyle of deadlines, commitments, and to-do lists might come in the form of a noisy, confining procedure such as a CAT scan or MRI.

We live in an increasingly fast-paced culture in which productivity is both honored and demanded. Yet this often exacts a cost upon our mental and emotional well-being. The words of Bob Seger's song "Against the Wind" capture the insidious nature of moving too quickly, a pattern that doesn't stop with age:

"Moving eight miles a minute for months at a time . . . I've got so much more to think about/deadlines and commitments/what to leave in, what to leave out/Against the wind/I'm still running against the wind" (1980, side 2 track 1).

We try to pack more into each day, neglecting the need for downtime. Even the weekends offer no reprieve. They are filled with shopping, chores, taking care of elderly relatives or young children. Social activities add even more events to our already overloaded schedules and can bring as much exhaustion as pleasure.

In both our homes and the workforce, our productivity is seen as a badge of honor. Most of us are sleep deprived. The lunch "hour" has been replaced by a quick snack at our desks or in our cars. In 2008, *The Boston Globe* reported that North Americans are allotted the fewest vacation days in the developed world, yet one-third of Americans use up less than half of their time off (Jackson, 2008). Even commutes to and from work become an opportunity for multitasking. The same *Boston Globe* article stated that nearly 70% of Americans eat while driving and 37% of those ages 19 to 27 text message while behind the wheel (Jackson, 2008). Stephan Rechtshaffen (1996), author of *Time Shifting: A Revolutionary New Approach to Creating More Time for Your Life*, estimates that 95% of us experience *time poverty*. The pervasive sense of time urgency can overwhelm your body and emotions and stimulate the nervous system with a cascade of chemical reactions that elicit symptoms of anxiety.

Time urgency and the feeling of working 24/7 aren't the only sources of the unrelenting stress that permeates our society. Chronic, unrelenting stress can take its toll on anyone. People who are overburdened with responsibilities, such as those who care for a sick family member or special-needs child, are particularly susceptible to chronic stress. People who work multiple jobs or put in 50- or 60-hour work weeks and support a family experience unrelenting stress. Employees who feel trapped in work settings with critical and demanding supervisors are vulnerable to such stress, as are people in marriages with abusive or narcissistic partners.

The time-honored notion that "you find out what you're made of" when under pressure has some truth to it. If you have an anxious temperament and/or a genetic vulnerability to anxiety, you are likely to be particularly vulnerable to chronic stress. Any significant unexpected stress, such as an illness, relationship problem, or job loss can trigger major anxiety. Knowing this, you need to be careful to limit the burdens you take on and to give yourself adequate time each day to rest and restore yourself.

Sleep Deprivation

Given the fast-paced nature and increasing time demands of today's society, it's no surprise that many of us are running on an insufficient amount of sleep. In general, most adults need an average of eight hours of sleep each night. It's easy to accrue a "sleep debt" as many of our daily activities and commitments push our bedtimes later and later. Sleep deprivation can also be due to the inability to fall asleep or to stay asleep once you actually do get yourself into bed. In Chapter 11, we will look at some of the factors that inhibit sleep.

Unfortunately, we now know that sleep deprivation can worsen or even start a cycle of anxiety. If you have an anxiety disorder, your body and mind are already overly responsive to fears or perceived threats. Sleep deprivation appears to further exacerbate this propensity for overreaction. One study (Yoo, Gujar, Hu, Jolesz, & Walker, 2007) suggested that emotional centers in the brain become hyperactive when the body is deprived of sleep. This is because the communication between the amygdala (a part of the brain that sends out an alarm signal in response to a perceived threat) and the pre-frontal cortex (a more rational, logical part of the brain) can become compromised.

In effect, when you are sleep deprived, your brain doesn't give you enough of a chance to evaluate the validity of the amygdala's alarm signals before stress hormones that mobilize you for action are released into your system. It's as if a section of your brain is crying wolf and rather than question the messenger, your body and brain immediately rally the troops in response. To treat an anxiety disorder, you often need to dampen your responsiveness to these alarm signals, not heighten them. Likewise, you often need to engage the very centers of the brain to which sleep deprivation appears to limit your access.

The flip side of this coin is that anxiety itself can lead to sleep deprivation. Many people with anxiety who have trouble falling asleep or staying asleep exacerbate this problem by worrying about their insomnia. If you have this problem, you might even find yourself dreading getting into bed at night. In this case, your worries and apprehensions rev your system so that rest is just about the last thing that your body is prepared to do when you turn in for the night. Thus, the restorative rest that you need to modulate your anxiety does not occur *because* of your elevated levels of anxiety. We will discuss how to combat insomnia in Chapter 11.

Zeitgeist: The Spirit of the Times

Remember how, right after 9/11, the media was full of commentary about the pervasive sense of fear and anxiety that was gripping the nation? In our discussion of the causes of anxiety, we mustn't overlook the effect of the zeitgeist, the spirit of the times, on each individual's consciousness. This affects us even when we aren't in severe turmoil as we were in the United States directly following 9/11.

Regardless of the time in history or one's place on the globe, each person belongs to a culture and a social order. Whether it be political change, an economic recession, or a fast-paced, technological revolution, societal stress impacts the spirit of the times and each individual in the culture. The 11 o'clock news reports a continuing recession, a political regime shift, a food recall. Individuals who are already genetically and temperamentally predisposed to anxiety are more vulnerable to experiencing societal distress at a more heightened level than the average viewer of the nightly news.

The Benefits of Understanding

Understanding the causes of anxiety gives you insight into your condition. Most anxiety disorders have multiple causes, like the ones Debby mentioned at the beginning of the chapter. Genetics might have made Debby susceptible, an illness may have stressed her resilience, worry about the economy may have been the final straw, or chronic insomnia may have set her on the path to anxiety. Gaining an appreciation of the multiple causes of anxiety, many of which were no fault of your own, can help to alleviate the shame and self-recrimination that you may have experienced. The objective fact is that anxiety is *not* a character flaw. You needn't blame yourself for your anxiety. Rather, knowledge in hand, you can now pursue a path of recovery. In the following chapters you will learn a variety of methods to treat anxiety disorders. The successful implementation of these methods does not always depend on knowing the causes of anxiety. However, knowing the causes of anxiety, as you do now, can support your treatment and give you a firm foundation from which you can begin.

CHAPTER 3

Treatment Approaches for Anxiety Disorders

"**H**ey, Carolyn, do you have a minute? I want to ask your advice about something," Marilyn, my neighbor, said to me as we met at the mailboxes outside our condos.

"How about we go for a walk and we can talk," I responded. "Just give me 10 minutes to change my clothes and I'll meet you outside."

As we started walking down the nature trail, I noticed Marilyn looked distressed. "It's about my daughter-in-law Natalie," she began. "She wants to get into therapy. Actually, we all want her to get into therapy. She's a darling girl but she's suffered from anxiety for quite a long time . . . lately it's gotten really out of control. Now she doesn't even want to leave the house. It's hard on my son, who is a pretty easygoing guy, but he's finding all her worrying and panic really hard to live with. She was in therapy with someone before they got married. Natalie said he was a very nice guy, easy to talk to, caring, but she said he wasn't all that helpful.

"So now we've been looking for someone else, and for a different kind of treatment than whatever it was that Natalie tried before. I thought it would be so simple: just go on the Internet, find the name of the treatment that works for anxiety, and find a list of therapists who specialize in it. Was I ever wrong—it's really confusing! There are so many different treatments out there, and so many different opinions on what works and what doesn't. And all these initials! CBT, EMDR, EFT . . . it's like an alphabet soup of options. I, for one, am more confused than before I began to research this. I finally told Natalie I had a friend who was a psychologist and would have some good advice that I could pass along to her. What do you think? Which is the best approach for Natalie?"

If you have spent any time exploring options for the treatment of an anxiety disorder, you too might have found yourself in Marilyn's quandary. As I told Marilyn, there are a lot of good treatment options out there, and it is important that you become aware of the range of treatments that are effective for your particular anxiety disorder. Unfortunately, there is no one best therapy approach. Likewise, it can be a bit overwhelming to figure out what is best for any given person, especially since a kind of combination of different approaches is often appropriate.

In your search for relief from anxiety, I strongly believe that you should be an educated consumer. Although reading about an approach isn't the same as experiencing it with a skilled therapist, it is a good place to begin. In this chapter you'll get a brief overview of many of the most common interventions that are used in treatment. It is a compendium of methods I've found effective over time. The upcoming chapters will then show how these treatments are used for specific anxiety disorders. Thus they will present more specific strategies that have arisen within each of the more general methods of approach presented in this chapter.

While the approaches presented are diverse, all the therapies included have the same end goal: to help you manage your anxiety disorder. Where they differ is in how they each go about doing this. Remember, there is no one "right" way to treat an anxiety disorder. As you will see throughout this book, I believe that effective therapeutic interventions come not from strict adherence to one single school of treatment, but from a willingness to select an eclectic mix of interventions that best fit you, the patient. Thus for the treatment of all of the anxiety disorders we examine you will find a wide variety of interventions applied to a wide variety of cases. But for now, we will begin with the basics.

Psychoeducation

Psychoeducation, an essential step of any treatment, involves the therapist's explanation of the nature of your specific anxiety disorder and the consistent patterns in which it typically manifests. This includes a discussion of the causes of your anxiety, the treatments available, and other resources, such as self-help books and support groups.

The information and knowledge gained through psychoeducation is both comforting and freeing. You learn that your experience of the disorder is shared by many others, which helps you to let go of shame and confusion. Suddenly your suffering makes sense. Psychoeducation continues throughout your treatment, particularly when the possibility of medications or other outside resources are introduced.

As I often inform clinicians,

> psychoeducation is an important component of all treatment. Clients need to be provided with an understanding of their styles of reactivity, symptoms, and the effect on their functioning. Frequently clients, particularly those with anxious temperaments, catastrophize their symptoms and fear dire outcomes if they don't diminish. They berate themselves for being weak and capitulating to their problems. These clients need to be reassured that their symptoms are not unusual and are common expressions of the right dynamics of genetics, temperament, and environmental factors . . . they must be assured that their condition is treatable and that they will learn specific strategies that have been successful with many others. (Daitch, 2007, p. 49)

Therapists should provide current, up-to-date information about their clients' specific disorders. You can recommend books to read, audio recordings, group therapy options, and self-help programs. (See Appendix for suggestions of such resources.) I have found it useful to include partners or other family members for at least one psychoeducation session as well. In these sessions, information about the disorder is provided and we address a partner or parent's role in his or her loved one's recovery. This is also the time to reinforce the patient's need to commit to at-home practice. As psychoeducation continues throughout treatment, other approaches such as pharmaceuticals, neutraceuticals, and methodologies such as biofeedback or neurofeedback may be introduced. However, it is important not to flood the patient with too much information at once, as this can become overwhelming. Remember that just as with other aspects of treatment, your timing and pacing are crucial during psychoeducation as well.

Treatment Approaches

Cognitive Therapy

Cognitive Therapy (CT) is based on the premise that identifying and changing your thoughts will change your beliefs and behaviors. Thus in cognitive therapy you will work to identify the thoughts that are fueling and maintaining your anxiety. This is generally done in a three-step process:

1. Your therapist will give you exercises to help you identify and record the thoughts that run through your mind, understanding

that your thoughts stem from underlying assumptions and beliefs that contribute to your anxiety. Often in these exercises you write down your worried thoughts and the beliefs that underlie them, rather than just stating them aloud to your therapist or letting them whirl around in your head.

2. Next, in collaboration with your therapist, you evaluate the accuracy and helpfulness of your thoughts and underlying belief structures.

3. Lastly, you can choose to replace them with thoughts and ideas that are more accurate and adaptive. By doing this you begin to change your underlying beliefs, and become less fearful. CT also helps you identify a new, more capable self-image.

I am indebted to the fine description of cognitive therapy offered by Aaron Beck and Marjorie Weishaar. They wrote: "The cognitive system deals with the ways people perceive, interpret, and assign meaning to events. . . . Cognitive therapy aims to adjust information processing and initiate positive change in all systems by acting through the cognitive system" (2008, p. 263). Notably, maladaptive conclusions regarding the nature of reality drive an anxiety disorder, and through cognitive therapy the therapist leads the patient to reevaluate these maladaptive conclusions by treating them as testable hypotheses.

For example, Anna was in CT because she had frequent, unpredictable panic attacks. Through CT, she realized that at the beginning of each attack the following thought entered her mind: "My shortness of breath means I must be in danger. I can't breathe! This is really bad!" (This is Step 1.) When she evaluated the accuracy of the thought with her therapist (Step 2), she realized that being short of breath is just a physical symptom that isn't necessarily linked to danger. So she replaced that thought (Step 3) with the thought, "I am short of breath. It's a symptom I don't like. But I know I'm not going to stop breathing or have a heart attack. So I will begin focusing on exhaling more slowly."

While altering fear-based thoughts and beliefs is crucial to overcoming an anxiety disorder, in my experience cognitive interventions alone are often not sufficient when addressing anxiety disorders. Individuals with anxiety disorders hold firmly engrained patterns of psychophysical overreactivity. I find that asking my clients to simply think their way out of these patterns of reactivity is akin to telling a driver's ed student to hit the brakes in a car with a faulty braking system. Knowing what to do is only half the battle. It is also important to provide clients with interventions that will actively help them to rewire their ingrained response patterns, in effect repairing their braking apparati. Therefore, you will note that most cognitive interventions in this book are paired with other techniques, such as behavioral interventions, which will be described below.

Behavioral Therapy

Behavioral therapy is based on the premise that changing your behavior will change your beliefs and thoughts. In effect, it is the converse of cognitive therapy in which you change your thought patterns to change your behavior. For example, rather than altering your thinking by telling yourself, "There's no danger when I go out on the balcony," you would change the behavior by actually going out on the balcony and having the *experience* of being safe. That experience would, in turn, help you to change your thoughts regarding the danger of heights, and resolve your fear.

In behavioral therapy, you confront your anxieties through exercises that expose you to the situation or object that causes you anxiety. These exposure exercises, also called *exposure therapies*, are powerful treatments for anxiety disorders. However, they are challenging to carry out because you have to be willing to endure the very situations and feelings that you find extremely distressing and seek to avoid.

Avoiding that which you fear, an instinct common to everyone who has anxiety disorders, actually strengthens the fear. Rather than continuing to engage in avoidance, exposure exercises force you to tolerate and even accept what you fear. They provide you undeniable experiences of surviving what you're afraid of, which challenge your fear-based thoughts and beliefs. For example, Jeff, who was terrified of public speaking, agreed to give a speech as an exposure exercise. His heart pounded and hands trembled the whole time, but he survived his presentation, amazed that his audience hadn't laughed at him. He began to wonder if it was possible that giving speeches wasn't as dangerous as he believed. As he did more exposure exercises, he gradually let go of his fear.

Behavioral therapy uses two types of exposure treatments: gradual exposure and flooding.

Gradual Exposure (GE)

Most people enter a swimming pool in one of two ways. In gradual exposure, first you dip a toe in, then take it out, then put your whole foot in to acclimate to the coolness; then you lower your calves into the water; then your waist; and so on until you lower your head into the water. That's how gradual exposure works with your anxieties. You expose yourself to a little bit of anxiety and get used to it before moving toward more discomfort. There are two types of gradual exposure. In *systematic desensitization*, the therapist combines relaxation exercises with exposure to facilitate this gradual "dipping" process. Exposure exercises that do not include relaxation are called *graduated exposure.*

Regardless of the type of GE you choose, to facilitate this gradual "dipping" process you and your therapist develop a list of situations that bring you anxiety. Then you put these situations in order from least to most anxiety provoking. Each successive step in the list would be akin to a successive step entering a chilly pool. This list is called a *desensitization hierarchy.* For example, Jack, who had a phobia of dogs, began his hierarchy with just imagining in his mind's eye the sight of a dog approaching him. Further along in his list he planned to watch his friend take her dog on a walk, but he would maintain at least a 20-foot distance from his friend and her dog as he observed. His final two steps, however, consisted of taking his friend's dog on a walk himself, and spending 15 minutes sitting in the fenced-in "dog park" area designated for off-leash play at Jack's neighborhood park. By the end of treatment, Jack would be fully immersed in that which he feared: he planned to sit in a neighborhood dog park. In flooding therapies Jack would have the same end result, but the process by which he got there would differ considerably.

Flooding

The other exposure technique, flooding, can be likened to cannonballing straight into the swimming pool. There's nothing gradual about it. The biting cold can be overwhelming at first, and you might feel a strong urge to leap out of the pool, but it doesn't take long to get used to the discomfort, and then for the discomfort to ease. For example, if Jack had chosen to do flooding he would head straight to the dog park for his first exposure experience. Unlike gradual exposure, flooding does not allow you to ease slowly into your discomfort, but instead forces you to confront it directly.

Occasionally, just one flooding experience is sufficient to eliminate a fear. This has been shown to be the case for the treatment of some phobias, such as those involving fears of animals, injections, or medical visits (Barlow, 2002). However, other research has found that most of the time several exposure sessions are needed to reach extinction (A. Alladen, personal communication, April 6, 2010). Despite various trends in research, I believe that in practice it is always important to remember that there are no absolutes. The number of sessions required to treat a specific client's anxiety is determined by the complexity of that client's disorder and the disorder's exact nature.

Some flooding techniques allow you to stop the exercise at any time, in effect swimming to the pool steps before you've gotten used to the cold water. Then you have to jump in again and try to tolerate the cold for a longer time. For example, Jack might flee the dog park after only a minute, only to regroup and go back in a few minutes later, this time for a longer amount of time. Other techniques encourage you to remain in the water until you acclimate to the cold, without the option to abort and try again. If Jack had chosen to do this type of flooding therapy, he and his therapist might have agreed that he would initially remain in the dog park for, say, five minutes. Jack would enter the park noting the time on his watch, and remain in the park until the five minutes had passed. Regardless of the flooding technique you use, if you do "take the plunge" and find you can tolerate the cold shock long enough to get used to the water, you become free to enjoy the pool as long as you please. Once Jack had remained in the park for a number of minutes, his body would learn that he would indeed not be attacked, and his nervous system would calm down. Despite the different methodology, flooding accomplishes the same result as gradual exposure: complete immersion in the feared circumstances.

Because flooding protocols are particularly intense, the flooding experience itself is likely to become a source of anticipatory anxiety for your clients. Thus it is very important that you adequately prepare your clients for this experience. Share reports of the efficacy of this approach, as well as what to expect during the exercise before initiating any flooding. Your enthusiasm and confidence in directing this technique will be infectious. It is also important that you evaluate whether or not a client possesses a sufficient degree of resilience to undergo this often-challenging course of treatment. Obviously, a strong therapeutic alliance also need exist.

For GE and flooding to be effective, you must give up your comfort and sense of safety in order to face the source of your anxiety. GE is less daunting than flooding, because its gradated levels of discomfort and its acclimation period let you learn to manage your discomfort over time. Flooding, on the other hand, is an intense, powerful method that can be hard to endure. However, it has its advantages. Some clients and therapists prefer it to GE because flooding takes less time to achieve the same goal as GE. In addition, some research indicates that the therapeutic gains achieved through flooding are sometimes retained better than those achieved through GE techniques (Barlow, 2002). As there is considerable support for the effectiveness of both techniques, choosing which type of exposure therapy is right for you depends a lot upon your personality style. Were you the kid who insisted that your Band-Aids be ripped off quickly, or pulled off slowly, centimeter by centimeter? Were you the one who cannon-balled into the deep end of swimming pools, or did you linger on the steps at the shallow end?

Research examining the benefits of GE versus flooding show varied and often conflicting results. For example, there are conflicting opinions and research regarding possible increased rates of dropout for exposure therapies, and flooding in particular. Some studies demonstrate higher dropout or noncompliance rates for flooding versus GE, and others show no significant difference between the two whatsoever. While the conflicting research could increase one's likelihood of using GE over flooding in order to minimize dropout and noncompliance, the jury is still out as to whether this is a valid contention.

Other research indicates that the outcome of some flooding therapies—a reduction of fear—was sometimes maintained more strongly than outcomes from GE (Barlow, 2002). When patients who successfully underwent either flooding or gradual exposure were polled five years after the end of their treatment, those who underwent flooding reported that less, if any, of their fearful symptoms reemerged than did those who underwent GE. Nevertheless, many patients and therapists do opt to use GE rather than flooding because GE offers a less concentrated means to the same end of immersion.

Cognitive Behavioral Therapy (CBT)

Cognitive behavioral therapy adds action to thought. A popular riddle goes: three frogs were sitting on a log. One decided to jump off. How many frogs remained on the log? The answer: three frogs. In this case, a decision (thought) is only half of the story. The decision does not do the frog any good until he actually takes the action decided upon (jumping). CBT is a highly effective treatment for anxiety disorders because it skillfully combines cognitive and behavioral approaches. On an intuitive level, this makes sense: if you ultimately need to change your thoughts and your behaviors, why not use both treatment modalities? Thus a therapist using CBT might have you create a list of your fear-related thoughts and then give you an exposure exercise to change your behavior *and* evaluate the accuracy of your thoughts and beliefs. In the following chapters, as you are reading through some therapeutic interventions, anytime you note that both cognitive and behavioral components are present within a single technique, you are reading about an intervention that uses CBT.

Relaxation Training

As you will learn in the next chapters, anxiety responses involve the entire body, triggering nervous-system activation and sometimes creating a prolonged state of hyperarousal. To counter the physical effects of anxiety and to interrupt the hyperarousal, many therapists offer relaxation training as part of treatment. This consists of a variety of techniques, such as breathing exercises or hypnotic interventions that allow you to calm your entire system—mind and body—when you are anxious or frightened.

In the next five chapters, you will learn many relaxation techniques. Some have been developed specifically for the anxiety disorder being discussed, and others are useful for any type of anxiety. They are listed below along with the chapters in which they are explicated in detail:

- Mindful breathing (see Chapter 4)
- 4 square breathing (see Chapter 4)
- Breathing words (see Chapter 4)
- Balloon breaths (see Chapter 4)
- Autogenics (see Chapter 4)
- Dialing down anxiety (see Chapter 4)
- Breathing in the light (see Chapter 5)
- Tight fist (see Chapters 5 and 9)
- Guided imagery/safe place (see Chapter 4)
- Progressive relaxation (see Chapter 4)

All the techniques are simple and easy to implement when you find yourself triggered by anxiety or fear.

The use of relaxation interventions to self-regulate when encountering acute anxiety or fear is a topic of debate, as it falls into the category of what some modalities such as particular types of CBT term *safety behaviors*. Safety behaviors appease one's anxiety. While this might sound like a good thing, some therapists feel that the use of safety behaviors such as relaxation techniques in response to anxiety actually prolongs the course of the anxiety disorder, as well as its treatment. Some argue that using strategies to calm the anxiety during exposure techniques only reinforces the client's belief in the power of his or her fears. Therapists in this camp, for example, would not use systematic desensitization as it pairs relaxation training with exposure as a client progresses through a desensitization hierarchy.

I, however, find that it is crucial to provide my clients with skills to quickly calm their bodies and minds when a fear response begins to erupt, and therefore often pair self-regulating techniques with exposure. Nonetheless, what is most important as you read this book is to identify the techniques and strategies that resonate with you and fit the needs and preferences of your clients.

I also recommend to many of my clients that they develop a daily relaxation regimen: a repertoire of relaxation techniques that they use on a daily basis. I think of it as an exercise routine for the mind, body, and soul. With sustained practice of these relaxation techniques and increasing skill, I also teach my clients that they are then able to utilize these relaxation techniques to diffuse anxiety as it arises both outside of the therapy room *and* while we are working through various other therapeutic interventions.

Mindfulness

Mindfulness is a mental attitude and a way of responding to problems. Thanks in large part to the contributions of Jon Kabat-Zinn, whose work has brought mindfulness-based approaches to the forefront, more therapists have recently been incorporating mindfulness as a part of treatment. At the heart of mindfulness is simple acceptance of your experience in each moment. The premise underlying mindfulness as it is used in therapy is that change can't occur when you avoid or suppress what's happening. Only by accepting each moment can your experience change.

Mindfulness practices teach you to simply observe the ebb and flow of your ever-changing emotions, feelings, urges, and desires, and to be aware of these states without judging them or trying to change them. Rather, in mindfulness you become open to what *is*. Mindfulness approaches typically include four components: attending to the breath; focusing attention on the body by "scanning" your body for current physical sensations; walking meditation; and incorporating mindfulness into your everyday life. These four components are discussed in more detail below.

Attending to Breath

This calming practice involves simply watching your breath, with no effort to control it. When the mind wanders off, you gently bring your attention back to it. Paying attention to the breath trains you to focus on the present moment in a relaxed way. If you have an anxiety disorder, you probably focus on your fearful thoughts, feelings, physical sensations, and fears about the future. Many therapists teach attention on the breath in order to train anxiety patients to pay attention to what currently *is*. When you focus on the present, you circumvent your tendency to worry about the future. When you pay attention to what is happening this very moment, no matter where you are or what you are doing, you inevitably become calmer.

The Body Scan

The body scan involves focusing attention on the body with the same non-judgmental attitude that you bring to your breathing. If you have an anxiety disorder, you are prone to holding tension in your body, so the body scan is an invaluable tool in your recovery. At first glance, this might seem paradoxical, because anxiety sufferers are often intensely aware of and focused on the sensations in their bodies. What's different about the body scan is that instead of worrying about the sensations, it teaches you an attitude of peace as you attend to the sensations in your body. You accept the sensations as a detached witness, without judgment, interpretation, or analysis of your physical sensations.

Often, the result of the body scan is that the physical sensations you notice soften rather than intensify, as they do when you worry and analyze them. When sensations such as tension, knots, and pain are observed with focused awareness and acceptance, you become less afraid of them.You learn to separate sensing *what is* from the catastrophizing thoughts and worries that you formerly paired with such sensations.

Walking Meditation

Walking meditation is another mindfulness technique that facilitates complete engagement in the present moment, this time by focusing on your footsteps and your breath. As you walk, you gently notice the sensation of contact between the ground and your feet, as each foot lifts from the pavement and makes contact again and again. You can also focus on the way your inhalation and exhalation naturally and rhythmically coincide with each step. You let go of thinking, judging, analyzing, and deciding, and instead simply experience the immediate sensations of walking.

Mindfulness in Everyday Life

Whereas you need time to yourself to practice mindful breathing, the body scan, and mindful walking, you can incorporate an attitude of mindfulness into all your daily activities. For example, when you are washing the dishes, you can focus your attention on the sensation of the warm water on your hands and the shape and colors of the soap bubbles as they glide across a dish. When you brush your teeth, you can attend to the tingling sensation of the brush on your gums, or the experience of your hand movements. Because mindfulness is simply focused awareness of the present moment, the possibilities for practicing it are endless.

Eating a meal mindfully, for instance, involves simply noticing the sensual experience of eating—the color of the food, its scent, the sensations of chewing, taste, and texture. When you practice mindful eating, you will not only enjoy your food more and digest it better because your mind isn't filled with worries, but you will also eliminate mindless overeating that contributes to weight gain.

Mindfulness is a way of training yourself to pay attention to life. Anxiety sufferers are consumed by fears and worry. With practice, mindfulness can decrease the impact of your anxiety disorder and greatly enhance your overall quality of life.

Miller, Fletcher, and Kabat-Zinn (1995) conducted a study of the effect of mindfulness meditation–based stress reduction interventions in the treatment of anxiety disorders. Clients who underwent mindfulness protocols experienced a significant reduction in the frequency and intensity of both subjective and objective measures of anxiety at both three-month and three-year follow-ups.

If your patients are interested in developing a mindfulness practice, you might suggest they join a mindfulness meditation group for support and reinforcement. The UCLA Semel Institute also offers some online resources for those interested in pursuing the practice.

Acceptance and Commitment Therapy

In recent years there has been an increasing interest in the therapeutic community in a comprehensive therapy approach called Acceptance and Commitment Therapy (ACT). ACT (pronounced as one word rather than as an acronym) incorporates mindfulness techniques and cognitive behavioral strategies to provide a three-part method for enhancing the quality of your life in the present moment. The goal of ACT is not to eliminate symptoms of anxiety, but to diminish their impact on your life. In his book *ACT Made Simple*, physician and psychotherapist Russ Harris wrote that the aim of ACT "is not to reduce [a patient's] symptoms but to fundamentally change his relationship with his symptoms so they no longer hold him back from valued living" (2009, p. 4). George Eifert and John Forsyth, authors of *Acceptance and Commitment Therapy for Anxiety*, came up with an alternate ACT acronym that succinctly captures the process: "Accept, Choose Directions and Take Action" (2005, p. 100).

Accept

This element of ACT is similar to mindfulness. When applied to anxiety disorders, ACT teaches you how to simply acknowledge and accept a worried or anxious thought with compassion and without struggle. Let's say you have to take a board exam and you catch yourself thinking, "I'm going to do terribly on my exam." To create some detachment from the anxious thought without fighting it, you simply say to yourself, "I'm having a thought that I'm going to flunk my exam." This separates you from your thought, and lets you give up the struggle to avoid the worry or fix it. With acceptance, you let go of the need to control and discover that your discomfort actually decreases.

Choose Directions

ACT emphasizes that quality of life is dependent on our living in a way that is congruent with our core values, or that which is most important to us. The choosing-directions component of ACT helps you to identify your core values. Eifert and Forsyth explained that "it is about [clients'] choosing to go forward in directions that are uniquely theirs *and* accepting what is inside them, what comes with them, and what accompanies them along the way" (2005, p. 7).

If you suffer from anxiety, you may be away of only one core value: to get rid of your anxiety. ACT helps you identify other aspects and qualities of life that you deeply value and that bring you greater fulfillment. Thus ACT encourages you to focus your mind and energy on more than anxiety reduction, and helps you embrace the full possibilities of your life.

Take Action

The last component of ACT emphasizes action: you are to walk the walk rather than just talk the talk. Once you have identified your core values, the ACT therapist helps you follow through with a commitment to action. This involves selecting a life goal congruent with your values and taking small but steady steps toward achieving the goal. For example, if good parenting is an important value to you, your goal could be becoming a more attentive parent. However, your anxiety might be interfering with your ability to be fully present with your children. For example, if you have OCD and obsess over germs, you might busy yourself with cleaning chores to calm your anxiety, leaving your children to get a snack and begin their homework while you are elsewhere in the house. An action step toward your goal might be postponing your cleaning ritual in order to give your children your undivided attention for the first half-hour they are home from school.

Eye Movement Desensitization and Reprocessing (EMDR)

EMDR was developed in the late 1980s as a powerful and efficient means of helping diffuse the fear and distress that people with post-traumatic stress disorder experience in the wake of trauma. Because EMDR helps *desensitize*, or decrease distress of anxiety-provoking situations, today many therapists also use it for the treatment of anxiety and anxiety disorders, including specific phobias, panic disorder, and agoraphobia. In the treatment of specific phobias, it can be used to help diffuse the fear and panic associated with encountering the feared situation or stimulus. In the treatment of panic disorder with and without agoraphobia, EMDR can diffuse the anticipatory anxiety associated with panic attacks, and the distress associated with the memories of previous panic attacks and phobic encounters.

While EMDR is considered an evidence-based treatment for PTSD, the little research that does exist suggests that it is not as efficacious in exposure therapies for the treatment of specific phobias, panic disorder, or agoraphobia. While exposure may still be the treatment of choice, you might consider EMDR as an adjunct. EMDR can be helpful in cases in which in vivo exposure is difficult because you only see patients in an office setting. For example, EMDR may be a more practical treatment than in vivo exposure for an individual with a phobia of flying on airplanes. Likewise, for a patient with a phobia of thunderstorms, a session utilizing EMDR would not require the occurrence of a thunderstorm, as in vivo exposure would. As EMDR has been shown to help alleviate symptomatology stemming from trauma, it may be especially helpful in the treatment of specific phobias that do have a traumatic origin.

EMDR not only helps by desensitization, it also allows you to *reprocess* the memory or association that is distressing to you. As the distress surrounding, say, your phobic object diminishes, you are also integrating a less distressing association with the memory and processing the association more fully.

Unlike most therapies, EMDR achieves these changes without your exploring your past fears, changing your behaviors or your beliefs. So how does it happen? That remains something of a mystery. EMDR makes use of bilateral stimulation, which alternately activates each hemisphere of your brain while you think of a distressing (or positive) thought or memory. When EMDR was first developed, this stimulation was done through left-to-right eye movements: hence the "E" and "M" in EMDR. Now EMDR therapists have various different techniques and equipment that can facilitate bilateral stimulation. Some therapists use creative visual stimulation with light boards in the shape of a ruler, on which a light travels back and forth as you follow it with your eyes. Others simply have you follow the movement of their finger back and forth in front of your eyes. Auditory and tactile stimulation also works. Some EMDR practitioners have you hold "tappers," two egg-sized pods that alternately vibrate as you hold them in your palms, or wear headphones that alternate their sound input between each ear.

EMDR's founder, Francine Shapiro, has postulated that the bilateral stimulation helps your brain process information and access related thoughts and memories. This diminishes distress and enhances a sense of resolution of the initial memory or association.

Emotional Freedom Technique (EFT)

EFT is a technique that incorporates aspects of traditional Chinese medicine, including acupressure, to stimulate the *meridian system*, or channels of energy throughout the body. According to Gary Craig, the founder of EFT, all negative emotions are caused by an energy imbalance in the body. Craig has developed an elaborate protocol for tapping particular acupuncture points depending on the emotions creating problems.

EFT therapists have you repeat a statement that names your problem (e.g., worry, rumination, phobia) with a positive affirmation (e.g., *Even though I have a phobia of heights, I deeply and profoundly accept myself*). As you say the statement, you follow a tapping protocol, tapping various acupuncture points, as directed by your therapist. Once learned, you can progress through this tapping procedure in under a minute. The procedure can quickly stop an unwanted fearful thought or emotional reaction, in some cases permanently.

Many people who practice EFT have found it to be powerful, effective, and efficient. There is, however, much skepticism as to the effectiveness of the technique, and some question as to how it works. We explore this issue in more detail in the therapists' box below, so if you are interested please do have a look.

Critics of EFT suggest that the helpful components of EFT lie not in the manipulation of energy fields by the mindful tapping, but in the distraction the tapping provides from one's negative thoughts. This doesn't explain why the procedure is often effective long after the tapping has stopped. Others attribute its effectiveness to the placebo effect, or to its more cognitive components: the identification of a negative thought or belief and the accompanying desire and intention to have this negative belief diminish and one's self-acceptance increase.

Unfortunately, it is not likely that this debate will subside any time soon. As clinicians, it is important that we keep an open mind to new treatment approaches and remember that just as our clients will resonate with some approaches over others, so will we. If you find EFT compelling or potentially valuable, I would not let the criticism regarding EFT deter you from pursuing training in this modality.

Despite the skepticism that exists and the unorthodox methodology, many of my clients have had success with EFT, and a number of colleagues whom I respect are champions of the approach. EFT can be incorporated easily into many treatments for anxiety disorders.

Hypnosis

Hypnosis is another powerful modality that can help you manage apprehension, fear, or worries by altering the cognitive, emotional, behavioral, and physical responses that accompany your anxiety. As such it can be a powerful adjunct to both cognitive and behavioral treatments. Beyond these two realms, hypnosis allows you to be receptive to many different strategies that you can utilize to enhance your recovery process. I often incorporate hypnosis into any treatment modality for anxiety disorders.

One meta-analysis found that the incorporation of hypnotherapeutic techniques into cognitive behavioral protocols significantly enhanced treatment outcome in comparison to clients who solely underwent CBT (Kirsch, Montgomery, & Sapirstein, 1995). In a review of current research on the efficacy of hypnosis, Schoenberger (2000) also found that hypnosis in combination with CBT produced greater anxiety reduction than CBT alone. Likewise, hypnotherapeutic techniques have been found particularly helpful in the facilitation of exposure protocols, as they can enhance a client's ability to engage in imaginal exposure via enhanced scene visualization (Deiker & Pollock, 1975). More globally, hypnotherapeutic techniques can enhance the likelihood of transfer and the maintenance of therapeutic gains, as clinicians may utilize post-hypnotic suggestion to facilitate behavior rehearsal.

People often have a misunderstanding of what hypnosis is. Hypnosis is simply a state of focused attention that is usually, but not always, accompanied by relaxation. Psychologist D. Corydon Hammond, a renowned expert in hypnosis, described hypnosis as " . . . the art of securing a [client's] attention and then effectively communicating ideas that enhance motivation and change perceptions" (1990, p. 2). This can be likened to imagination training, in which you are guided to use your imagination to experience changes in emotions, physical sensations, attitudes, and behaviors. To facilitate this process of imagination, hypnosis typically involves the five sequential phases below:

- Hypnotic induction
- Deepening

- Therapeutic suggestion
- Post-hypnotic suggestions
- Alerting

Hypnotic Induction

The first phase of a hypnotic experience is the *induction* phase. During the induction, you are encouraged to get comfortable, to let go of external stimuli, and to attend to the therapist's voice. Your therapist might say something like: "As you sit in the chair, you can notice the chair supporting your body; your head resting on the head rest; your leg, supported by the leg rest. You might start to focus very carefully on your breath. You don't need to change your breathing . . . simply attend to it and see what you notice . . ." While there are many different approaches to induction, all induction techniques serve to narrow and focus your attention. Usually, during the induction phase, clients experience eye fatigue and naturally close their eyes, though hypnosis can occur with your eyes open.

Deepening

In the deepening phase, you are led into a relaxed state in which conscious, analytical thinking and processing are diminished and you become more open to suggestion and to accessing memories, insights, and internal resources. Common deepening techniques utilize peaceful and pleasant visual imagery and direct suggestions to relax or envision yourself descending down a stairway or elevator. Some hypnotherapists also use indirect approaches to deepen a hypnotic trance, such as telling stories of everyday examples of relaxation that engage you.

Sometimes clients worry that they are not going "deep enough," or far enough into a state of hypnosis, when they are undergoing hypnotherapy for anxiety reduction. After the trance session they may comment, "I must not have been hypnotized because I was aware of everything you were saying." Luckily, research shows that "little hypnotic depth is required to reduce anxiety" (Barabasz & Watkins, 2005, p. 187). Thus the degree to which your client has entered into a hypnotic state is less relevant with this client population. Only 40% of people experience hypnotic amnesia, or some degree of a lack of conscious awareness of what has been said during the session (Hammond, 1998).

Therapeutic Suggestion

The third phase, therapeutic suggestion, is really the meat and potatoes of hypnotic interventions. Now that you are in a highly relaxed, focused state, you have an increased capacity to change, grow, and challenge your old, anxiety-producing patterns of thinking and behaving. As Dr. Corydon Hammond noted, when suggestions that are compatible with a client's goals are given when the client is in a state of absorbed, focused attention, the suggestions seem to "have more impact on the mind" (1998, p. 6). Thus, in this phase of hypnosis, a clinician usually presents suggestions that help you increase your impulse control, enhance your ability to calm yourself, and learn to better modulate your emotions.

Post-Hypnotic Suggestion

The goal of post-hypnotic suggestion is to increase the likelihood that you incorporate into your daily life the tools and skills learned during hypnosis. For example, let's say that during your hypnotic session you learned to calm your anxiety through the use of a deep-breathing technique. In a post-hypnotic suggestion, the therapist might suggest that each time you notice your anxiety levels rising, you initiate this deep-breathing technique. While it might seem obvious that you need to apply the therapeutic tools you learn to your daily life, it can be a challenge once you leave the therapy office. Post-hypnotic suggestions help to ensure that the transfer of a newly-learned skill set to the outside world actually happens. The therapist can also encourage increased responsiveness to hypnosis with a post-hypnotic suggestion that you will enter each session of hypnosis more quickly and be more responsive to suggestions that diminish your anxiety.

Alerting

In the alerting phase, the therapist gradually guides you back to a state of alert awareness, in which your conscious mind is fully engaged. Typical instructions to come out of hypnosis involve counting forward or backward. It is important, however, that this process is not abrupt. Your therapist is likely to inform you of the transition that is about to occur. An excellent example of one such preparatory statement was given by Harold Golan, DMD: "In a few moments, but not just yet, you'll be opening your eyes. You'll be feeling great just like you have had a pleasant nap. . . . Everything about you will feel comfortable and relaxed. . . . " (1998, p. 55). Once you are prepared to transition, an activity like counting might occur.

Self-Hypnosis

The term "self-hypnosis" simply refers to your entering into a hypnotic state of focused attention and absorption independently, in the absence of your therapist. Indeed, many clinicians believe that all hypnosis is self-hypnosis and that the therapist is just a facilitator and guide for the process. Although you may feel as if you are not going as deeply into a hypnotic state without a therapist guiding you, self-hypnosis can be effective and can bring about desired results. Practicing self-hypnosis can reinforce the relaxation techniques and therapeutic tools that you learn in therapy. By reinforcing these tools, you can substantially decrease your anxiety.

In order to conduct a self-hypnosis session, write down your goals and the suggestions you want to give yourself to meet those goals. Then narrow your attention by focusing on a spot on the wall or ceiling, or on your breathing. You can deepen the hypnotic state by doing progressive relaxation or imagining a safe place (see Chapter 4 for specific techniques for focusing attention and inducing relaxation). You might also make self-suggestions such as "I am relaxing deeply now," or "with each exhalation, I am getting more and more relaxed."

Once you have achieved a state of relaxation, you can give yourself suggestions to help you with your anxiety, such as facing fears, releasing tension, building positive expectations, or developing other healthy attitudes or behaviors. Then you can re-alert by counting backward from 10 to 1.

While some clients learn to slip easily into self-hypnosis, you might find it easier to go into self-hypnosis if you listen to audio recordings. If you are interested in this option, you can ask your hypnotherapist to make an audio recording of the stages of hypnosis that you can listen to at home. Thus there are many ways to make self-hypnosis work for you. By becoming proficient in self-hypnosis you can practice hypnosis at any time, thus making this practice a more portable self-management resource.

Can Hypnosis Work for You?

If you have an anxiety disorder, you might assume you are too anxious to be hypnotized. On the contrary, *because* you are anxious you probably have several qualities that make you highly hypnotizable, naturally able to go into a hypnotic state easily and to respond particularly well to hypnosis. First, you probably have a vivid imagination. OK, you use it to imagine all the awful things that could befall you, but you can use it as a resource when you learn hypnosis. Second, if you have an anxiety disorder, you tend to be sensitive to your body sensations (OK, perhaps too sensitive). In hypnosis, you can use that sensitivity to alter how your body experiences stress. Finally, you have a great ability to focus your attention (OK, you focus mostly on your worries or fears). You can use that skill for the hypnotic state, which calls for focused attention and absorption.

Many common misconceptions about hypnosis come from TV and movies. Contrary to inaccurate representations of hypnosis, you *cannot* be hypnotized against your will, nor can you be made to think or imagine anything you don't want to. While you are in a hypnotic state of focused attention, your conscious mind observes the process. If anything in the experience is uncomfortable or undesired, it comes to the forefront. At no point in hypnotherapy do you surrender your ability to make decisions or advocate for yourself. Just as in any therapeutic endeavor, hypnosis is a collaboration between client and therapist. You are free to intervene at any time and can bring yourself out of this relaxed state at any moment. Indeed, I have found hypnotherapeutic approaches to be invaluable in my treatment of all of the anxiety disorders.

Depth/Insight-Oriented Therapy

Another approach to treating anxiety comes from a very different philosophical orientation than the interventions we have been discussing. Depth/insight-oriented therapy consists of an array of approaches that take into account conflicts that are thought to exist within the psyche—our minds. Specifically, there is an emphasis on unconscious conflicts: conflicts that exist within you but are not in your conscious awareness. Some anxiety disorders may have their root in unconscious conflicts that have been with you since childhood or later. It can be essential to some people's recovery to develop an awareness and resolution of these conflicts or negative experiences.

The goal of depth- or insight-oriented exploration is to elicit conscious awareness of these conflicts, repressed/suppressed memories, and unacceptable thoughts, feelings, and urges that can underlie anxiety. Depth approaches believe that bringing these experiences to your awareness will help you get past your anxiety. In order to do this, you need to gain insight regarding your unconscious conflicts, in effect making the unconscious conscious. Depth therapies can be helpful when such internal conflicts contribute significantly to the manifestation of anxiety.

My own approach is that I tend to be guided by the concept of parsimony: the simplest, most direct route is the one I try first. However, I have found that sometimes when these approaches don't yield sufficient results, some type of insight-oriented treatment is indicated. In these cases, getting to an underlying conflict or trauma that set off a phobic reaction, for example, can be paramount in the successful alleviation of symptoms. Many people with a history of childhood abuse or trauma manifest symptoms of anxiety. In this population in particular, I find it necessary to incorporate some type of uncovering work to help resolve these traumas. Insight-oriented therapies can be an important component of an integrative treatment approach. Whereas this book does not delve into the complex and rich world of depth psychology, a number of the approaches, including hypnotherapy and EMDR, do involve some uncovering work. (See Chapter 7 for a case illustration integrating hypnosis and uncovering.).

Biofeedback

Biofeedback is an intervention that trains you to control body responses that are typically outside of your conscious awareness. For an anxiety disorder, you would use biofeedback to gain conscious control over heart rate, blood pressure, skin temperature, sweat gland activity, and muscle tension—all physiological processes that are routinely overactive if you suffer with anxiety. For example, your heart might race, your skin might become cold and clammy in response to an anxiety reaction, or you might feel your face flooded with heat. You might experience cold sweats or hot sweats. In biofeedback, electrodes feed information to machines that monitor these body processes. The machines, in turn, actually give you moment-by-moment "feedback" regarding the body process being measured. They do so by displaying the levels of activity on a monitor that you view, and some machines also give you auditory cues by using different tones to indicate whether you are nearing optimal ranges of arousal. In effect, the biofeedback process is similar to the children's game in which a person is led to find a hidden object by receiving feedback from a knowing onlooker who says "you're getting closer" or "you're getting farther" as the "seeker" moves about a room. Of course, in the case of biofeedback, you would be the seeker, and the knowing onlooker would be the machine.

In response to the feedback from the machine and the helpful facilitation from your biofeedback clinician, you can learn to make internal shifts that alter the readings from the electrodes. Through trial and error you can learn how to bring the machine's readings into optimal ranges. For example, if a machine is measuring skin temperature, you can gradually learn what it *feels* like when you are in an optimal range, and learn strategies to willfully guide yourself into this optimal temperature range. To return to the analogy of the children's game, once you have received enough feedback from "the knowing onlooker" (the machine), you will know internally how to locate the desired level of arousal, just as the "seeker" will retain the internal knowledge of where the desired object is hidden. Thus biofeedback is a safe procedure that can give you the much-needed feeling that you can be in control of the physical reactions associated with anxiety—responses that previously felt *out* of your control.

Biofeedback works using principles of operant conditioning in which the feedback given by the machines acts to shape the participant's behavior. Thus the "reward" in this shaping paradigm consists of getting the dial, tone, or vibration in the desired range. Subjects engage in trial and error until the ability to get the reward indicator in the desired range comes under conscious control. Research has yet to demonstrate that the learning process in biofeedback follows established response curves present in operant conditioning, so biofeedback cannot be definitively defined as a form of operant conditioning. I look forward to the knowledge that research in the years to come might offer.

How Do You Learn Biofeedback?
You can learn biofeedback from a professional who has been trained in this methodology. There are also a number of relatively inexpensive monitoring devices that you can use at home on your own (see Appendix for a list of professional organizations that can provide you with a referral for biofeedback or biofeedback equipment). While some people opt to purchase home-use devices and skip initial training with a professional, I would advise receiving training, at least initially, for best results.

As biofeedback and neurofeedback involve the monitoring of the body's natural electrical currents, it is important that you ascertain whether a patient has a heart condition, pacemaker, implanted defibrillators or other electrical devices before pursuing this type of therapy. While individuals with these conditions are still candidates for bio- and neurofeedback, Lake (2009) noted that it is important to exercise caution with these clients. I would recommend that clients who fall into the abovementioned category address any concerns with a biofeedback specialist before initiating treatment.

Neurofeedback
Our nervous systems are affected not only by hormones and chemicals but also by electrical activity. Neurofeedback is a particular type of biofeedback that measures the electrical activity in the brain in the form of brain waves. There are four different categories of brain waves. Using electrodes that feed into an electroencephalography (EEG) machine, you can learn to identify which type of brain waves you are currently experiencing. Just as with other forms of biofeedback, you can also learn to consciously alter the frequency of your brain waves as you see fit. You will learn below that different frequencies of brain waves are associated with different states of attention and that one type, the beta wave, is specifically associated with anxiety. If you have an anxiety disorder, you can use neurofeedback to train your brain to produce more calming brain waves and thus operate in a more stable way.

As mentioned above, electrical activity in the brain is expressed by four main types of brain waves, which each have a different frequency. They are listed here, in order of quickest to slowest frequency:

- beta (fastest)
- alpha
- theta
- delta (slowest)

Beta waves, which are faster than the other brain waves, are needed when you wish to be actively engaged in a mental task, say studying for an exam, but are also associated with stress and anxiety. Too many beta waves can interfere with attempts to relax or make you feel that you are on alert, even in non-stressful situations. If you are anxious and easily stressed, you may generate beta waves frequently.

Alpha brain waves are associated with physical and mental relaxation, while theta waves are associated with drowsiness, meditation, dreaming, sub-conscious states, and hypnosis. Delta waves are the slowest of the four brain-wave frequencies, and are associated with deep sleep.

Riding the Waves: The Process of Neurofeedback

One of my early teachers in hypnosis, psychologist D. Corydon Hammond, enthusiastically supports using neurofeedback with his clients to help train their brains to function more optimally. He reports observing that neuro-feedback has had a positive impact on many of his clients who have anxiety disorders.

Initially a few electrodes are placed on the scalp along with a few on the earlobes. Once the electrodes are in place, the electrical activity of your brain is recorded on a computer. Just as with the other biofeedback machines, you are given real-time feedback on your actual brain wave activity by seeing it via video or audio display. As you observe your brain activity, you engage in the slight internal shifts described above with the other biofeedback techniques. Also similarly, you engage in a trial and error process. In this process you use the machine's feedback as an indicator until you reach a point where you can consciously guide your brain waves into the desired frequency without the aid of the EEG equipment. For example, if you notice you are experiencing an excessive amount of anxiety and recognize you are operating at a beta wave frequency, you can choose to alter to, say, alpha. If your heightened anxiety is making getting to sleep a challenge, you can volitionally shift into theta and then delta frequencies as you lay in bed. As with other forms of biofeedback, neurofeedback can help provide you with a sense of mastery over aspects of your anxiety that were previously out of your control.

Integrative Approaches

Good psychotherapy incorporates creativity. Throughout this book you will find many interventions that pull from a variety of treatment approaches, incorporating two or three of the modalities listed above into a single intervention. For example, in Chapter 9 you will find Schwartz's four-step approach for the treatment of obsessive–compulsive disorder. This approach incorporates components of mindfulness and cognitive therapy. You will then see how hypnotherapeutic techniques can complement and enhance this treatment. In this way, there are endless possibilities for the creation of a multifaceted and individually crafted treatment plan. As you proceed through this book you will hopefully gain an understanding of what therapeutic techniques and adjunctive approaches you might wish to investigate and discuss with your therapist. Should you choose to seek out therapy, you will be well prepared to be an active participant as your treatment team develops an integrated treatment approach to best suit your individual needs.

Adjunctive Methods

Another part of the development of an integrated treatment plan is the incorporation of many different adjuncts, or add-ons, to psychotherapy. At some point in your treatment you and your clinician might want to collaborate with a psychiatrist, family physician, or integrative medicine physician. You might also want to consider altering your exercise habits and diet. Thus in the final chapters of this book we will discuss several adjunctive approaches that have been very helpful to clients with anxiety disorders.

Choosing a Treatment

While it is important to remain open-minded to trying different therapeutic approaches, some types of interventions and therapists will fit better with your personality style and needs than others. Luckily, there is a wealth of different therapeutic modalities *and* therapists out there for you to work with. The downside to this plethora of opportunities is that not every therapist you work with will be trained in all of the therapeutic modalities you might be interested in exploring. If you are working with a therapist who does not have training in a methodology that you are interested in, I encourage you to talk about this with your therapist. There may well be another therapist to whom your current therapist can refer you.

If this is the case, you might agree to put your current therapy on hold while you have some sessions with another practitioner. Alternately, if all involved agree it is a good idea, you can arrange to continue to see your primary therapist for supportive psychotherapy while undergoing treatment in the alternate modality with the other practitioner. Whereas it is traditionally not standard practice to see two therapists concurrently, I have found that it has not been a problem for my clients to continue to see their primary therapist while getting more specialized treatments for an anxiety disorder. Many therapists are eager to see their clients benefit from the range of treatments available to them.

I make a great effort to tailor my interventions to match both the symptomatology and personality of my clients. If my initial intervention does not show results, I keep working to find what does work for that individual client. To this end, I have found it a professional asset to continually expand my repertoire of therapeutic tools. I encourage you to keep abreast of new and even "alternative" therapeutic interventions and capitalize on a wide range of professional development opportunities.

Evidence-Based vs. Non-Evidence-Based Therapies: An Ongoing Debate

There is much debate among psychologists regarding the use of therapeutic techniques that are not evidence based. The term denotes treatments whose efficacy for specific disorders has been tested by researchers. Some therapists feel that they shortchange their clients if they use an intervention that has not been demonstrated by research to be effective. Other therapists feel they are shortchanging their clients if they eliminate interventions from their repertoire just because their effectiveness has not been adequately or conclusively researched.

There are many reasons that a therapeutic treatment might not be evidence based. Some interventions, by their nature, do not lend themselves well to clinical research. This is especially true of modalities in which interventions are individualized for each patient. Also, the process of empirical research takes a lot of time and funding. This is all to say that just because a technique has not been empirically validated does not mean that it does not work, or cannot work for you. Likewise, there is never any guarantee that *any* intervention will be the right one for a particular client. Neither you nor your client should feel like you have failed in therapy if, despite giving your best efforts to an intervention, it has not been highly effective.

In the chapters that follow, you'll learn all about the different anxiety disorders, the day-to-day problems they cause, and the treatments that are commonly used for them. Each chapter includes recovery stories of people who have been diagnosed with the disorder and details of their treatment. You may find it useful at first to return to the overview of information about different treatments in this chapter until you become more familiar with each.

CHAPTER 4

Relaxation Techniques for Everyone

In the previous chapter, you discovered that a wide range of therapeutic treatment options is available to people suffering with anxiety and that I recommend an individualized approach integrating diverse treatments. There is one constant, however—the bedrock of all approaches for treating anxious clients—and that is relaxation techniques. Early in the treatment process, I teach clients a variety of techniques for calming the physical revving up that comes with anxiety. By practicing the techniques on their own, outside our sessions, my clients become skilled in the relaxation techniques that work best for them and can use these techniques as needed. You will see these techniques pop up time and time again as part of the treatments for particular disorders in the following chapters.

This chapter describes relaxation techniques that are applicable to all the types of anxiety disorders presented in this book. Even before entering treatment for anxiety, you can try them on your own. (These are also useful tools for more generic, situational anxiety that everyone experiences now and then.) There's no reason for you to go even another day without getting the relief these tools can offer.

Many of the techniques include scripts that guide you through the exercise. You can have a friend or spouse read the script to you as you practice an exercise, or you can record the scripts before beginning the relaxation exercise. Of course, you can also learn and practice them with the help of a therapist. This is exactly what the clients you'll meet later in the book do.

You might find that you prefer some relaxation techniques over others, that some of the techniques aren't a good fit for you while you take to others right away. Individual preference is normal. It is for this reason that I offer many different anxiety-reduction techniques to work with. Only through trial and error will you find the ones that really work best for you. That being said, I also encourage you, as I do my clients, not to give up if a particular exercise doesn't immediately feel like a good fit. The effectiveness of each of these techniques increases with practice. I have found that sometimes a client's most powerful relaxation tool turns out to be one that he or she didn't immediately take to. Even with the techniques that initially work well for you, it is important that you practice them regularly, because with repeated practice any tool will become all the more powerful.

I now encourage you to sit back, relax, and try out the anxiety-reducing techniques below. Don't wait to start getting relief from your anxiety.

The ABCs of Breathing

Normally, we breathe without thought or effort. It is so fundamental that we often overlook the *way* we breathe. For individuals with anxiety disorders, certain breathing patterns cause the body to hold a lot of tension. Learning the ABCs of breathing—Attention to Breathing and Calming—is of great benefit to anyone experiencing anxiety.

Simply attending to the breath or consciously slowing the rate of breathing is a simple but highly effective way to reduce tension and calm the nervous system. When experiencing heightened anxiety or when the body is stressed, people often breathe quickly and shallowly, which causes the body to lose the carbon dioxide needed to think clearly and stay relaxed. Slow, steady, deep breathing, on the other hand, is associated with emotional equilibrium and serenity. Because breathing exercises are concrete, easy to remember, and remarkably effective, it is easy to establish the practice of mindful, slow, deep breathing.

A variety of simple but powerful breathing techniques, several of which are outlined below, are drawn from mindfulness approaches as well as from Buddhist teachings and Eastern martial arts and yoga. You can try the exercises listed below, seek out others, or create your own. The key is finding breathing techniques that work best for you.

One note of caution: for a minority of individuals, such as those with panic disorder who experience shortness of breath (see Chapter 6), breathing exercises can actually increase tension and anxiety. (If you are in the midst of a panic attack, which may cause you to breathe too rapidly, rather than observe your breath you should attempt to slow your respiration rate. To help accomplish this see the two breathing exercises below, *four square breathing* and *breathing words*.) If you experience greater anxiety while trying out these exercises, honor your experience, taking what works and leaving the rest. There are no shoulds or absolutes in overcoming anxiety.

Mindful Breathing

This gentle, non-intrusive breathing exercise involves training yourself to simply pay attention to your breath without trying to alter it. This in itself serves to slow the respiration rate.

> Take a moment to focus on your breath. You don't need to change it; simply notice it. As you do, notice sensations that accompany your breath. With a gentle curiosity, you can notice the texture of your breath, the rhythm of your breath, and even the temperature of the breath. Now take a deeper breath in without straining, and hold it for a moment; as you exhale, notice a letting-go of tension, concerns, expectations, judgments.

Four Square Breathing

This is a particularly good method if your mind easily wanders during less structured breathing approaches such as mindful breathing.

First try this sitting in a comfortable chair. Once you master it, you can do this exercise just about anywhere. All it requires is the ability to count to four.

Sitting comfortably, breathe in to the count of four, hold to the count of four, exhale to the count of four, hold to the count of four. Continue this exercise for about four minutes.

After you have practiced this for awhile, you might find it helpful to incorporate a visual component. As I suggest to my clients, imagine drawing a box. As you breathe in to the count of four, imagine drawing the first side of the box, with the line beginning at the bottom of your visual field and progressing vertically upwards. Then, as you hold your breath to the count of four, imagine the line progressing horizontally from left to right, making the top of the box. Next, while you exhale to the count of four, imagine the line progressing downward to form the right side of the box. Finally, as you hold to the count of four, complete the square by drawing the base line horizontally from right to left.

Breathing Words

Adding words to the breathing process can help in two ways: it gives your mind something to focus on besides your breathing, and it gives you a message you need to hear. Simply think the words as you breathe, rather than actually speaking them.

Sit in a comfortable chair and breathe in the word "I." As you hold the inhalation, think "am re-"; and as you exhale, think "-laxed." Make sure that you take your time going through each of these steps. In particular, exhale slowly.

A variation on this is to think, with every inhalation, "I breathe in safety." With every exhalation, think the phrase, "I breathe out fear."

Balloon Breaths

This exercise involves the deep, diaphragmatic breathing that research has linked with states of relaxation. You may do this in a comfortable chair or lying on the floor. The advantage of having your back against the floor is that you can feel the deep breaths more easily.

Put one hand on your stomach and one on your chest. Inhale (think "in") and notice your diaphragm (just below your ribcage) expanding, like a balloon. Exhale (think "out") and imaging the balloon flattening as your diaphragm draws in. Let your breathing be relaxed and without strain. Repeat this cycle 10 times. Once you've become comfortable with this technique, you can even do it standing up. Because it is inconspicuous, this is a useful technique to do in public when you notice that your breathing has become shallow.

The ABC breathing techniques can be done just about anywhere, at any time. I encourage you to incorporate them into breaks throughout the day: when booting up your computer; at red lights; when waiting in line at the grocery store; the list can go on and on. Even two minutes of focused attention on your breathing can relax your system and create more resilience to stress.

More Tools for Relaxing

Most people who have a severe cold know that just taking Vitamin C isn't enough. They also need to drink lots of fluids and perhaps get extra rest. If you suffer from anxiety, relying only on breathing exercises is like only taking Vitamin C for a cold. Helpful, yes, but why stop there? Let's learn some more.

Guided Imagery: Your Safe Place

Using guided imagery to create a "safe place" is a great tool to relax an overly revved nervous system. It is useful to reduce anxiety that arises in the moment and to ease the physical discomforts that result from chronic anxiety.

Whether you use guided visualizations led by your therapist, recorded on a relaxation CD, or created in your own mind, they help you identify and develop sensory images of safe places—real, imagined, or a combination—evoking the sounds, smells, sights, and sensations of the place that feels utterly safe for *you*. You are the expert on what images work best for you and you are free to create or to change whatever you need in your safe place.

In the guided imagery exercises, you identify the particular images and sensations that you find most soothing. Some people are comforted by images of beaches, sun, and water. Others turn to images of woods, mountains, a garden, or even a cozy room for relaxing. What's most important is that you practice making your visualization so vivid that it seems real.

Once you've chosen a safe place, with all its sights, sounds, smells, and sensations, in an imagery exercise, you will learn to elicit the safety and sensations associated with the safe place any time or place. The more senses you use, the easier it will be to elicit the soothing sensations in the heat of the moment.

The following is an example of a guided imagery exercise that I often use with my clients. To try it out yourself, I suggest reading the script over a few times so that you can guide yourself through it without having to consult the book. Before beginning, do some slow, deep breathing, as described above, to relax. Once in a calm, relaxed state, you are ready to begin.

Focus your attention on developing an image of a pleasant, safe place, a safe haven that represents peace and security to you. Perhaps of a wonderfully sheltering, soothing place in nature, or a place you've visited before; or perhaps you would prefer to go somewhere that you are creating now. Just let your mind drift off to a warm and welcoming place. Let your intuition be your guide. It really doesn't matter where you go, all that matters is that you allow yourself to float off to your special place, allow yourself to be enveloped in the cocoon of safety and security.

Once you are at that safe place, look around. What do you see? What images? What colors? Is the light dim or bright? Are the colors bright or subdued? What smells do you notice? The fragrance of flowers, perhaps, or salt air, or freshly mowed grass, or pine trees? What do you hear? Water lapping at the shore, or birds chirping, or maybe there's a still, soothing silence. What's under your feet? Sand or grass or something else . . . Are you walking or sitting or lying down? Or maybe you feel you are kind of floating there.

Allow yourself to experience being in your safe, secure place fully, with your whole body and mind, all your senses. Let it become even more real to you; you feel so secure, serene and comfortable. You can rest in this place of quietness, of safe solitude, resting your mind, resting your body, deeply down into the quiet. . . . Appreciate the stillness, the absolute stillness that allows you to retreat from the world in your safe place.

Now give your safe place a name, whatever name comes to your mind, a name that you can use as a cue to re-elicit this feeling of comfort, peace, relaxation and rest whenever you wish. You can return to this scene again and again, several times a day, so that it becomes easier and more automatic for you to reconnect to this feeling of comfort. If anxious images come to mind, they can be quickly replaced by the sweet, soothing sensations of just the right images that you created today.

Guided imagery exercises such as this one tap the extraordinary power of the human mind to create positive or negative emotions. With patience and practice, you'll become adept at entering a safe place at will. The skill you gain in imagery will also be useful in the many visualization exercises that are focused on relieving particular aspects of your anxiety disorder.

Visualization for Bodily Distress: Breathing in the Light

If you suffer from anxiety, you probably are all too familiar with the ways anxiety manifests in your body. You might experience stomach pains or cramping, tightness in your chest or tension in your neck and shoulders, hot sweats, shakiness in your arms and legs. There are countless ways anxiety affects the body. In this exercise, you identify the places in your body where tension or anxiety manifests and place a "virtual" compress of sorts exactly where relief is needed. By imagining soothing, colored light being absorbed through deep breathing into places that are uncomfortable, you create an imaginary salve. This calming, soothing light can relieve physical pain or tension and alleviate mounting anxiety. Besides imagining the light, you also place your open palm on the affected region of your body, so your touch can be therapeutic in itself, promoting relaxation and comfort.

Sit in a comfortable chair and focus your attention, with acceptance and curiosity, on your body.

Begin by scanning your body. Notice any tension, tightness, or strain. Pay particular attention to your head, shoulders, neck, chest, and stomach, places where people often hold tension. . . . Once you notice where your body is holding tension, slowly and gently place your hand on that part of your body. If there are two places that are tense, uncomfortable, or painful, place one hand on each of the spots.

As your hands cover these places of tension, feel the warmth from your hand covering the discomfort. Now imagine a soothing light coming toward you, a translucent, colored light, gentle, comforting, peaceful. The light can be cooling or warming, whichever feels best to you. It can be whatever color you choose, a color that is soothing, calming, healing for you.

As you inhale, breathe in that colored light. Let it spread all around that area of your body where your hand rests and imagine the light softening

Anxiety Disorders

the tightness, smoothing the tension, and soothing and easing any strain.

And as you breathe in this soothing light, know that you can breathe it in at any time, whenever there is a place or a space that needs calming or healing.

(Adapted with permission from Daitch, 2007, p. 138–139)

This is a simple yet fundamental exercise, alleviating tension within the body in order to relieve a tensed emotional and mental state of being.

Progressive Relaxation

Progressive Muscle Relaxation (PMR) is a widely used and easy-to-learn method for stress reduction developed in 1939 by American physician Edmund Jacobson. A two-step approach to tensing and relaxing various muscle groups, PMR is especially effective for people whose anxiety is accompanied by muscle tension. The objective, as the person works the various muscle groups, is to become aware of the relaxation of the muscles when the tension is released. (A professionally prepared recording can be used as a guide while learning the technique.)

In this exercise you will consciously tense and then relax the various muscle groups. It is important that you relax the muscle groups for longer than you tense them. I generally suggest that you tense the particular muscle for about 10 seconds and then relax for about 20 seconds. Although in the following procedure we begin by tensing the hands, there are multiple versions of this approach. Some begin with the tensing of the head, progressing downward through the body. Conversely, other versions begin at the feet and progress upward through the body toward the head.

You can begin by sitting in a comfortable chair, reclining, or lying in bed or on the floor. And perhaps you may wish to close your eyes. You might wiggle around a bit until you feel comfortable. . . . Now let's start with the muscles in both hands. Make fists; hold them tightly for about 10 seconds; now let go. Notice how your hands feel as they release tension. You may find that your hands feel warmer as they relax. Repeat this one more time.

Now, tense and relax your wrists. Starting with palms down, pull your fingers up toward the ceiling; hold for about 10 seconds; now relax. Notice the warmth coming into your hands and fingers. Repeat this one more time.

Next, tense your upper and lower arm muscles. Do this by bending both your arms at the elbow and tensing your muscles as you bend. Hold this position for about 10 seconds, and then release the tension as you straighten your arms. Repeat this one more time.

Now move on to the shoulder and neck muscles. Shrug your shoulders high; hold for 10 seconds or so; now let them go. Notice the warmth and relaxation coming into your shoulders and neck. Again, tense, let go, relax. Do each of these exercises twice.

Next, push your head against whatever is supporting your body. Tense the muscles in your neck, hold them tight for 10 seconds and then let go.

Now, pull your chin in toward your chest. Tense, study the feeling, and then let go. Wrinkle the muscles in your forehead, tensing the muscles. Hold the tension for five seconds, let go and do it again.

Next squint; hold for about 10 seconds and let go. Notice the relaxation.

Tighten your jaw by opening your mouth widely; hold for about five seconds; now let go. Do that twice. Press your tongue hard against the roof of your mouth; notice the tension, hold for a few seconds and then let go. Repeat. Don't forget to do each exercise twice.

Now move to your chest. Arch your back slowly as you inhale and tense the muscles around your ribcage. Hold the tension for about 10 seconds. Now let go. Study how the tension is released as you let go. Do this again. Inhale and hold for 10 seconds, release, now let go.

Tense the muscles in your lower back and stomach by pressing your buttocks against the chair, recliner, bed, or floor. Press them down as far as you can, and hold for 10 seconds, noticing the tightness in your lower back. Let go. Feel the tension leaving your body. Now focus on the warmth and well-being that has entered your lower back and stomach. Rest for about 20 seconds and then do that again.

Now tense the muscles in your upper legs as tight as you can. Hold for 10 seconds, and relax. Repeat. Feel the warmth and the sense of well-being that the relaxation brings.

Now, raise your toes toward your body. Aim for your chin. Note the tension in your calves. Hold for about 10 seconds, then let go and relax. Do that again, noticing how your legs feel. Now push your toes away from your body (if you are lying down), or into the floor (if you are sitting). Hold for 10 seconds, now let go. Do that again. Notice the warmth that has flowed into your feet and toes. Imagine all the tension that you have harbored in your body is now released out from your toes. Relax, let it flow out.

Now scan your body from head to toe. Notice which muscles are more relaxed and which muscles might still hold some tension. First, simply notice the difference. Then, if you wish to proceed, you can perform more tensing and relaxing repetitions on the muscles that remain tense.

Each time you practice PMR, notice first the tension, then the warmth and well-being you feel when you let go. Each time you will become increasingly relaxed and more adept at the process. Eventually, as you master PMR, you will be able to relax your muscles at will, anywhere or anytime. You will simply scan your body to determine which muscles are tight and causing you anxiety, stress, or pain, then tense and relax them twice. Progressive muscle relaxation will become second nature.

Autogenics

In the 1880s, German physician Oskar Vogt researched and pioneered a method of self-hypnosis for stress reduction. Decades later, Johannes Schultz, a Berlin psychiatrist and neurologist, expanded Vogt's technique into a therapeutic approach called Autogenic Training that promotes physical relaxation and enhances well-being. Schultz discovered that imagining feelings of warmth and heaviness in the body (especially in the arms and legs) evokes a deep state of peacefulness and lowers one's reaction to stress.

Autogenics uses "self-talk" to help you invoke tranquil sensations in your mind and body. There are several variations and approaches to autogenics, but most have fundamental similarities. Each approach includes directives, in the form of outlined steps, to elicit specific responses. The steps are taught sequentially; you learn and master one step or phase at a time. Typically, there are six steps in the autogenic method. The goal is to create heaviness and warmth in the arms and legs; slow and regular heartbeats; slow, deep breathing; warmth in the abdomen; and a sensation of coolness in the forehead—all responses associated with relaxation or self-hypnosis.

In order to accomplish these objectives, autogenics incorporates self-statements and imagery that relate to the response you want to elicit. As the exercise below illustrates, to help develop a steady heartbeat, you might repeat to yourself the phrase, "My heart beats slowly and regularly." Using imagery to elicit a feeling of warmth in your hands, you might imagine sun shining on your hands or holding a hot beverage. Likewise, you might imagine lead weights on your wrists and sandbags on your legs to promote a feeling of heaviness.

Dealing with anxiety through autogenics is similar to self-hypnosis without the need for a formal hypnotic trance. Like hypnosis (described in Chapter 3), the effectiveness of autogenics is increased by an attitude of receptivity and passivity. In other words, you *allow*, rather than force, the desired response and let go of concern about the outcome or response.

An Autogenics Exercise

Sit in a comfortable position, take a few deep breaths, and scan your body for tension. Imagine exhaling into any areas that feel tense or tight. You can continue to calm your body by breathing slowly and deeply, with the exhalation longer than the inhalation, for about two minutes. Once your body is calm, you are ready to begin the autogenics training.

Step 1: Heaviness

Focus on your right hand and say to yourself, "My right hand is getting heavy." Repeat six times. Now focus your attention on your left hand and say to yourself six times, "My left hand is heavy."

Next, imagine that there are lead weights on your wrists, making your hands very heavy. As they become so very heavy, you feel more and more relaxed. Feel the heaviness spread up to your arms. First focus on your right arm and say to yourself, "My right arm is heavy." Repeat six times, and then focus on your left arm: "My left arm is heavy." Repeat six times, then say, "Both my arms are heavy . . . heavy and relaxed," and repeat this six times as well.

After you finish the last repetition, take a moment to feel the heaviness; really feel it. As you do this, say to yourself: "My arms are heavy and I feel calm and relaxed. My arms are heavy and I am relaxed. Both my arms are heavy and I feel so very calm."

Now allow that heaviness to spread to your legs . . . nice heavy legs, and repeat these phrases: "My right leg is heavy" (six times); "My left leg is heavy" (six times); "Both my legs are heavy" (six times); "My arms and legs are heavy" (six times). Feel how heavy your limbs are, so heavy that it would be difficult to move them. You could if you wanted, but they can stay so nicely heavy and still.

Step 2: Warmth

Focus your attention on your right hand again and say six times to yourself, "My right hand is warm." Let that warmth spread to your right arm and say, six times, "My right arm is warm." Then repeat six times each for your left hand and arm. Finally, say, "Both my arms are warm" (repeat six times). Imagine holding a nice, warm cup of coffee or tea, or if you would prefer, imagine that your hands are submerged in a warm tub or warmed by a soothing fire—use whatever images work for you. Repeat six times, "My arms and legs are heavy and warm and I am calm and relaxed."

Step 3: Heartbeat

Repeat six times: "My heart beats slowly and regularly. And I am calm and relaxed, so calm and at ease." Imagine your heart slowing down as you repeat your phrase, "My heart beats slow and regularly." Imagine a metronome that creates a slow and steady tempo, and imagine your heart beating as regularly as a metronome.

Step 4: Warm Abdomen

Repeat six times: "My stomach is warm and soft. I imagine that a warm and golden light is shining on my stomach now. My stomach is warm and soft, and I am completely calm and comfortable and composed." Feel soothing warmth spreading through your stomach and abdomen.

Step 5: Breathing

Repeat six times: "My breath is slow and deep, and I feel completely calm and composed." Feel your breath slowing and deepening. Next, repeat six times: "My body breathes me, and I feel so at ease."

Step 6: Cool Forehead

Imagine that a breeze is cooling your forehead, and with this coolness comes your ability to think with a clear, cool head. As you imagine this coolness, repeat the phrase "My forehead is cool" six times.

Note that after each step in the autogenics exercise, you can follow up with self-statements, such as the following, that minimize distress and reinforce your goals:

- I am calm and centered and relaxed.
- I have all the time I need to accomplish what I need to do.
- I can handle it.
- I am in charge of my reactions.

Tight Fist

Another relaxation technique, the tight-fist technique, can also be done discreetly in public to release fear and tension. The exercise works by combining the physical release that comes from tensing and relaxing your hand with a visual image of releasing fear. You can imagine the fear being transformed into a colored liquid and released out of your body. Many people apply the metaphor of releasing toxins, finding it helpful to visualize the earth as capable of absorbing any fear- or tension-filled toxins and cleansing them. To practice the tight-fist technique, follow the exercise below.

Imagine that all your worry, fear, and muscular tension is going into one of your hands. Make a fist with that hand, squeeze it tightly, feel the tension, magnify it, and tighten that fist even more. Tighter and tighter. Now imagine that tension becoming a liquid in a color of your choice; the liquid represents your distress, worry, any uncomfortable feeling in your body. Imagine your fist absorbing all of the colored liquid, all the fear, all the discomfort.

Now gradually release your fist and imagine the colored liquid flowing to the floor and through the floor to ground, to be absorbed deep into the soil . . . where it will be cleansed and released far away from you in the earth . . . far away from you. If you like, you can repeat squeezing your fist and releasing the liquid again, noticing the difference between tension and relaxation.

(Adapted from Daitch, 2007.)

Dialing Down Anxiety

Often people with anxiety disorders experience anxiety like an internal engine suddenly revving up. Have you ever driven on the highway, glanced down at the speedometer, and been startled at how fast you were going? "75 miles an hour! I better slow down!" And you do slow down, without any effort. You know without thought just how much pressure to release from the gas pedal to slow to the exact speed you want. As you retract your foot from the gas and ease down a little on the brake pedal, your eyes probably shift from the road to the speedometer to monitor the downward arc of the needle. When it reaches your desired speed, say 65 mph, your attention fully returns to the road, you lightly return your foot to the gas pedal, and you go forward on your way.

Your internal responses to life events or stressors can gain momentum unexpectedly like a speeding car. Regardless of the stressor that sets you off, your racing thoughts can rev your nervous system until it feels like you're speeding. Wouldn't it be nice if you could just apply the brakes until your worries reached a desired level? Dialing down anxiety uses imagery to trigger the physical and mental processes that let you put the brakes on an overly activated, racing system.

To use this imagery tool, first imagine your safe place, which you identified and practiced in the guided imagery exercise earlier in this chapter. The following dialing down anxiety exercise is one I developed and described in my earlier book (Daitch, 2007), and I have adapted it here.

In your safe place, you imagine a dial with a needle that points to your current level of tension (or reactivity) on a scale of 0 to 10. Now imagine a shaded area on the part of the dial that represents a zone of comfort; perhaps the shaded range goes from 0—or no anxiety—to 2 or 3, the small amount of tension needed to handle any situations that may arise. Now create a red zone on the dial signifying excessive anxiety, tension, or intense reactivity, perhaps from 8 to 10.

Now, look at the dial, and, if the needle is not in that optimal range, if it's on a middle-range number and should be in the low range, or if it's in the red zone and should be in the middle range, imagine dialing the number down, moving the needle into that optimal range.

Now think of some event, situation, sensation, or thought that causes you anxiety. Perhaps it is just an inconvenience or an aggravation, yet you experience it as something much greater, with too much intensity. Now concentrate on the dial, and notice what number the needle is on. Ask yourself what just the right level of reaction is for you to be effective, focused, yet relaxed and in control. Imagine using your fingers to turn the knob to move the needle down to that desired level.

Now slowly take three deep breaths. You become more and more deeply relaxed, and you see the needle moving down now to where you want it. Notice how much more in control you feel.

Each time you dial down your anxiety, it will become easier and easier to feel in charge. You can make a commitment to dial down your reactions daily and as you do, you may say a supportive statement, such as "I am in charge of my response." Repeat that phrase now three times, and as you do, allow yourself the satisfaction that comes from being in control.

By using the image of a dial you can calibrate the level of activation to just the right intensity, knowing you are no longer at the whim of runaway anxiety. An affirmation such as "I am in charge of my response" is a reassuring, empowering way to complete the dialing down exercise. Eventually, simply stating these words along with imagining the desired number on the dial will be all you need to diffuse worry or anxiety.

The more you practice breathing exercises, guided imagery and visualizations, autogenics, progressive relaxation, and the tight fist exercise, the easier they will become and the more tools you'll have to quickly relieve the physical and emotional symptoms of anxiety. The key, again, is practice and persistence. Now that you have experienced what I consider to be the foundational techniques of anxiety reduction, we will move on to examine anxiety reduction interventions that are specific to particular anxiety disorders.

CHAPTER 5

Generalized Anxiety Disorder

"I worry about everything—my kids getting kidnapped, my husband getting into a car accident, the chemicals in our food," 37-year-old Emily, a full-time homemaker, told her friend Julie over coffee. Emily leaned forward on her kitchen chair, rubbing her temples with quick, sideways swipes. "My parents said that I was nervous as a kid, and I know I've always been high strung. But it wasn't a problem until recently, when Rick started going out of town so much. I get irritable and impatient with the kids, and I'm afraid it's hurting them."

The mother of four young children, including eight-month-old twin boys, Emily had good cause to be stressed. Her husband, Rick, a sales rep, traveled for work, so Emily was frequently alone with the kids for days at a time. Born with an anxious temperament, Emily watched her anxiety intensify into chronic worry as her life became more and more demanding. The anxiety began causing physical problems, too, including stomach pain, tension headaches, and occasional heart palpitations. Insomnia left her frequently exhausted. Besides her fears for her children, Emily worried about her own health and felt a constant sense of impending doom.

"I went to the doctor last month to see what was wrong," Emily said, after a gulp of coffee. "He did some tests and told me it was my nerves. He suggested that I go into therapy."

"Are you going to?" Julie reached for Emily's hands. "I think it's a great idea. I know someone good."

"Thanks, but there's no way that's going to happen. No time, no money. I'll have to figure it out myself." Emily smiled thinly. "Just one more thing to do."

Pieces of the Puzzle

Everyone worries occasionally. It's no big deal. However, anxiety becomes a problem when the worry becomes frequent and intense, as it did in Emily's case. When the constellation of symptoms such as those Emily described over coffee lasts consistently for six months or more, the condition is known as generalized anxiety disorder (GAD).

GAD creates problems on three levels: cognitive, physical, and emotional. On the cognitive or thought-related level, GAD results in excessive, unrealistic worry focusing on issues such as health, finances, career, and the well-being of loved ones. Emily worried excessively about all of the above topics, catastrophizing, predicting a grave outcome for each. Emily's body bore the burden of her runaway train of dismal thoughts.

The physical, or *somatic*, symptoms of GAD include trembling, muscular aches, insomnia, abdominal upsets, dizziness, and feeling wired or keyed-up. Many of the somatic features of this disorder result from the presence of excessive levels of stress hormones circulating throughout the body for prolonged periods of time. Like Emily, many people with GAD seek out the help of their general practitioner or even medical specialists before they find that the cause of their physical distress is GAD. These physiological symptoms often form a vicious cycle in which anxiety snowballs: cognitive worry fuels somatic disturbances, which fuel even more cognitive worry, which then heightens the chronic somatic complaints, ad infinitum.

GAD takes its toll emotionally as well. The physical and mental effects of GAD usually result in a pervading sense of being revved up, irritable, or on edge, inescapably vulnerable to a world of distressing possibilities. While Emily was managing to keep her head above water in taking care of her children, the work life, social life, and family life of individuals experiencing GAD often suffer. Already Emily's physical symptoms, irritability, and dire outlook were straining her ability to parent her children.

Although Emily was not planning to seek treatment—adding one more item to a list of bills that threatened to mount as high as Jack's beanstalk—therapeutic interventions can be very helpful to individuals experiencing GAD. It is possible to get off the runaway train of worry and regain mental calmness and physical health.

The Differences Between the Disorders

All of the anxiety disorders have one major thing in common: the experience of heightened anxiety. What makes the disorders differ, however, is the way the anxiety manifests. Distinguishing GAD from the other anxiety disorders can be particularly tricky because with GAD, you tend to worry about and fear some of the same things that trouble people with other anxiety disorders. If your child is playing with a neighbor's dog, you might worry excessively about your child being bitten. A person with a specific phobia of dogs will worry excessively about being bitten by a dog too. If you are about to give a public speech, you might worry excessively about your performance. Likewise, the person with a specific social anxiety disorder will worry about giving a speech. If it's the start of flu season, you might worry excessively about getting sick and stock up on hand sanitizers and Vitamin C. The person with obsessive–compulsive disorder that centers around fear of contamination will also worry about catching colds.

However, the hallmark of GAD is not a *particular* type of worry, as it is with the other disorders. Furthermore, the intensity of anxiety experienced when confronted with feared situations generally isn't as intense when you have GAD as it is with many of the other anxiety disorders. For example, the person with a phobia of dogs experiences terror when facing a dog. He or she does not experience the sustained, chronic levels of anxiety that are typical of GAD. The person with obsessive–compulsive disorder experiences such intense anxiety in response to an intrusive, fearful thought, such as germ contamination, that he or she needs to engage immediately in some ritual to quiet the fears. If you have GAD, you are not likely to, say, use hand sanitizer 100 times in response to your worries over germs, the way someone with obsessive–compulsive disorder might.

The key word to remember when thinking about generalized anxiety disorder is "general." One of my clients once playfully remarked, "I was at a seminar this morning about the importance of embracing cultural diversity in the workplace. It got me thinking: if there's one thing I can say about myself, when it comes to worrying, I'm an equal-opportunity employer. I'll worry about anything. I don't discriminate one bit." I couldn't have said it better myself.

People with GAD not only produce more somatic sensations of agitation, they also scan their bodies more frequently and imagine catastrophic implications of these sensations. Thus, they show greater somatic stress reactions. While their misinterpretation of what they're feeling does not spark panic, as it does in individuals with panic disorder, it does maintain and even increase the chronic levels of physiological stress they experience. It is important to note that this increased somatic awareness and distress differs from somatization disorder. In the latter, the multiple physical complaints generally involve several different organ systems and the disorder centers around these physiological concerns. People with GAD typically display a much more limited range of physical symptoms, all of which can be attributed to a dysregulated nervous system. Their worries are also much more *generalized,* so somatic complaints are but one of the many concerns that trouble these clients.

Who Develops Generalized Anxiety Disorder?

In a given year, over 3% of the adult population in the United States has a diagnosis of GAD. As with many of the anxiety disorders, GAD does tend to run in families. Some of this is due to the influence of our early role models: as children, we tend to internalize the ways our parents view and respond to the world. Thus if your mother was a chronic worrier, you probably grew up with a heightened sense of the problems and pitfalls that might lurk around every corner. You would be more likely to take on the worry-based thought patterns typical of GAD and develop the disorder yourself. More recent studies, however, have demonstrated that GAD also has a genetic component. Some of the genetic traits that make one susceptible to major depressive disorder have been linked to the development of GAD. Studies have also shown that women are more likely to be diagnosed with GAD than men. Anywhere from 55–65% of individuals with GAD are female.

It is common for individuals with GAD to report that they have felt overly anxious and nervous for the majority of their lives or that the worrying started during adolescence. This is the case for about half of the people diagnosed with GAD. The other half tends to develop it in adulthood. So unlike some of the other anxiety disorders, in which the onset of the disorder tends to cluster around specific age ranges, the typical age of onset for GAD varies quite considerably.

Once you have GAD, however, it doesn't tend to go away on its own. Without treatment, you are likely to maintain the disorder, and during times when you experience considerable life stressors, your GAD symptoms will tend to worsen. With the right treatment, however, this can all turn around.

The Good News

Having GAD doesn't doom you to being a chronic worrier for the rest of your life. While it may seem like worrying is a basic part of your personality, with therapy you can change this. I encourage you to embrace some of the many options in this book that can bring about growth and recovery. In the following sections, you will learn about the therapeutic interventions that can teach you to look beyond your worries, so that you can curb your anxiety and experience more pleasure in your life.

The Goals and Gains of Therapy

- Develop skills to interrupt negative, irrational, or obsessive thoughts
- Diminish worry and fear of the future
- Develop the ability to calm and self-soothe
- Build resilience in the face of short- or long-term stress
- Diminish physical symptoms, such as a racing heart or stomach distress
- Diminish restlessness, irritability, and insomnia
- Cultivate a sense of hope about recovery
- Cultivate a sense of well-being, capability, and resilience

How to Get There: Therapeutic Techniques and Interventions

Although this chapter focuses on the treatment of GAD specifically, the techniques outlined are applicable to all of the anxiety disorders addressed in this book. Indeed, it can be argued that the symptoms of generalized anxiety disorder are a part of every other anxiety disorder. On occasion, individuals with a specific phobia, such as a fear of public speaking, may not have chronic anxiety, but even these individuals will find the following techniques helpful in overcoming their particular fear.

The good news is that many people over many decades have developed successful approaches, all with the same general goal in mind: to reduce or even remove the problematic symptoms of GAD. However, each technique arises from a different theory about how to treat GAD. Some focus on first changing thoughts, others emotions, others the physical sensations related to anxiety. I believe that when dealing with anxiety disorders, it is essential to teach people first to calm the instantaneous physical revving that comes with anxiety. Everyone knows it is hard to calm your mind when your heart is racing a mile a minute and your shoulders are tense. Let's look at interventions that help people with GAD relax and put on the brakes.

Lessening Bodily Distress: Progressive Muscle Relaxation and Visualization Techniques

If you suffer from generalized anxiety disorder you probably are all too familiar with stomach pains or cramping, tightness in your chest, and tension in your neck and shoulders. These sensations are common occurrences, their intensity increasing with worries or daily stressors. A vast array of relaxation techniques can reduce both the distress of these physical symptoms and the physical sensations themselves. The anti-anxiety techniques presented in the previous chapter, as well as those that follow, can all be applied to the treatment of GAD to accomplish this purpose.

For Emily, I chose three techniques with the goal of softening the particular GAD-related physical symptoms that she experienced: stomach pain, heart palpitations, tension headaches, and a sensation of heat that often flooded her face. The first intervention was the progressive relaxation tool, exactly as taught in the previous chapter (see pages 63–65).

The second technique I chose for Emily was *breathing in the light*. This exercise employs both visualization and kinesthetic self-soothing to accomplish two goals: (1) increase awareness of where the body holds tension when stressed; and (2) facilitate the release of this tension. I guided Emily through this exercise as it is presented in the previous chapter (see pages 62–63). Once Emily had mastered these two techniques, I created a version of safe-place imagery to alter her reaction to the uncomfortable warmth that she sometimes experienced when she was stressed.

Guided Imagery: Safe Place

Underlying the chronic worry that is a hallmark of GAD is the underlying assumption that threat lurks around every corner: the world is not a safe place. For this reason, I find the use of guided imagery to develop a "safe place" to be especially helpful for my clients with GAD. As you'll recall from Chapter 4, once you develop your "safe place," thoughts of this safe place can bring about feelings of safety, security, well-being, and serenity.

Through the safe place guided imagery exercise presented in Chapter 4, Emily developed her own safe place: a small cove on an imaginary beach touched by the warm, soft breezes of the South Pacific.

Once you have this safe place established, you can utilize it frequently for other therapeutic purposes. For example, if you have GAD, you are most likely sensitive to your body's reactions to stress. Emily, for example, didn't like the excessive heat in her head and chest that sometimes accompanied her anxiety. We used the following exercise to help her reframe that experience.

Emily returned to her safe place and once again experienced the sense of security and well-being it brought her. This time I suggested that she associate the *warmth* of the beach and sun with comfort, thereby creating a positive association for the feeling of warmth that she could use on later occasions when her body naturally became warmer when it was stressed.

In order to do this, I first guided Emily into a relaxed state in which she called up the imagery and sensations of her safe place on the beach. Then I reframed the sensation of heat:

Not only imagine yourself lying on the beach towel, begin to feel the sensations of warmth, hear the pounding waves, and smell the salty air. Imagine basking in the sun, feel your body sinking into the warmth of the sand underneath your towel. You might even notice a softening of the tense muscles in your back and a calming of the pounding in your chest.

As you lie on the beach in your sunny spot, feeling so relaxed, you can enjoy the developing warmth that you feel as you lie back in the sun. And isn't it nice just to drift away and feel yourself melt, melt, melt away on a beautiful beach (pause).

From time to time, everyone experiences increasing body heat. Many people feel flushed and hot when they become anxious. It's normal and natural to feel warm when you're anxious. You've told me that in the past you haven't liked that feeling, that you wanted that feeling of warmth to go away . . . but there's a way to think differently about that sensation of warmth. Imagine that instead of being distressed by the heat as soon as it arises, you think of a time when warmth felt wonderful, at the beach, for example. The tense situation and the beach both create heat in your body but you respond quite differently. Contrast the prickly, nervous sweat and burning in your chest with the relaxing warmth as heat from the sand rises through your beach towel to soothe your back, and the sun blankets your face, eyelids, and forearms. With practice, the soothing experience of the beach will become a powerful resource you can call on in tense moments.

The above intervention employed reframing. Reframing helps a client to find something positive in an event. In Emily's case, we reframed the sensation of warmth as something normal, natural, and even necessary when the body is preparing for action. In addition, we linked a positive association to the feeling of warmth, giving the suggestion that she can associate warmth with relaxation. In this way she could replace her formerly held negative reaction.

Minding the Mind with Cognitive Therapy

Cognitive Therapy (CT) has been shown in research to be an effective treatment for all of the anxiety disorders. Aaron Beck (2005), a psychiatrist well known for his treatment of anxiety and depression and a founder of cognitive therapy, found that CT is especially effective in treating generalized anxiety disorder. (I always include CT as part of a comprehensive treatment plan, but recognize that some clients prefer other approaches.)

CT is based on the understanding that our thoughts, rather than our behaviors, emotions, or physical tensions, are the doorway to therapeutic change. When used for GAD, it works to identify thoughts, such as "There's probably salmonella in the chicken I'll cook for dinner tonight"; underlying assumptions, such as "Harm is just around the corner"; and core beliefs, such as "The world is an unsafe place."

Once the immediate thoughts have been identified, CT helps you delve down to identify *core beliefs*, which Beck believes are the driving force behind anxiety disorders. Beliefs such as "The world is an unsafe place" fuel anxiety. Changing these core beliefs and the rant of thoughts that go with them through CT can alter behavior, emotions, and physical tensions and imbalances that come with anxiety disorders. Changing thoughts and thought patterns sets off a chain reaction that reduces anxiety. CT offers many ways to create such change.

A common exercise in CT, done in the therapist's office and at home by the individual, involves creating a list of worries versus reality-based thoughts. In this exercise, you write down your worries in one column and in the column next to them write thoughts that are more reality-based and adaptive. You ask yourself the question: how likely is it that the outcome I'm fearing will really happen? This evaluation is intended to help you identify and alter some core beliefs. Here is an example of a chart that Emily made:

WORRIES/ASSUMPTIONS	REALITY
I've heard there's salmonella in chicken. Someone talked about it on TV. There could be salmonella in the chicken I'll cook for dinner tonight.	It's highly unlikely that the chicken I bought from the grocery store is contaminated. I buy food from that store every week, and it's always been OK.
If I serve bad chicken to my family, we could all get sick. One of us could even die. I can't let my children die.	If anyone in my family becomes sick from eating contaminated food, we'll go to the hospital, get medical help, and end up OK.
Even if we don't die before we make it to the hospital, doctors make all kinds of mistakes. People die every day from hospital mistakes. Or we could catch something else at the hospital. Sick. One of us could even die. I can't let my children die.	Hospitals help more than harm. It is likely that if we go there with a medical problem, we will get better rather than worse. I can always call my parents to come be advocates at the hospital if we're all too sick to talk.

As we can see, Emily assumes not only that bad things will happen, but that the results of these bad things will be catastrophic. Food poisoning will result in death rather than a trip to the hospital and a cure. A trip to the hospital will result in a calamity in which adequate treatment will not be received, rather than a cure to the presenting condition. With this catastrophic thinking, it is easy to see how mountains of anxiety arise from thoughts. By getting in the habit of writing down thoughts and then challenging them, you can elicit a more healthful chain reaction based on the core beliefs "I am not always in harm's way," and "I have skills and strength to cope with any of the adversities that might come my way."

In his book *The Complete Anxiety Treatment and Homework Planner* (2004), psychologist Arthur Jongsma, Jr., laid out a very effective anxiety-reducing exercise that takes the list-making technique above a few steps further. The steps of the exercise below are simple.

1. Write down the specific fear.

2. Rank the likelihood that the fear will be realized on a numeric scale (I usually use a scale of 1–100). Emily wrote down her fear that her family would get food poisoning. When she thought about it, however, she rated the likelihood of its actually happening as only a 20 out of 100.

3. Write down the self-talk messages (all the negative thoughts) that reinforce the fear. Emily's self-talk statements included: "I can't let my family get sick," "Food I buy from the grocery store might be dangerous," and "If we get sick a hospital would just make everything worse."

4. Write down the consequences if the feared events were to actually take place. Emily thought her family members would get deathly ill, and that one might actually die.

5. Ask yourself if there is anything you can do to affect the outcome. Emily strategized about ways to avoid food poisoning: cook meat fully, wash hands when switching from preparing one type of food to another, shop at the big grocery store chains that keep up with inspection standards, and contact a doctor if anyone in the family gets stomach cramps or diarrhea lasting for more than 24 hours.

6. Respond to the final two questions: what's the worst possible scenario if the bad outcome comes to pass, and how would you and your family's life be affected if that actually happened? Could you live with it? How could you cope, or function? After some discussion, Emily and I concluded that even if the poisoning was severe, the affected family members would go to the hospital, get medicine, and recover fully within a couple weeks. All family members would experience some short-term emotional or physical discomfort, but all would come out OK in the end.

I encourage individuals who are anxious to practice this exercise whenever they have a worry that causes distress. They can do this with or without a therapist. Therapists can train their anxious clients to identify exaggerated worries, develop a concrete method to talk back to them, and put the brakes on unrelenting fearful thoughts.

While cognitive therapy does yield great results, it presupposes that we have control over how we think. Part of the challenge in training people to change their thoughts and their self-talk is to catch unhealthy thoughts and correct them *quickly*. This is not easy, because thoughts occur suddenly and often without our conscious awareness. Psychologists David Barlow and Jerome Cerny, renowned experts in anxiety disorders, stated that "maladaptive cognitions are automatic; and they are very discrete predictions or interpretations of a given situation" (1988, p. 122). In other words, they are quick, hard to catch, and often include "very specific interpretations and predictions about the situation" (p. 123). Because of this challenge, many therapists have merged cognitive techniques for GAD with other types of psychological approaches, as the following interventions demonstrate.

Cognitive Behavioral Therapies: "The Worry Box" and "Worry Time"

The Worry Box
As we've seen above, list-making exercises frequently used in CT can aid you in identifying irrational worries and recognizing that you have the resources to cope with imagined adversity should it ever materialize. However, when you have GAD, irrational thoughts have a tendency to pop up all over the place. Like the gophers in the arcade game, they just keep rearing their heads no matter how many times you bonk them back down into their slots.

The worry box adds action to the cognitive work of list-making by giving you a physical place to put your worries—a place outside of the mind. When a worry pops into your mind, you write it down on a slip of paper and put the slip into a container, a box, or basket. Rather than leaving a thought in the mind, where it will simply pop up again and again, action puts the thought *outside* of the mind, so it is well contained elsewhere. Like traditional cognitive exercises, with the worry box you are writing your worried thoughts onto paper. But unlike traditional exercises, you are not attempting to evaluate the validity of your worried thoughts; rather, you are using the writing activity to distance yourself from your worries. Thus if and when the thought pops up again, you can immediately picture the slip with the worry contained within your worry box and then direct your thoughts elsewhere.

Emily chose to slip an envelope into her purse that would serve as her worry box throughout the day. While this worked well when she was stationary, she often found that she didn't have time to stop and jot down her worries while she was busy watching her young children. "If I still had my old office job, this worry box would have been perfect," Emily remarked. For this reason, the following "worry time" intervention was more helpful, as it is with many of my clients whose days are quite active.

Worry Time

While the worry box involves assigning fearful thoughts to a box, basket, or envelope, worry time entails *postponing* unwanted thoughts to a later time. You are probably familiar with the concept of delayed gratification: *I'll watch an hour of TV at 6 P.M. if I get the dishes done. If I get my billing done, I'll take myself out to get ice cream after dinner.* If you have intrusive, fearful thoughts, you can use the framework of delayed gratification to postpone your worries. Rather than delay a pleasurable trip to the movies, you dictate when and where you will attend to your worries: you set yourself a "worry time."

In order to do this, you literally set a time (or multiple times) through-out a day or week—say, from 6:00–6:20 P.M. each night—to entertain all the worried thoughts that you have at other times. If a thought pops up in the midst of the day, you stop it in its tracks and set it aside for later, when your worry time is scheduled. The energy needed to let go of the worry and move on to another thought is minimal, because you are simply shelving the thought for later rather than trying to expunge it permanently.

Worry time is one of the few at-home assignments that can be rewarding to clients whether they practice it or rebel against it. It can feel tedious and unpleas-ant to deal with the stressful thoughts and worries during the scheduled worry time. Often, clients find that they do not want to keep worrying for the entire allotted time, and the fearful thoughts become less urgent. When clients file away worries for later but then shirk the allotted worry time because they'd rather be doing something else, this is success! They are not only choosing but desiring not to worry!

Emily found that adhering to worry time worked much better for her given her schedule. She set herself a 20-minute worry time each night, just after she put her kids to bed. She reported that shelving her worries for a later time felt strange at first, but she stuck to her commitment.

Soon, Emily and I agreed to decrease her prescribed worry time to 10 and then 5 minutes a night. She often found that by the time she reached the end of the evening, many of her previous worries just didn't seem rele-vant anymore. "All my worries seem so pressing and important when they come up in a given moment," Emily remarked to me after she had been doing her worry time nightly for about two weeks. "But by the time night rolls around and I let myself go back and think about what I was so concerned about, I can see that most of the things I was worried about never even happened. I never thought I'd say this, but worrying has actually begun to feel like a big waste of my time!"

Mindfulness and Acceptance

Although the worry time and worry box techniques focus on controlling and shifting your attention away from your worries, acceptance and mindfulness-based approaches offer a very different but highly effective way to manage your GAD. Mindfulness was first introduced in Chapter 3 and will be discussed again in the chapters on panic disorder (Chapter 6) and OCD (Chapter 9), as mindfulness is an approach that can apply broadly to many different disorders. When you practice mindfulness, you become engaged in the present moment. Rather than shelving a worried thought until later or writing it down to get it out of your mind, mindfulness techniques encourage you to accept and even welcome *all* your thoughts and sensations, including worry.

A simple mindfulness exercise, which I used with Emily, involves thinking, or writing down, your thoughts and sensations, as below:

I notice my _____ (fill in with the words that describe your thought or feeling, e.g., my worry, my heartbeat . . .).
I welcome my _____ (worry, heartbeat, etc.).
I accept my (worry, heartbeat, etc.) _____ with compassion.
Then ask yourself:
What do I notice now?

You may discover that your experience changes when you simply accept it rather than trying to stuff it down. It may not change, and that's another experience to notice, welcome, and accept.

As I have mentioned throughout this book, I try to offer a variety of therapeutic interventions. Neither I nor the client knows ahead of time which interventions the particular client will like, or which interventions the client will adhere to over the course of time. While it may seem paradoxical to offer both mindfulness interventions and postponement, I feel it is incumbent upon the therapist to offer a variety of strategies that I have seen to be clinically effective. I suggest you try an array of different kinds of interventions with each client. You never know which one will do the trick.

Hypnosis Using "Parts of Self"

Although not all therapists practice hypnosis, I regularly use hypnotherapeutic interventions in my practice. One intervention that I have found particularly helpful for clients with GAD involves the identification of different "parts of self." All of us have many different components of our personalities. For instance, when you get together with an old high-school friend, you may find you act younger: you are energetic and carefree, laughing at things you haven't found funny since you were in high school together. This friend brings out an aspect of yourself, or "part of self," that exists within you, even if you are not often in contact with it.

Likewise, all of us also have wise and resourceful parts of self. When you are in the midst of worry, you most likely are not in touch with this calmer, more grounded part of yourself. I often use hypnosis to help my clients with GAD access these more developed parts of self. Like them, you already possess much of the wisdom and strength that can help you manage your anxiety. It's just a question of enhancing your ability to access this sense of strength and capability.

I used a parts of self intervention to help Emily manage and reduce her worrying. When Emily had successfully moved into a hypnotic state (see Chapter 3 for more on hypnosis), I gave her the suggestion that even if she found herself worrying, she could recognize that the worried part of her was only one part of herself, and that there was, in fact, a stronger part of her that could comfort and manage the worried part. Then I suggested that she put the worry on the chair, which created a visual image of detachment and separation from her worry. I gave her the following suggestions to cement these ideas:

Now see yourself putting your worried self on a chair across from you . . . And you can decide how far away you wish to place the chair upon which your worried self sits . . . connecting to her first with compassion and understanding . . . without judgment . . . with acceptance, accepting her discomfort, accepting her anticipation that something bad could happen, accepting all the sensations in her body . . . good or bad. And would you like to have the satisfying experience of helping that worried part of yourself manage her fears . . .

Now, imagine talking to that worried part, from a wise, healthy, strong part of yourself . . . reassuring the worried self . . . You can access a mature, strong part of yourself that can not only comfort the worried part of self, but reassure her. There is always a part of you that is strong, balanced, mature, and even brave . . . Though you might temporarily forget that this strong part is there, it is always there.

And from this strong part of self you can offer wise words to your worried self . . . sitting over there . . . letting her know that most of what is worried about doesn't come to fruition . . . And even in the unlikely event that it does, that you have the resources to manage whatever comes up . . . And now I'd like you to have a pleasant experience . . . the experience of holding that wonderful feeling of being in control, of feeling calm, composed . . . feeling your body relaxed, feeling healthy, handling the children with humor and enjoyment . . . and at the end of each day, feeling comfortably, even satisfyingly tired, not from stress but from a day of productive activities, and getting into bed, feeling the smooth, silky sheets and the comfy pillow, and falling asleep easily. Now let these satisfying feelings intensify . . . and really hold onto them . . . And I'm going to be quiet while you have the pleasure of these comfortable feelings . . . (Pause for one to two minutes.)

Next I re-alerted Emily by counting backward from 10 to 1 and suggesting that each time she went into hypnosis in the future, she could look forward to being even more responsive to the process.

The abridged script above draws from concepts of Ego State Therapy. *Ego states* reflect the notion that various organizational states, or personas, exist within each person (Watkins, 1992; Frederick & McNeal, 1993). Notably, these different organizational states can be associated with different stages of a person's development and are also linked to various life experiences. When communicating this concept to your clients, it is important to convey that the existence of multiple ego states is not indicative of psychopathology. Rather, the existence of these multiple personas is a component of the healthful psychological functioning of any individual.

The identification of ego states can enhance a client's ability to identify with a part of him- or herself that is resourceful, developed, and resilient. Psychologist D. Corydon Hammond wrote that in using ego states in therapy, one can "selectively amplify or diminish parts of [a client's] experience in order to achieve a higher purpose" (1990, p. 322). Thus the more developed parts of the self can guide, comfort, and advise the more vulnerable and fearful aspects of the self. When working with a GAD client, parts of self can be used to help the client access and empower a stronger part of the self to help manage worry.

Medication

While medications are by no means a necessary part of treatment for GAD, they have helped many of my clients overcome their generalized anxiety disorder. Remember, GAD takes a toll on the body. If you have GAD, your body is most likely used to being in a constant state of heightened stress. Your body may continue to release an excessive amount of stress hormones and neurochemicals on a daily basis. Antidepressants, such as selective serotonin reuptake inhibitors (SSRIs) and serotonin norepinephrine reuptake inhibitors (SNRIs), can help your body learn to re-regulate itself, and not always run on "high alert" (for a more detailed description of these medications, see Chapter 10). Buspirone can be used on a daily basis as an alternative to antidepressants to aid this recalibration. However, some researchers and doctors think it is not as helpful as some of the antidepressants.

Benzodiazepines, a fast-acting family of anti-anxiety medications, can also be helpful when you find yourself particularly stuck in a cycle of worry and in need of a quick de-escalation. However, benzodiazepines are not intended for long-term use. I have found that once my clients have learned the calming techniques I teach in therapy and as they become experts in de-escalating their worries and anxiety, benzodiazepines are usually not needed.

For GAD, many combinations of medications and therapy can be helpful. Some clients only use the longer-acting antidepressants or buspirone; some use a benzodiazepine for a short period of time. Other clients use both, while still others don't take medication at all. Working with your therapist, you can explore your options and find out what types of treatment are best suited for you.

Recovery: Emily's Story

Emily was highly motivated and established regular, at-home practice sessions immediately. At my suggestion, she joined a yoga class, which not only reinforced the therapeutic teachings but also gave her much-needed time for herself away from the house. She initially tried taking the SSRI Lexapro, but discontinued it after three months because she didn't like the weight gain and sexual side effects that accompanied it.

She chose not to try another medication. "At first I didn't think I could get over my worries," Emily said when we discussed whether she would go on a different medication, "but after working with you these past three months, I think all the tools I'm learning will give me everything I need to let go of my worrying."

Emily was correct. After about five months of weekly therapy, in which we used the techniques described in this chapter, Emily tapered down to seeing me twice a month. She also joined a support group for sufferers of anxiety disorders, which reinforced her practice of the techniques and gave her emotional support and friendship. She continued bi-monthly therapy with me for a year and a half.

One unexpected benefit of her recovery is that Emily is more relaxed with her children. She reports that she no longer hounds them with admonitions to be careful and avoid getting hurt. Now, in fact, she encourages them to take small risks.

Emily no longer needs regular appointments because she can handle most of the anxiety she experiences by using the techniques she's learned. If she has a particularly difficult event, however, she does schedule an appointment, but these are few and far between: Emily's just not that worried anymore.

CHAPTER 6

Panic Disorder

Cynthia and Jan had been meeting up for Saturday shopping trips and coffee almost weekly throughout the 10 years since they had graduated college. However, over the last 10 months, their jaunts to Macy's and Starbucks went from frequent to nonexistent. Whether Cynthia canceled in advance or at the last minute, she always had an excuse. Finally, one Saturday Cynthia again called off their arranged meeting, but Jan insisted on seeing her friend.

"Well," Cynthia responded hesitantly, "why don't you come over here instead? I'll make coffee. I really have missed seeing you."

Jan did go to Cynthia's for coffee that day. She skipped the small talk and begged her friend to tell her what had been going on for the past six months.

After a bit of coaxing, Cynthia explained. "Well, last September this crazy thing happened. I was standing in an aisle at the grocery store and suddenly I thought I was having a heart attack. At first, I just couldn't catch my breath, which was a nightmare in itself. Then my whole chest clamped up, and my face was pouring sweat; I thought I was about to faint." Cynthia kept her eyes glued to the floor as she quietly spoke. "It was all I could do to keep standing, and everything started looking so hazy that it must have taken me 10 minutes to find the exit. I'm so glad I finally got out of there. I thought they were going to have to call the paramedics. It was awful."

Jan took her friend's hand. "That sounds horrible. Do you remember if you were stressed about something? Wasn't that when your mom was in the hospital?"

"That's right, it was when Mom was having the surgery for her colon cancer and Jeff was traveling. I'm relieved that mom came through all that OK, but I haven't gotten over what's been going on with me. It wasn't a heart attack, but whatever it was, it keeps happening. The attacks just come up out of the blue, and I never know when another one's going to happen. You can't even imagine what it's like. It's this huge fear, terror, like I'm either dying or going completely crazy—you know, not knowing what's wrong with me and not being able to stop it from happening." She looked at Jan with tears in her eyes. "I just hate going out now. It's too stressful. That's why I've been canceling my shopping trips with you."

Pieces of the Puzzle

The terrifying episode Cynthia described to her friend is a classic example of a *panic attack*, one of the hallmarks of panic disorder (PD). Panic attacks are exactly what their name suggests: onslaughts of intense fear that, to the individual having the attack, often seem to come from nowhere with an intensity that feels unmanageable and unstoppable. They can occur as you are going about your day, or they might begin as you are asleep and startle you awake. Likewise, they can also occur in response to a stressor, such as hearing the news that your company will be laying off 60 employees. Whatever the cause, many people experience a panic attack once or twice in their lives. However, unlike Cynthia, do they not go on to develop panic disorder.

What made Cynthia's case different? After one episode of panic, Cynthia worried all the time about whether, or *when*, the next panic attack would occur. Cynthia became especially afraid to be in crowded, public places for extended periods of time, for fear of having an attack there. These worries and apprehensions about the possibility of another panic attack are a hallmark of panic disorder called *anticipatory anxiety*. When Franklin Delano Roosevelt uttered the now-famous words "The only thing we have to fear is fear itself," he probably did not realize that he was describing the experience of panic disorder sufferers quite well. Unlike people with generalized anxiety disorder, who have an extensive, concrete list of worries, people who have panic disorder are afraid of experiencing fear itself.

Because of her anticipatory anxiety, Cynthia did her best to avoid the setting in which she experienced her first attack. Avoidance is a third hallmark of panic disorder. "Why would I want to risk being there again for any length of time, or in any big store, for that matter, when at any point, it could happen again, and I'd be stuck there again?" Cynthia pleaded with her friend.

Cynthia didn't stop going into grocery stores or shopping centers immediately after her first panic attack. Initially, she began writing grocery lists, so she could speed in and out of the supermarket as quickly as possible. But soon that strategy proved unacceptable, as the wait in the checkout line became too much to bear. With each passing second, Cynthia became more afraid that the torrent of panic was about to begin; she monitored her body for any sensation indicating the start of an attack. In the first two weeks after the first attack, Cynthia had two panic attacks as she stood in a checkout line. In the first, she had finished paying by the time it started. She was able to get the groceries to the car and then slip into the back seat for the five-minute duration of panic.

However, when the second panic attack hit, Cynthia had to leave her groceries and race for the door. The attack subsided within seven or eight minutes, but she was too fearful and embarrassed to return to the store. Her husband, Jerry, picked up take-out for dinner that night. After that, grocery shopping was abdicated to Jerry, and weekend shopping jaunts with friends avoided.

In the most severe cases of panic disorder, individuals so severely limit their activities that they don't leave their homes or they venture out only with a trusted companion. At this point, they suffer from panic disorder with agoraphobia (*agora* being the Latin word for marketplace). Agoraphobia is a fear of public places.

When Cynthia began to limit the range of her activities so she didn't have to venture out of the house, her panic disorder included agoraphobia. She expressed what many agoraphobics experience when she tearfully confided to her friend, "I know you're going to think I'm being ridiculous, but I just hate going out anywhere now. It's too stressful. I feel safer being at home. I'm so sorry that I haven't been honest with you, but that's the truth about why I haven't been meeting you to go shopping."

The terror and heartache that Cynthia had been keeping from her friend are typical of people who suffer from panic disorder. Again, not all individuals who experience a panic attack go on to develop PD, and not all individuals who have PD go on to develop PD with agoraphobia. The good news is that if you have PD, a complete recovery is possible with treatment regardless of where you fall on the panic disorder continuum.

Components of Panic Disorder

In order to understand treatment options for PD, it's important to understand the disorder itself. The three main components of PD, which I'll explain in more detail below, are:

- Panic attacks—the experience of panic that seems to just pop up out of nowhere, having no discernable trigger.

- Anticipatory anxiety—a preoccupation with the fear that another panic attack might occur.
- Avoidance—the subsequent avoidance of situations and places where panic attacks might occur, as well as places where an easy escape is improbable. When the level of avoidance increases to include all situations that require venturing out of your home, you have developed agoraphobia.

Panic Attacks: The Fight / Flight Response

In her first panic attack, Cynthia experienced many typical physical symptoms (rapid heartbeat, hyperventilation, sweating, etc.) and thoughts ("I'm having a heart attack," "I'm about to faint," "I'm going crazy"). While the symptoms were quite real, they were not the result of a medical condition, as Cynthia thought. These physical sensations were elements of an adaptive response to danger that we all possess: the fight/flight response.

The fight/flight response results from the interplay of two branches of your nervous system that can be likened to a car's gas pedal and brakes. When you sense you are in danger, your *sympathetic* nervous system kicks in, flooding your body with the fuel it needs (hormones/chemical messengers such as adrenaline and norepinephrine) to respond instantaneously to a threat and protect itself. The *parasympathetic* nervous system serves as the brakes, slowing and calming your body to counteract the revving of the sympathetic system. Together, the two systems give you the ability to rev up in response to danger and then slow down when the threat is gone. These processes occur without any thought on your part. They are part of our make-up and reflect the innate wisdom of our bodies.

We have all experienced the fight/flight response to various degrees. Consider the experience of Elise, who was home alone and settling into bed one night. As she was about to drift off to sleep, rustling outside her bedroom window caught her attention. Immediately she jumped up, her heart rate quickening, her breathing speeding up, her ears focused on picking up any sounds that were out of the ordinary. Her sympathetic nervous system (the gas pedal) had revved up to mobilize her body to protect itself in case of danger.

She flipped on the bedroom lights and crept to the window. In an instant she saw there was no intruder to fear—just a raccoon climbing the tree by the window. Immediately the tension in her neck and shoulders eased; she took a sigh and relaxed. Now her parasympathetic nervous system was putting the brakes on, slowing and calming her system.

During panic attacks, people experience the same physical manifestations of the sympathetic nervous system. The heart rate increases to give the body more oxygen. Blood flow is redirected to the muscles and organs that will help you defend yourself in case of an attack, so your extremities—

skin, lower arms, fingers, and toes—receive less blood flow than usual. This is why your hands and feet might look pale and feel cold or numb during a panic attack.

Your breathing also quickens, which can result in sensations of breathlessness or choking, because your brain is actually getting less oxygen. This is why people often feel dizzy, light-headed, or confused during panic attacks. It also accounts for the sense of unreality that some people report, as well as the slightly blurred vision and hot flashes. Blurred vision can also be caused by the dilation of the pupils—another fight/flight response. The dilated pupils account for the phenomenon of seeing spots that some people experience during panic attacks.

The physical symptoms of panic disorder don't stop there. In conjunction with the revving-up, saliva production and digestive activity decrease. This can cause the mouth to become dry and accounts for feelings of nausea, heaviness, or butterflies in the stomach. Muscles also tense, which can result in sensations of tightness or even muscle cramps, as well as trembling or shaking.

Along with all the physical changes, the flooring of the sympathetic gas pedal also revs your mind. While the body is primed to either fight or flee, your mind scans the environment for sources of danger. Say, for instance, that you are hiking and your system goes on high alert because you hear a rattlesnake rattling its tail. Your body mobilizes to run and your sharpened mind scans your surroundings to locate the snake. That's the fight/flight response to actual danger. But what if your body goes on high alert while you are in the grocery store? There are clearly no outward threats, so the physical sensations of danger cause you to turn the search for danger inward: you become afraid you are having a heart attack or that you are going crazy— some kind of medical emergency. You cannot find a rational reason for your extreme symptoms, but you also can't stop the overwhelming panic.

Besides the physical changes in your body, the revving of the sympathetic nervous system triggers an intense urge to flee. If you have ever had a panic attack, you may remember feeling desperate to make a mad dash for the nearest exit. Again, this urge to escape makes sense when you are confronted with a rattlesnake in the woods. Unfortunately for panic-attack sufferers, it is a hardwired response that kicks in whether you are in the woods or the grocery store.

Panic Attacks: Fear and Escalation

So the question arises, why does this powerful survival response of fight or flight kick in when you are in no danger? How does a physiological response meant for survival become a liability, as it does in panic disorder? Dr. David Barlow and his colleagues, international experts in the treatment of panic disorder, suggest that what gets a panic attack going full throttle is the fear of fear. Individuals who experience panic attacks are particularly afraid of the physical symptoms of the fight/flight response. Even one or two mild symptoms occurring randomly can start the panic attack. The individual's subsequent interpretation of those sensations then launches the fight/flight response, which snowballs out of control. Let's examine how this happens.

In her bestselling memoir, *The Middle Place*, Kelly Corrigan described being on a job interview the first time she felt the unanticipated and terrifying experience of panic: "I sat in a conference room on the twenty-first floor, chatting over coffee, while we all waited for someone important named Mark, who was running behind. During that short delay, I went from predictably jittery to uneasy and self-conscious." Very quickly Corrigan's uneasiness manifested itself in unsettling symptoms in her body. "My stomach tightened, I had a sudden chill. My head felt constricted, like I was wearing a hat that was too small. Then there was another bad feeling, something respiratory . . . *Was this a heart attack . . .*" (2008, pp. 138–139).

Although Corrigan survived the interview without succumbing to the temptation to escape, the panic attack had a dramatic impact on her. Like most panic attack sufferers, Corrigan initially concluded that the cause was strictly physical and she was in need of a complete medical evaluation. "I was sure I needed testing and an overnight stay and probably some medication." Soon the panic attack expanded beyond physical symptoms. She came up with distorted interpretations to which she could attribute her distress. She later told her mother: "I mean I felt insane today. I felt like I was gonna run into the street screaming, I felt totally out of control . . . if it happens again, I mean, it just can't happen again, Mom. I can't take it. It was unbearable and I can't stand it and if it happens again, you're gonna have to take me to the hospital . . . " (2008, p. 140). The snowballing, vicious cycle these sensations and thoughts create is seldom evident to the individual experiencing the panic attack.

David Clark (1988), a researcher on panic at Oxford University, developed a clear model that explains this cycle of escalation. Clark emphasized how easily the physical sensations that often accompany anxiety, such as a rapid heartbeat, can be misinterpreted and lead to an escalation of the panicky feelings. Once the first symptom of a physical panic reaction (fight/flight response) is underway, such as Corrigan's sensation of being chilled, a panic sufferer automatically goes through four stages of response:

1. Focuses intently on the physical sensations ("I'm breathing more quickly than usual, could something be wrong?"; "Wow, my hands are tingling too!")

2. Experiences amplification of the physical sensations because of the focus on them ("Oh my gosh, I'm breathing faster and faster—it's getting worse"; "My hands are about to go numb")

3. Misinterprets the symptoms as catastrophic ("I can't catch my breath! My chest is clamping shut!")

4. Panics, experiencing a devastating loss of control, and returns to stage 1, beginning the cycle over again *starting* with hyperventilation and chest pains

Even though the arrival at full-blown panic may seem instantaneous to the panic sufferer, Clark's point is that once the panic stage is reached, the physical sensations worsen and the cycle begins again. This cycle usually repeats several times until the level of panic experienced in a panic attack is reached.

According to Clark's cycle of escalation, Corrigan's initial observation of respiratory difficulty could have played out many different ways. If she had thought, "Wow, I'm a little out of breath—must have been walking a little more quickly than I thought," and not paid it another moment's attention, a panic attack would not have ensued. Or she might have reasoned, "Wow, I'm a little out of breath and jittery. Maybe I shouldn't have had that second cup of coffee this morning." Again, this more reasonable interpretation would have prevented further escalation.

Your interpretation of your physical sensations can make all the difference—even if those sensations begin while you are asleep. For example, you might wake up during the night and notice that your heart is racing a bit or that you are a bit hot, maybe even sweating. If you notice these physical sensations and think, "Wow, my heart is racing . . . I must have been having an exciting dream," you will not be alarmed. The cycle of escalation will not begin, and a panic attack will not ensue. If you have panic disorder, however, you will interpret these same physical sensations quite differently and spark a cycle of escalation that will quickly lead to a full-blown panic attack.

Unfortunately, if you experience a panic attack and go on to develop panic disorder, you will become more and more prone to the insidious cycle of escalation that Clark outlines. This is due to anticipatory anxiety, which is the second component of panic disorder, and hypersensitivity to any physical sensation that resembles a component of the fight/flight response.

Panic attacks are very unpleasant when they occur in the daytime. However, they can seem all the more alarming when your client wakes from a sound sleep in the midst of panic. Approximately 25% of people with panic attacks experience at least one such *nocturnal panic attack*. In reality, they are identical to waking panic attacks, and the intervention strategies you have in place for the treatment of daytime panic attacks can be applied to nocturnal panic attacks with positive results.

Anticipatory Anxiety: The Movie in Your Mind

The second major component of panic disorder is anticipatory anxiety. Many people experience a panic attack or two, but do not go on to develop PD. Cynthia was not so fortunate. If you're like her, you have a movie theater in your mind that replays the scene of your panic attack over and over again. And you are the movie critic, giving a running commentary: "I looked ridiculous; I couldn't control the panic; I had to bail and run out of the store; I couldn't handle it . . . " As you watch the internal movie, your thoughts cement the negative outcome and your inability to cope; you might even experience some of the panic symptoms all over again.

Next, a new, distressing thought comes to mind: *what if this happens again?* Scene after scene plays out on the screen, and you watch, powerless, as the panic overwhelms you. In your imagination, you watch coming attractions of even worse panic attacks: *Return of the Panic Attack, Parts 2, 3, and 4.* You become convinced you won't be able to tolerate the impending panic attacks that you are sure are waiting for you.

Anticipatory anxiety actually sets you up to experience a panic attack. Your expectation of fear and danger puts your entire system on high alert, and you become hypersensitive to any physical sensation associated with panic. As Cynthia stood in line at the grocery store, she was scanning her body for any sensation that might indicate a panic attack was on its way. Her expectation of catastrophe primed her sympathetic nervous system to rev the body and search for danger. It is not surprising that after a minute or two of this heightened tension, Cynthia's heart began to beat faster. While this initial symptom was not really an indication that a panic attack was about to occur, Cynthia's interpretation of the symptom was enough to set Clark's cycle of escalation into action, and Cynthia was off to the races.

Avoidance

The third component of panic disorder is avoidance. After anticipating the horrors of new panic attacks, it's natural to conclude that you only have one course of action: avoid the places where your panic attacks occur. For some, this may simply mean avoiding the specific venue. (Cynthia began to avoid grocery stores.) However, the fear often generalizes to places similar to the original venue, such as, in Cynthia's case, shopping malls or department stores. The avoidance expands to environments that are crowded and enclosed, places from which a speedy exit is difficult. Some people eventually develop panic disorder with agoraphobia, becoming afraid to go anywhere outside of the home.

The Differences Between the Disorders

While all the anxiety disorders have many similarities, they also each differ in significant ways. Panic disorder is different than generalized anxiety disorder, because the worry associated with GAD typically focuses on specific problems of daily living, such as worries about family, career, school, or finances. In panic disorder, it is the fear of having another panic attack that perpetuates the condition.

Panic disorder is also different than the specific phobia conditions discussed in the last chapter. While both phobias and panic disorder involve avoidant behavior, the purpose of the behavior differs. If you have a specific phobia, you avoid the object or situation that elicits the fear, such as snakes or driving on bridges. If you have panic disorder, you avoid panic itself; you avoid situations where you may experience the physical symptoms of panic and the distorted thinking that follows them.

It is also important to note the distinction between panic attacks and panic disorder. If you have had a panic attack, you do not necessarily have panic disorder. For some people, a single panic attack, say, right before speaking to a big group, does not lead to the fear of fear and its accompanying avoidant behavior. It is only when recurring panic attacks are coupled with anticipatory anxiety and avoidance that panic disorder is diagnosed. Why do some people have a few panic attacks and develop the disorder, while others don't develop PD? It may be that some people are more vulnerable to developing panic disorder. As we noted in Chapter 2, some people are simply less stress resilient. The following section might help to answer more of these questions.

Who Develops Panic Disorder?

If you have panic disorder, you are not alone. In the United States, six million people, or 2.7% of adults, share your condition (Kessler, Chiu, Demler, & Walters, 2005). PD typically develops in early adulthood, but you can develop it at any point in your life. Even when panic disorder doesn't appear until early adulthood, however, people with PD share similar childhood traits and experiences. Most of my clients who suffer from PD report that they were high-strung children for whom new situations, particularly those in which their parents weren't present, were especially stressful. Some avoided sleepovers at friends' houses and hated going away to summer camp. Others had school phobia—an intense fear of going to school. These manifestations of separation anxiety don't always end in childhood.

Indeed, in some cases, an initial panic attack as an adult is preceded by a significant separation, such as going to college, the death of a loved one, one's children leaving home, or a divorce. In Cynthia's case, her initial panic attack occurred while her mother was undergoing cancer treatment.

It is also common for people with untreated PD to develop depression. The more your life is run by your fear of panic, the more you lose to your disorder. It is understandable that depression would ensue, if you feel you are constantly at the mercy of your panic. But panic disorder is treatable, and your hopelessness and helplessness needn't last. The remainder of this chapter is devoted to the solution: the road to recovery from panic disorder.

When panic disorder is not treated or is treated unsuccessfully, it often leads to feelings of demoralization, hopelessness, and depression. Although findings have varied, research has found that anywhere between 10% and 65% of individuals with panic disorder also have major depressive disorder (MDD). In about two-thirds of such cases, the onset of MDD occurs concurrently with or soon after PD develops (APA, 2000). Intuitively, these findings make sense, given that people with PD limit their activities to avoid panic attacks and often withdraw from friends to avoid embarrassment. The isolation that follows is a common element of depression. Several of my clients who had PD became so depressed that they had quit their jobs or dropped out of school before they finally entered treatment. It is important to keep this possible comorbidity in mind during your treatment of this client population.

The Good News
If you suffer from panic disorder it is important to know that there is good news. Although the symptoms of panic disorder are overwhelming, with the right tools you can have a complete recovery from panic disorder. I assure you that you won't be a victim of panic disorder forever.

The Goals and Gains of Therapy
- Cultivate an expectation of recovery
- Gain knowledge about the nature of the disorder
- Gain an understanding of the cycle of panic escalation
- Learn to disengage from the thoughts that escalate the panic
- Learn to tolerate the initially mild symptoms associated with the anxiety response
- Develop ways to quickly release anxiety
- Gain understanding of the impact of anticipatory anxiety

- Learn to diffuse anticipatory anxiety
- Overcome avoidance of situations and places previously associated with panic

How to Get There: Therapeutic Techniques and Interventions

Psychoeducation: Knowledge Is Power

While it is important for you to learn about the nature of any physical or psychological disorder that you might have, this is especially true if you have panic disorder. Remember, mistaken assumptions and ideas about the causes of your panic symptoms and your ability to cope with them form the basis of this disorder. By understanding these misattributions, you open the door to new, more adaptive ways of thinking. Thus it is essential that you remember that your panic is triggered by the fight/flight response, rather than any real, life-threatening condition. Naturally, then, you need to learn, as we did in the beginning of this chapter, what physical sensations and responses the fight/flight response induces. Once familiar with those, you will be less likely to misinterpret them as signs of real danger when you are having a panic attack. More importantly, knowing the fight/flight symptoms prevents you from overreacting to them and generating a panic attack in the first place.

The duration of a panic attack is another aspect of panic disorder that often gets blown out of proportion. While panic attacks feel like they last forever to the person experiencing the attack, they are actually short-lived, generally lasting less than 10 minutes, and only rarely as long as an hour. Remembering that the panic attack will quickly subside may reduce its severity and your suffering.

By understanding the fight/flight response and the physical symptoms it creates and by reminding yourself that your discomfort won't last for long, you gain significant control over your panic attacks. Recall the example given earlier in this chapter in which one individual's observation of slight breathlessness led to hyperventilation, chest pains, and the misperception of a heart attack. In contrast, another individual noticed the same breathlessness, attributed it to walking quickly, and did not give it another moment's attention.

To gain power over your panic disorder, you need to take into account all the things that fan the flames of an overreaction. Educate yourself about stimulants and depressants and their impact on the body. Since panic disorder involves an overreaction to physical sensations that mimic the fight/flight response, caffeine and stimulating drugs are the last things you want to take in. A far less obvious culprit that can worsen panic is alcohol. When the depressant effects of alcohol wear off, many people experience a rebound reaction of agitation and physical shakiness. These are the same symptoms that individuals with PD both misinterpret and seek to avoid. Alcohol and caffeine are discussed in greater detail in Chapter 7, but since their use can easily trigger panic attacks, their mention here is all the more pertinent.

Charney, Heninger, and Jatlow (1985) reported in their research that caffeine consumption increased anxiety in 54% of clients with PD and actually triggered panic attacks in 17% of clients. Assessing caffeine consumption and recommending a gradual curtailing is one of the first things you should incorporate into your treatment plan.

Daily Relaxation Regimen

Regardless of other treatment approaches you decide to use, I recommend that you gain a firm grounding in relaxation training. For a detailed description of relaxation techniques, see Chapter 4.

Minding the Mind with Cognitive Therapy

Cognitive therapies for PD often begin with psychoeduation. The therapist teaches what PD is and how it works, in much the way I did in explaining the three components of PD: panic attacks, anticipatory anxiety, and avoidance. A major goal of cognitive therapy is to create change by identifying and then altering the thoughts and beliefs that lead to panic and avoidance. Cognitive therapies teach you to recognize the symptoms of a panic attack for what they are: components of the fight/flight response. This re-education provides the base from which you can change your beliefs and subsequent attributions.

In their book *Mastery of Your Anxiety and Panic,* Craske and Barlow (2007) listed five commonly held beliefs regarding panic attacks that cognitive therapy works to reframe: you are going insane; you are losing control; you are having a nervous collapse; you are having a heart attack; or you are fainting. In cognitive therapy, you learn to counter these fears with the use of more adaptive, more accurate self-statements. In response to each of the five fears noted by Craske and Barlow, you might tell yourself the following:

- Fears of going insane: *I'm not going crazy. I'm just having a panic attack.*
- Fears of losing control: *My body is safe. I am safe. I'm uncomfortable, but I can handle it. I'm still in control.*
- Fears of having a nervous collapse: *This agitation is time limited. In a*

matter of minutes, my body and mind will go back to normal.

- Fears of having a heart attack: *Even though my heart is beating quickly, I am not having a heart attack. This is just a panic attack.*
- Fears of fainting: I'm in the middle of a panic attack. *My blood pressure is elevated, which will keep me from fainting.*

Homework Assignments in Cognitive Therapy

In order to help you identify the thoughts, behaviors, and beliefs or attributions related to the panic, cognitive therapists often assign their clients simple tasks to be done between sessions. For example, Craske and Barlow give their clients a wallet-sized panic attack record to keep track of their panic attacks, the date and time each occurred, what triggered it, and whether the attack was unexpected or anticipated because of a stressful event. Clients can also record the thoughts and behaviors that accompanied the attack and rate their level of distress during the attack on a scale from 0–10.

Homework has many benefits. Identifying and documenting the conditions related to your panic attacks helps you put them into perspective. Simply writing down when panic attacks occur gives you accurate information about their frequency. It's common to think they occur more often than they do, feeding the misperception that the attacks occur *all* the time, at the drop of a hat. Recording where the attacks occur and what was going on when they started helps you identify the conditions associated with the panic attacks. The more you know about the *what, when, where,* and *why* of the attacks, the better equipped you and your therapist will be to address and extinguish them. Having a record of your panic attacks also helps you evaluate the progress of your therapy; how nice it is to look back and see that now you are rating your attacks as less distressing, or that they are occurring less frequently.

The So-What Question

Another approach to your thinking, inspired by cognitive therapy, is to ask yourself, "So what if I have another panic attack?" Then answer this question realistically. What's the worst thing that can happen if you actually do embarrass yourself during a panic attack? Maybe a handful of strangers you don't know will notice that you are sweating, breathing quickly, or racing for the nearest exit. So what? You've learned that you're not going to faint, so you don't have to worry about that. In the worst-case scenario, that you really are having a heart attack, you'll get medical attention. Of course, you don't *want* to experience humiliation or physical or emotional discomfort, but understand that even if all of these scenarios happened, you would be OK. Then you can escape from the big black hole of fear surrounding your panic attacks.

Exposure Therapies: Graduated Exposure

As you will recall from Chapter 3, exposure therapies involve, as their name suggests, *exposing* you to the situations or sensations that you fear and likely avoid. In graduated exposure, you experience what you fear in small, incremental steps, without the aid of relaxation techniques to buffer your anxiety. When used to treat panic disorder, graduated exposure involves incremental exposure to the places or sensations associated with panic attacks. This treatment helps you discover that you needn't fear the places and sensations you have been dreading. Thus you learn to replace fear and panic with a sense of mastery. This exposure process has two steps:

1. Create a *desensitization hierarchy*: you and your therapist brainstorm a list of anxiety-provoking scenarios and situations associated with your panic attacks, and order the list from least to most anxiety-provoking.
2. With the support of your therapist, you progress through each step on your desensitization hierarchy. One by one, you encounter and overcome each of the scenarios you fear.

Step 1

First, you and your therapist construct a list of your fears regarding your panic attacks and then put them into a hierarchy from least to most anxiety-provoking. Usually, you will end up with a desensitization hierarchy list of 10–20 exposure scenarios or steps. The exact number will vary for each person. Like most of my clients, Cynthia did not have any trouble listing the different situations that brought about significant fear and anxiety for her. Brainstorming together for 20 minutes resulted in the following desensitization hierarchy:

1. Drive to the parking lot of a convenience store and observe people entering the store.
2. Go to a strip mall for five minutes (with a friend, husband, or sister).
3. Enter a convenience store with a support person for five minutes during non-peak hours (e.g., mid-morning).
4. Enter a convenience store, alone, during non-peak hours.
5. Enter a convenience store alone at a busy time (e.g., 5:30 P.M.). Stay inside five minutes.
6. Go in the convenience store and purchase five items at a non-peak time.
7. Go in the convenience store and purchase five items at a high-traffic time.

8. Go to a small grocery store with a shopping list at a non-peak time and purchase the groceries.

9. Go to a small grocery store with a shopping list at a busy time (e.g., 5:30–6:00 P.M.) and purchase the groceries.

10. Go to a strip mall alone and purchase one item.

11. Go to a shopping mall with a companion on a weekend when it is crowded.

12. Go to a big grocery store alone when it is crowded. Take a shopping list and purchase the groceries.

13. Go to the shopping mall alone on a weekend when it is crowded. Buy yourself a gift as a reward!

While the above list encompasses only in vivo exposure, some therapists find it helpful to precede the in vivo exposure with imaginal exposure. In the safety of your office, the client can imagine the anxiety-provoking experiences in the hierarchy before actually performing them. This can also be accomplished using systematic desensitization, in which in vivo and imaginal exposure trials are paired with relaxation training. For an example of a systematic desensitization protocol, see Chapter 7.

Step 2

Once you have constructed your desensitization hierarchy, you are ready to begin progressing through your list, step by step. It is normal to initially experience heightened anxiety as you try each step for the first time, just as you initially feel a shock of cold water when you first step into a pool. With each new step, you will feel a brief shock of cold. But if you remain in the pool and give your body time to acclimate as you go down each step, the once-cold water begins to feel fine, if not warm. Just like gradually entering a pool, in graduated exposure you remain on the current step in your list until it no longer brings about a burst of anxiety—until what once felt like ice-water feels lukewarm and tolerable. Amazingly, with enough repetition, steps that once provoked high anxiety rouse little-to-no anxiety.

Cynthia and I agreed that, with the exception of the final few steps in her list, she would attempt to progress through one step in her hierarchy each week. Between her weekly sessions with me, she would engage in that week's step repeatedly until she felt the anxiety triggered by the step diminish significantly. If she did not feel that her anxiety had decreased significantly by the end of that week, she would remain on that step.

While gradual exposure techniques can play a pivotal role in the alleviation of your panic disorder, exposure techniques that involve flooding can be just as valuable. One such flooding treatment is discussed next.

Exposure Therapies: Panic Control Treatment

Panic Control Treatment (PCT), developed by David Barlow and colleagues, is a flooding technique that provides exposure to internal, *interoceptive* fears. In the treatment of panic disorder, these interoceptive fears refer to the fear of internal sensations associated with the fight/flight response. Thus interoceptive exposure involves creating sensations such as shortness of breath, dizziness, or rapid heartbeat in the therapist's office and then riding and evaluating the wave of panic they cause. There are four main steps in this process:

1. Understand the physical symptoms of the fight/flight response.
2. You and your therapist create a two-columned thought inventory (illustrated on the following page). Fill out the "perception" column, listing your fears during your panic attacks.
3. Trigger a panic attack in the therapy room by doing an exercise such as "over-breathing" for a few minutes.
4. While having the panic attack, test the assumptions listed in the "perception" column of your thought inventory. As soon as the panic attack subsides, fill out the "reality" column in the inventory with information learned from testing your perceptions.

Step 1

You and your therapist first discuss the fight/flight response and Clarke's cycle of escalation to make sure that you understand what is happening when you have a panic attack. Knowledge is power, and in this case, it is the first step in gaining power over your fears.

Step 2

You and your therapist create a thought inventory to log perceived versus real threats to your physical safety during a panic attack. Begin by filling out the "perception" column, listing your assumptions regarding components of your panic attacks. (You fill in the "reality" column in Step 4.) The table on the following page is Cynthia's perception column of her thought inventory.

Step 3

Once the "perception" column is filled out, you and your therapist test your assumptions by inducing a panic attack in the office. A few common meth-

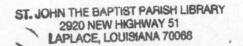

PERCEPTION	REALITY
I'm so dizzy I'm about to faint!	
My heart is racing and my chest aches. I'm having a heart attack!	
My throat is clamping shut; I can't breathe; I'm suffocating!	

ods used to induce an attack are breathing quickly and shallowly for a number of seconds; shaking your head from side to side for a number of seconds; or jogging in place to elevate your heart rate. For this example, let's say you choose to breathe quickly and shallowly for 60 seconds. The forced hyperventilation brings on all the symptoms of a panic attack right there in your therapist's office.

Step 4

Once the panic attack is in full swing, you and your therapist test your previously listed assumptions. If you think you are about to faint, stand up; you won't faint, because your blood pressure is actually elevated during the panic attack, which prevents fainting. Write this new information in the *reality* column of your thought inventory. Cynthia filled out her reality column as follows:

PERCEPTION	*REALITY*
I'm so dizzy I'm about to faint!	*I'm dizzy because I'm breathing quickly and shallowly. I won't faint because my pulse is elevated, not depressed.*
My heart is racing and my chest aches. I'm having a heart attack!	*My heart is beating rapidly because I'm revving into fight/flight mode. This is a healthy response to a threat, not a heart attack.*
My throat is clamping shut; I can't breathe; I'm suffocating!	*I'm feeling this because I'm breathing quickly and shallowly. If I can calm down, my breathing will return to normal.*

Through this exercise you learn that the fears that fuel your panic attacks are simply misattributions. Most notable is that every "life-threatening" symptom is simply a result of shortness of breath and the ensuing fight/flight reaction. They are not life threatening at all. This flooding technique can be likened to Dorothy's pulling the curtain open to expose the Wizard of Oz toward the end of the movie. Once Dorothy saw the reality of the little man at the switchboard behind the curtain, all the smoke, bells, and whistles lost their power to frighten her.

Flooding is a powerful technique because it allows you to quickly and decisively identify and understand your misattributions, which, as Clark taught us, fuel a panic attack's cycle of escalation. Flooding experiences can replace the fear of the Wizard's mysterious power with a calm understanding of the man behind the curtain.

More notably, flooding can accomplish in one session what gradual exposure might accomplish in weeks. Of course, treatments that include flooding can be very challenging to undergo, and for this reason you, like many clients, might feel that gradual exposure might be the best fit for you. There is no need to feel that you are "not strong enough" to weather a therapy, or too fearful to benefit from a possible source of health. This simply means that flooding is not the right therapeutic tool for you.

If you and your therapist do choose to incorporate flooding into your treatment, remember to be extra kind to yourself while you are going through the therapy: flooding is a very powerful, high-intensity experience. Make sure you set aside extra time between sessions for rest, relaxation, and maybe even a little pampering. While good self-care should accompany any therapy, I emphasize it for those who choose to do flooding.

Craske and Barlow addressed the causes of failure to desensitize to interoceptive fears (2007). They suggested that failure to desensitize is related to insufficient exposure. It is essential that you encourage your clients to face their dreaded reactions and situations for extended and frequent periods of time. Try to have your clients initiate exposure exercises daily, if possible, lasting from 15 to 90 minutes a trial. Also, if you're using flooding, the theory is to have your client temporarily abstain from any self-soothing or anti-anxiety medication (e.g., Xanax) that will diminish immediate distress during the flooding exposure itself. The goal is to help your client learn that his or her reactions, albeit uncomfortable, are not catastrophic.

Mindfulness
We are beginning to see more evidence that some treatments with roots in

Eastern spiritual traditions are helpful in the treatment of anxiety disorders in general and panic disorder in particular. Mindfulness is one such treatment. Mindfulness is the practice of calm, detached, and focused attention on your experience in the moment. It is particularly helpful when you feel emotional, because it helps you develop objectivity. You learn to be aware of your emotions and thoughts without judgment, without trying to change them, and without worry about the future. This is non-judgmental acceptance of whatever is happening in the present moment. With practice, this new perspective—that in this particular moment, everything is OK—steadies your emotions.

For people with anxiety disorders, who are typically worried about the future, this gentle approach is very effective. In my book *Affect Regulation Toolbox* (Daitch, 2007), I described how I used mindfulness to help a client who suffered from panic disorder. In the guided meditation below, I have adapted this mindfulness meditation for Cynthia.

> *Now, while you are anxious, you have an opportunity to learn a process called mindfulness . . . that involves standing back and watching your feelings. . . . Ask yourself what feeling is coming up for you right now. And as you identify that feeling, simply observe it, without judgment, without self-recrimination, like a detached observer, like a scientist observing an interesting phenomenon. What do you notice? (Adapted from Daitch, 2007)*

Because you become a witness simply observing your thoughts and emotions, mindfulness usually results in a release of anxiety. You feel less vulnerable, which eases your panic.

Acceptance

Since mindfulness rests on acceptance, you may wonder how it is possible at all. Acceptance is the opposite of what you usually experience when you are having a panic attack. Besides, should you really *accept* panic? Let's get clear about what acceptance means in this context.

Georg Eifert and John Forsyth, psychologists and writers on acceptance and commitment therapy, explain that "acceptance means to 'take what is offered,'" (2005, p. 138). This echoes the "so what?" question asked in cognitive therapy. When you make a commitment to accept what is, to say "so what?" to yourself, you begin to soften your suffering. Psychologist Marcia Linehan speaks of an attitude and practice of *radical acceptance* as an important component of healing. She writes, "Freedom from suffering requires acceptance from deep within of what is. Acceptance is the only way out of hell" (1993, p. 102). Thus even if you are not in therapy, you can practice mindfulness to powerful ends.

Techniques Using Mindfulness

Riding the Wave

Since panic usually emerges quickly, sometimes the best strategy is to utilize mindfulness and acceptance tools to ride the panic wave until it's over. Cynthia created a self-help ritual of repeating phrases that reminded her to accept, self-soothe, and release her symptoms: "I am aware of the panic. I breathe through the panic. I flow through the panic and I release the panic."

Developing a Dual Perspective

You can use mindful observation of the physical symptoms associated with panic to reduce your reactivity to them. Mindfulness develops an awareness that you can tolerate (accept) the temporary discomfort of anxious episodes (Brown & Fromm, 1986). So even if you are experiencing a host of physical symptoms—feeling like you are choking, dizzy, about to faint — you can remain mindful, observing and accepting the feelings as being in the moment.

Hypnotic Fast-Forwarding

On the flip side of staying in the moment, another effective strategy is to mentally fast-forward to the immediate future when the panic attack is over. And it *will* be over, often in just a matter of minutes, although it may subjectively feel longer as it is happening. When Cynthia was in the midst of a panic attack, she reminded herself to look at her watch and say to herself: "In 10 minutes—or at least in 30 minutes—I'll probably feel better. I can tolerate almost anything for a half an hour, can't I? What can I do to distract myself until it *is* over?"

The fast-forwarding technique is based on a hypnotherapeutic intervention called age progression. The technique was developed by psychiatrist Milton Erickson, generally considered the father of modern hypnotherapy. Dr. Erickson would direct his clients to a time in the future when their symptoms were resolved. Further, Erickson would encourage his clients to experience the feelings of satisfaction that would accompany symptom relief (see *Pseudo orientation in time as a hypnotherapeutic procedure* in Rossi, 1980; also, see Daitch, 2007, pp. 165–168, for illustrations of the use of age progression in the treatment of panic).

For clients with panic disorder, age progression can be used to fast-forward just minutes (rather than months or years) into the future. First, the client is guided to imagine having a panic attack. The short duration of the typical panic attack is emphasized: "Surely, you can tolerate being uncomfortable 20 minutes, of course you can . . . " Second, the client is guided to fast-forward to the end of the panic attack and notice that she or he has indeed lived through it. The therapeutic goal is to develop in clients the belief that they can survive a panic attack and thereby enhance self-efficacy.

Cynthia found that she could distract herself by playing music and singing aloud if she was home or in the car. When an attack occurred in public, Cynthia would slowly clench and release her hands, imagining the panic becoming a bright-colored liquid that her fists absorbed. She would close her fists for 10 seconds, then slowly relax her fingers and imagine that all her panic was slowly releasing itself outside onto the lawn or pavement, where it evaporated.

Medication

I recommend that some clients also consult a psychiatrist for anti-anxiety medication in conjunction with psychotherapy for the treatment of PD (for a more thorough discussion of medications, see Chapter 10). Medication can play a key role in breaking the cycle of panic. For many clients the onslaught of panic can be so disruptive it interferes with their functioning. Some medications reduce the intensity of the symptoms quickly, so that the intense suffering diminishes and clients can concentrate both on their treatment and their lives.

However, taking anti-anxiety medications without also being in therapy is not a good idea. Studies have shown that in the long run, psychotherapy focused on anxiety management is more effective than medication alone. While medication can reduce symptoms for a time, you need therapy in order to learn the coping strategies to combat panic in the long run, to learn to better interpret your physical sensations, to recognize a cycle of escalation, and to address the underlying cause of your panic disorder. With effective treatment, you have the added benefit of gaining a sense of competency and control. It is empowering to retrain your thoughts and reactions and gain mastery of your condition through your own diligence.

That said, medication *can* reduce your body's proclivity for revving into fight/flight mode. The quick-acting benzodiazepines, such as Xanax, Ativan, and Klonipan, can be useful at the onset of treatment or to use as a safety valve in a crisis. (Recommendations and cautions on the use of these drugs are discussed in Chapter 10.)

It is reasonable to consult a psychiatrist if you are not responding to therapy or if your symptoms are severe. I agree with Margaret Wehrenberg (2008), author of two books on anxiety, who recommends that her clients consult a psychiatrist if they are having panic attacks several times a week. My experience is that, except for those with a history of substance abuse, PD clients seldom abuse anti-anxiety medications, some of which can be habit-forming.

Recovery: Cynthia's Story

Cynthia entered therapy and learned how to be mindful of the physical symptoms of panic. With practice, she was able to observe and accept the sensations in her body that were present in the moment and to let go of worrying about what might happen to her body in the future. In other words, she learned to stay in the *now* and to identify and label the reactions in her body as sensations that were definitely not dangerous.

Cynthia initially tried a trial of the medication Lexapro, but under her psychiatrist's supervision she discontinued it within three months because it caused her diminished libido. She did get a prescription for Xanax, which she took if she had a panic attack that became unbearable. During the course of her treatment, this only occurred two times, but Cynthia still keeps one Xanax in her purse just in case.

A major part of Cynthia's treatment included exposure therapy. She was often frightened and didn't think she could do it, but she forced herself. Within two months' time, she could attend family functions; within four months, she was able to go to the grocery store and, yes, resume her shopping expeditions with her best friend.

CHAPTER 7

Specific Phobias

"**W**hy don't you at least *try* driving on the freeway again," Nina's mother pleaded over the phone. "What harm could it do? I'll sit in the passenger's seat right next to you. You can do this. You used to drive on the highway every day."

What Nina did not want to tell her mother was that even the thought of getting on the freeway's onramp got her heart racing and her palms sweating. The five minutes she spent on the freeway six months ago, dizzy, heart pounding, fearing she would faint or lose control of the car and crash, was nothing she ever wanted to repeat again.

"It's really not that big a deal, Mom. I just leave an hour earlier for work, and it takes me an hour longer to get home. I listen to books on CD, which I really enjoy. Let's talk about something else."

"But honey, you can't let what happened one time six months ago rule your life. This isn't the Nina I know. Besides, you're a great driver. You've never even had a fender bender. You have nothing to be worried about."

Nina couldn't disagree with her mother more. Not only was she worried, she was petrified.

A 28-year-old paralegal, Nina had developed a specific phobia. Unlike people with panic disorder, who experience intense episodes of panic in many different situations, Nina's excessive fear was confined to one thing only: highway driving. She could tolerate being a passenger in a vehicle on the expressway, but after her experience six months before, Nina vowed never to drive on the highway again.

Pieces of the Puzzle

Specific phobias (SPs) are intense, persistent fears of specific objects, situations, or things. Adults and adolescents with a phobia know that their fear is excessive and illogical, but that doesn't subdue the intense alarm they experience when confronted with the phobic object or situation. Just the thought of the feared situation triggers agitation, and actual exposure to the feared object or situation usually induces extreme fear and, for some, even a panic attack (see Chapter 6 for a detailed description of panic attacks). As will be explained later, in certain SPs, exposure to the feared situation can even result in fainting.

SP is diagnosed when the phobia has existed for at least six months and the fear interferes significantly with a person's lifestyle or daily routines, as in Nina's adding two hours to her daily commute to avoid freeways.

Specific phobias manifest in a variety of different ways. People can develop a phobia of just about anything and can have more than one phobia at a time. The object of phobias generally falls into one of five categories, which are explained below:

- Situational
- Natural environment
- Animal
- Blood/injection/injury
- Other

Situational

In situational phobias an individual fears a specific set of circumstances related to the man-made world, such as buildings, planes, trains, and automobiles. Nina feared driving on highways. Other common situational phobias include driving or walking over bridges or through tunnels, being in enclosed spaces such as elevators, flying, and taking public transportation, such as busses, subways, or trains.

Natural Environment

As the name suggests, this category of phobias involves situations encountered in nature. The most common phobias include fears of storms, water, and heights. Heights and bodies of water are much easier for people with these phobias to avoid than are storms. Indeed, many of the situations in natural-environment phobias are relatively easy to avoid encountering.

Thus it is less common for individuals with these phobias to seek out professional treatment.

Such was the case for Tom, a retired tax attorney from Virginia. Tom and his wife, Angeline, had made minor accommodations for Tom's fear of heights for nearly 40 years. When the issue arose in social settings, Tom would often quip that his version of *Nightmare on Elm Street* would be having to live and work in Manhattan. Angeline would chime in: "Good thing I never wanted to live in a penthouse, or anywhere in the mountains, for that matter," giving her husband a wink and a nudge.

Like many individuals living with a phobia, Tom did not seek help. He and his wife just worked around it. For vacations, the couple went to the beach and golf courses rather than mountain resorts. When Angeline went to the Grand Canyon, it was with the grandkids.

Making small adjustments to accommodate a phobia in this category can be an effective response most of the time. However, consider what happens when individuals with a phobia are unexpectedly confronted with their most dreaded situation. For their 40th wedding anniversary, Tom and Angeline visited California for the first time. They had no idea what lay in store for them when Tom booked a daylong bus tour of the Hollywood Hills. He didn't know they would be winding through one-lane, cliffside roads like Mulholland Drive. After only 15 minutes on the bus, Tom's fists were clenched so tightly his fingernails cut into his palms. He told Angeline that he was too sick to continue. She asked the bus driver to drop them off somewhere they could call a taxi. The entire tour group watched as the bus driver pulled to the side of the road and radioed for a taxi to pick up Tom and Angeline.

One unexpected encounter with the full force of phobic terror can convince people who had managed to avoid their phobic situation for years that accommodation and avoidance are ultimately unwise. Unfortunately, following the aborted Hollywood Hills bus tour, Tom only vowed to research his vacation plans more thoroughly. Had he decided to pursue therapy for his phobia, his need to constantly curtail his activities to avoid heights would have most likely become a thing of the past.

Animal

Animal phobias are intense fears of any of the many creatures in the animal kingdom. Fears of snakes, spiders, or other insects are a common type of animal phobia and are actually thought to have a genetic or evolutionary component. Some researchers believe that the tendency to fear these creepy-crawlers is hardwired into our DNA. It makes sense: insects can be carriers of diseases, many spiders and snakes are poisonous, and some snakes are our predators. To survive, our early ancestors had to avoid these creatures. Their survival reinforced this propensity and it was passed down to us. Many of us find creepy-crawlers to be, well, a bit creepy. But for some people the natural aversion to these creatures reaches the level of full-blown phobia.

Consider Jackie, who suffers from arachnophobia, the intense fear of spiders. Jackie came to therapy at the insistence of her husband Vic.

"Boating is Vic's passion. He loves that boat of his like it's his child," Jackie told me in her first session. "But do you *know* how many spiders can be on a single boat? I just can't do it. I tried to tolerate it to be with Vic, but I gave up. Vic does his best to help. He cleans out the boat before I get there. He has an insecticide he douses the entire deck with, and he even offers to inspect the area before I get on. I know he's trying so hard, but even he admits that it's impossible to get rid of all of them. So now, we spend most of our weekends apart, Vic on the boat and me at home."

I asked Jackie if her spider phobia affected other areas of her life. "Well, yes, actually, it has gotten worse. Lately, I've stopped gardening in the summer, which I used to love. Now that I think about it, I don't really enjoy summers much anymore because I live in absolute terror that I'll see a spider when I go outside." Jackie's eyes teared up. "Do you think you can really help me?"

Blood/Injection/Injury

Blood/injection/injury phobias are the most common of the specific phobias in this category. Blood phobia consists of an intense fear of the sight of blood or bleeding. Injection phobia is a fear of needles and receiving or even witnessing injections. The lesser-known injury phobia is an extreme fear of sustaining or seeing physical injuries.

Most phobias get the heart racing and the blood pressure rising. Blood/injection/injury is the only category of phobia in which, for a subset of individuals, the fear can lead to a significant *decrease* in heart rate and blood pressure, sometimes resulting in fainting. Researchers theorize that for these people, an intriguing genetic component is at play.

Like the fear of creepy-crawlers, evolutionary theorists propose that blood/injection/injury phobias that include a drop in blood pressure and heart rate have a genetic component that has been hardwired to aid our survival. Think of the soldier on the battlefield or the hunter–gatherer out in the woods who has sustained a serious injury. To increase chances of survival, he needs to lose as little blood as possible. Say the hunter–gatherer has been attacked by an animal and seriously injured. If he loses lots of blood, he dies. A decrease in his blood pressure so extreme he passes out will minimize blood loss, possibly saving his life. Supporting this evolution- ary theory is the finding that the predisposition to this particular phobia is genetic and passed down among blood relatives.

Other researchers, however, have found that some people develop blood/injection/injury phobia in the absence of any apparent genetic pre- disposition. Rather, the phobia tends to originate following a traumatic experience in childhood or adolescence, such as getting a shot or blood test. This would help to explain the subset of individuals who do not experience decreases in blood pressure when exposed to their feared situation. Whether genetic or not, it is not easy to accommodate these phobias in everyday life.

Many people with these phobias avoid medical care due to the intense fear of injections, the sight of blood, or the heightened possibility of seeing others with injuries. They avoid getting shots, dental work, blood work, or invasive medical procedures. Visiting family or friends in the hospital is often out of the question. But even with the most painstaking avoidance of medical environments or procedures, it is hard to completely avoid con- frontation with the feared situation. This was the case for Ryan, a 21-year- old college student who was working at a restaurant one summer.

"I've got to get in to see you before next Friday, if you can work me in," Ryan pleaded over the phone. Luckily I had a cancellation and he was in my office the next morning.

"My mother said you helped her out a lot, that now she can get shots and blood tests and all that," Ryan began, nervously interlacing and unlacing his fingers as he spoke. "I've been terrified of needles for as long as I can remember, but it's never gotten me in a bind like this. Yesterday the Health Department came to the restaurant to give the wait and cook staff TB tests. I have to get the test to keep my job, so I got in line. I rolled up my sleeve and looked at the ground. I was really jumpy and clammy. The next thing I knew, I came to on the floor. I flat-out fainted! The nurse said they'd come back in less than two weeks! I don't know how I'm going to go through with it. I thought about just getting another job, but I need a TB test to do my practicum in the public schools this fall, too. I need to do this. Last winter, I gave up plans to go to Costa Rica for the term because I didn't want to deal with the vaccinations. This has to stop getting in the way in my life."

Others

"Others" is a catch-all category that includes the many specific phobias that do not fall neatly into the other four groupings. A few phobias in this cate- gory occur frequently enough to merit their discussion. One is the fear of falling and having nothing to hold onto. To avoid this situation, sufferers try to make sure they are always near walls, railings, or other kinds of physical supports. Other phobias in this category include fears of choking, contracting an illness, and vomiting.

Allie, a 19-year-old college freshman, appeared to have everything going for her. She was bright and energetic, and best of all, she was in love for the first time. Things were going great until her boyfriend, Adam, invited her out to dinner to meet his parents. At first Adam accepted her excuses for not going, but eventually he suspected something else was going on. What Allie hadn't told Adam was that she had a phobia of vomiting in public places, known as emetophobia. She avoided meeting his parents because she was afraid she'd be sick.

That wasn't the first time that her phobia had affected her day-to-day life. Allie usually steered clear of eating in restaurants and avoided foods that she thought might make her nauseated. She also avoided contact with anyone who was ill.

Allie's phobia even affected her choice of colleges. Most of her friends went away to school, but Allie chose a local school so she could live at home. She was afraid to eat in the college dining hall and risk vomiting in public, afraid of being exposed to all the other students in the dorms during cold and flu season, and afraid of having to share a bathroom with them.

Adam knew his girlfriend was a picky eater, but he found Allie's insistence on having meals together in the privacy of her home romantic. However, Allie's consistent refusal of his parents' dinner invitations was straining their relationship. She didn't want to risk losing Adam. Finally, Allie became fed up with the restrictions her phobia imposed on her life. She didn't feel that her phobia was something she could "work around" any longer. In desperation, Allie came to see me.

It is important to note the key role that avoidance plays in the maintenance of phobias. Although this avoidance might ensure that people like Allie do not encounter their feared scenario, it does nothing to diminish phobic fears.

People who suffer from emetophobia exhibit the following avoidance behaviors:

- Avoidance of people who could be ill, particularly children
- Avoidance of alcohol (and the vomiting that results from overindulging or a hangover)
- Avoidance of people who drink excessively (and might vomit as a result)
- Avoidance of restaurants and eating in public

- Avoidance of certain foods (that are thought to be more likely to induce vomiting)
- Avoidance of becoming too full when eating
- Avoidance of becoming pregnant (and having to deal with morning sickness)
- Avoidance of long car rides or airplane travel (due to fear of becoming nauseated and vomiting or watching fellow travelers do so)

There are an infinite number of things and situations that people can fear at such an intense level that they become specific phobias. The next question to examine is who might develop these phobias.

The Difference Between the Disorders

Specific phobias bear similarities to both social anxiety disorder (see Chapter 8) and panic disorder (PD) with and without agoraphobia (see Chapter 6). People experiencing all three of these disorders often avoid feared situations or endure them under extreme duress. If you have any of these disorders, you are also prone to panic attacks. Many of the behaviors and symptoms of the disorders are similar, if not identical. The *reasons* for the behaviors and symptoms distinguish the disorders.

For example, if you have a *specific phobia*, you fear only the particular object or situation. You might not have a panic attack, but if you do, it is in response to exposure to the phobic object or situation. On the other hand, people with *panic disorder* (rather than a specific phobia) often experience panic attacks, which seem to pop up out of the blue rather than be triggered by something in particular. Their fear is of having the panic attack itself, which leads them to avoid any situations where they might be likely to have a panic attack.

Someone with PD might fear driving on the freeway, just as Nina does. However, Nina suffers from a specific phobia, not from PD, because she *only* fears driving on the freeway. She does not avoid other situations out of fear of having a panic attack. People who go on to develop panic disorder may well have their very first panic attack while driving on the freeway, but their fear *generalizes* to having another panic attack *in any situation,* rather than highway driving specifically.

Specific phobias may also outwardly appear the same as some social anxiety disorders. For example, both Allie and someone with SAD might avoid eating in restaurants, but again, the reasons behind their fear and avoidance distinguish the two disorders. Allie, who has an SP of vomiting, avoids eating in public settings out of the fear she might vomit in these venues. Someone with social anxiety disorder avoids eating in restaurants out of a fear of being seen or judged by others. In fact, this is the case for Andrew, as we will see in Chapter 8.

The avoidance of specific objects and places due to SP also looks similar to the avoidance demonstrated by people with post-traumatic stress disorder (PTSD) or obsessive–compulsive disorder (OCD; see Chapter 9). People with PTSD and SP might develop an intense fear of an object or situation because those objects or situations are reminiscent of a past trauma. But for people with PTSD, this fear is also accompanied by many other symptoms related to the trauma. Although the symptoms of OCD might look similar to SP, what distinguishes OCD is that the fear of certain objects or situations stems from the individual's underlying obsessions, such as an obsession with germs and a fear of contamination. Jackie, on the other hand, avoided gardening because she had a specific phobia of spiders.

Who Develops Specific Phobias?

Just as different categories of phobias have different rates of occurrence, some also have different patterns of onset and duration. Animal and natural-environment phobias tend to begin in childhood. However, height phobias, which are in the natural-environment category, can develop in adulthood as well as childhood. Situational phobias also tend to begin in childhood, with another significant peak in their onset occurring in the mid-20s. Generally, however, specific phobias are most prevalent in people between the ages of 25–54 (Bland et al., as cited in Barlow, 2002) and seem to decrease in frequency and intensity with age.

If you have a specific phobia, you are not alone. Specific phobias are relatively common. Some surveys have found that anywhere between 4% and 9% of the population has an SP at any given time (APA, 2000). However, a relatively small number of people with SPs, 12%–30%, choose to get help in treating their phobia (APA, 2000). The more a phobia interferes with your daily life, however, the more likely you are to seek out treatment. Thus someone with a fear of heights who lives in Manhattan amidst high-rise buildings is more likely to seek treatment than someone with the same phobia who lives in a small town in Iowa, with neither high-rises nor mountains.

Clients frequently ask if many other people share their specific phobia. While specific phobias are relatively common, some of the categories of phobias occur more commonly than others. In samplings of people who are under the care of therapists or psychiatrists, situational phobias are the most common, followed by those pertaining to the natural environment, blood/injection/injury, and lastly animals. Community samplings—that is, information collected from the general population—reveal a different ordering of these categories. They have found that situational and animal phobias are most common: specifically, phobias of heights, spiders, mice, and insects.

Sometimes a phobia develops because of a bad association with a situation or object. For example, if you were bitten by a dog, it makes sense that you would develop a fear of dogs that would persist throughout your life. Since such a traumatic event could happen at any time, phobias that develop in response to a traumatic experience do not have a typical age of onset. (Remember, for PTSD to be diagnosed, additional responses to the trauma also need be present.) These phobias do, however, tend to develop rather rapidly following the trauma. As these types of precipitating traumatic events are widespread, these phobias can also fall into any of the five phobia categories.

Along with differences among the categories of phobias, there are also significant differences between men and women regarding the rate of diagnoses of SPs. Women are diagnosed with SPs approximately twice as often as men, and for some of the categories of specific phobias women are diagnosed up to nine times more often. Some surveys have found rates of diagnosis between genders to be somewhat closer to equal for the blood/injection/injury category and specifically for fear of heights: about 55%–70% of people with these diagnoses are female. Yet no matter how you cut it, women who are polled report having SPs far more often than men.

One explanation for the preponderance of women with phobias was proposed by Barlow (2002). He suggested that because boys are encouraged to take more risks than girls typically are, boys may become more resilient facing commonly feared environmental triggers. However, there are other hypotheses that could account for this phenomenon. For example, boys and men might not necessarily become more resilient in response to a cultural expectation. Rather, they may simply be less willing to admit they have phobias because of the stigma. Can you imagine John Wayne, Bruce Willis, or Vin Diesel jumping in fear at the sight of a spider? Men are expected to be more like Superman than Woody Allen. The debate about the influence of culture on gender strengths and vulnerabilities continues.

The development of a phobia earlier on, in adolescence, has not been found to predict the development of any other psychological disorders, although it does increase the chance that you might develop another specific phobia later in life. This brings up another important point: often individuals have more than one phobia. While you are most likely to develop another phobia in the same category as the one you already have, it is not uncommon for people with more than one phobia to have phobias in different categories.

When making differential diagnoses, it is important to note that multiple avoidance responses can be associated with a single phobia. For example, a client with emetophobia (fear of vomiting) might avoid flying in airplanes. At first glance the avoidance of plane travel might appear to be a separate, coexisting phobia. But this "fear of flying" might simply be an avoidance response resulting from emetophobia. Understanding both the cognitions and the behaviors that signify a phobia is crucial for your diagnosis. If your client informs you that he or she refuses to fly out of the fear of vomiting on the airplane, only one phobia—emetophobia—is present. However, if the client communicates that he or she avoids flying out of a fear that the plane will crash and all the passengers will die, a separate phobia exists.

Other anxiety, mood, and substance-abuse disorders also commonly co-occur with specific phobias. In fact, people often initially seek treatment for another disorder and end up receiving treatment for their phobia(s) as well. This additional treatment can be an unexpected benefit of therapy, which is particularly important because most phobias persist throughout one's life if treatment is not sought. So if you do have a specific phobia, I urge you to seek out therapy: you needn't live with your phobia any longer.

Many of the clients I have treated for a specific phobia actually came to therapy for other reasons. Often these clients do not even think to mention their phobias, or if they do it might come up later in treatment. Thus it is especially important that you screen new clients for the existence of phobias, even if they are not directly related to the presenting problem. Conversely, when a specific phobia is the *primary* presenting problem, it is often not associated with other psychological disorders (Barlow, 2002). One study reported that 47% of clients with specific phobias did not have any co-morbid psychological conditions (Sanderson, DiNardo, Rapee, & Barlow, 1990).

The Good News

Whether you endure your feared object or situation on a daily basis or manage to avoid that which you phobically fear, there are many treatments available to you. Because phobias are, as their diagnostic name suggests, very specific, treatments for SPs can even be relatively brief in duration. You can, with the right help and the right treatments, overcome your fears.

The Goals and Gains of Therapy
- Gain an understanding of the causes and treatments of your phobia
- Master relaxation techniques
- Develop a hierarchy of the least-to-most anxiety-provoking situations related to your fear
- Establish a plan of exposure treatment to take on each challenge in your hierarchy
- Develop cognitive statements that counter negative beliefs and responses

How to Get There: Therapeutic Techniques and Interventions

Minding the Mind with Cognitive Therapy
Cognitive therapies for specific phobias focus on identifying and changing the thoughts that accompany the phobic fear. As has been discussed already, cognitive therapy (CT) is based on the premise that identifying and changing your thoughts changes your beliefs and behaviors. The majority of people who have phobias would admit that their fears are blown far out of proportion. Cognitive therapies can help you take an in-depth look at the thoughts that accompany your fears. You and your therapist will brainstorm new thoughts that you feel are more appropriate and desirable responses to the situations you fear.

Thought Inventories
Many cognitive therapists use a thought inventory list to help clients who suffer from specific phobias identify the thoughts that reinforce their phobias. Discussing such a list, psychologists Martin Antony and Peter Norton identified a number of questions that can help you evaluate the validity of the beliefs surrounding your phobic object or situation. Regarding your phobic fear, they suggested you ask yourself:

- "What am I afraid will happen?"
- "What am I predicting will occur?"
- "What am I imagining will occur?"
- "What will happen if I encounter a [insert your phobia]?" (Antony & Norton, 2009, p. 87)

To create the CT thought inventory, you and your therapist create two columns on a sheet of paper. In the left column, labeled "Fearful Thoughts," you enter your answers to the above questions. However, it is important to not only identify the thoughts that fuel your fear, but to have new thoughts to replace them with. So, in the right column, labeled "Reality-Based Thoughts," you write down more reasonable responses to the fearful object or situation. These become a new script to say to yourself when your phobia strikes. Below are examples of thought inventories that Jackie (fear of spiders) and Allie (fear of vomiting) might have made.

JACKIE'S THOUGHT INVENTORY FOR HER FEAR OF SPIDERS	
FEARFUL THOUGHTS	**REALITY-BASED THOUGHTS**
I can't handle even the sight of a spider. If I see one, I'll lose it.	I might not like seeing a spider. It might feel very, very uncomfortable. But this discomfort isn't anything I can't deal with.
If I see a spider, I need to run away from it or it will crawl on me.	If I see a spider, there's no need to run from it. I can just step out of the way if it appears to be headed in my direction, or calmly move to a different area if I don't want to be around it. The spider isn't out to get me or crawl on me.
I couldn't stand it if the spider crawled on me.	A spider crawling on me might send chills up my spine, but I can just brush the spider off or have someone else brush it off of me.
The spider will bite me.	Very few spiders would end up biting me. Usually, the spider would just crawl on me without biting and I could brush it off.

ALLIE'S THOUGHT INVENTORY FOR HER FEAR OF VOMITING	
FEARFUL THOUGHTS	**REALITY-BASED THOUGHTS**
If I eat in a restaurant, I could throw up.	It's true that I might throw up if I eat in a restaurant. It's pretty unlikely that that would happen, though, and even if it does, it would be OK.
If I threw up in front of my friends, I couldn't face them.	If I threw up in front of my friends, my friends would be understanding and want to help me and make sure I was OK. They wouldn't judge me. I wouldn't need to be embarrassed or ashamed. It wouldn't be the end of the world.

Cognitive Statements That Reinforce Your Strengths and Resources

We've just seen how cognitive interventions can help you identify the fearful thoughts that frequently run through your mind. Cognitive therapy can also help you learn to broadcast more positive messages to yourself throughout the day. In addition to replacing fear-based thoughts with more adaptive ones, you can develop your own affirming and reassuring inner voice. Just imagine how different you might feel if you told yourself "I *can* handle _____," rather than "I can't." I offer my clients the following intervention to turn their negative self-talk around.

In our therapy together, Nina, Jackie, Ryan, and Allie each identified instances in their lives in which they had successfully faced a challenge. Nina recalled overcoming her testing anxiety and scoring well on her SATs. Ryan recalled summoning the courage to ask a girl he liked out on a date, despite his fears of rejection.

Next we brainstormed a list of personal attributes each client demonstrated when facing each challenging situation. Words and phrases such as *brave, courageous, capable,* and *willing to take on challenges* frequently made the list. Once this list was made, all the clients composed a list of affirmative thoughts to repeat to themselves in fearful situations. Nina wrote: "I am courageous. I am feeling fear right now, but I can tolerate it." Ryan noted: "I am capable. I can access the resources to challenge my fear."

Likewise, you can also think back to a challenging situation that you successfully faced, and say to yourself, "I did _____, so I can also do _____." For example, Nina wrote: "I was terrified of taking the SATs, but I took them and did well. I did that, so I can also face my fears of driving on the highway." I have found that most people with anxiety underestimate their own resources. Identifying and using affirmative self-statements can help remind you that you have indeed successfully faced and overcome daunting challenges in the past. Likewise, you have the ability to overcome your anxiety disorder.

Although changing your thoughts can be very helpful, some therapists and clients find that cognitive therapy alone is not enough to combat a phobia. When cognitive interventions are paired with other interventions, however, they become all the more powerful.

Exposure Therapies

Exposure therapies are generally considered the gold standard for the treatment of specific phobias. As its name suggests, exposure involves *exposing* you to aspects of what you are fearing or avoiding. For SP sufferers, this means exposure to your phobic object or situation. If you seek therapy for an SP, you and your therapist will most likely use some type of exposure technique to lessen your intense, seemingly knee-jerk fear of your phobic object or situation.

In general, there are two types of exposure treatments: gradual exposure and flooding exposure. (For a more detailed description, see the section on exposure therapies in Chapter 3.) To understand the difference between the two, recall the different ways of entering a chilly swimming pool mentioned in Chapter 3. You can either take the pool's steps, gradually introducing a foot, then a calf, and so on into the water, or you can cannonball right into the deep end. The former is an example of gradual exposure; the latter is flooding.

Both gradual exposure and flooding can be used to treat specific phobias. Recall also from Chapters 3 and 6 that gradual exposure involves creating a desensitization hierarchy—a list of exposure activities that progress from least to most aversive, akin to the gradual submersion of your body into the pool. The exposure activities on the list usually progress from simply imagining encounters with the phobic stimulus to encountering the stimulus itself. When the gradual exposure is intertwined with relaxation exercises, it is called *systematic desensitization;* when it is done without relaxation exercises, it is called *graduated exposure.*

Nina, Jackie, Ryan, and Allie did exposure therapy in their phobia treatments with me. As I have found with many of my clients, after we discussed the different exposure treatment options, all four chose to do systematic desensitization. Even though that took more time to implement than flooding and involved learning more skill sets (i.e., relaxation training), all felt it was the least aversive intervention.

The importance of incorporating relaxation techniques is debated in the literature. Barlow (2002), for example, notes that the incorporation of relaxation techniques in flooding protocols has not been found to affect the treatment outcome, and is thus an unnecessary component of exposure therapy. Furthermore, while clients undergoing in vivo exposure report experiencing more distress than clients who undergo systematic desensitization, their treatment is no less effective, and sometimes more so. As current efficacy studies do not suggest that one method is significantly more effective than the other, I gear the type of exposure treatment to the client's preference: some prefer "fast and furious," and others the more gentle route. In fact, because of the "fast and furious" nature of flooding treatments, many clients do not complete this therapy. In these cases, gradual exposure may well be effective, even if flooding was not.

While in vivo is more time efficient, and relaxation training not "necessary," I feel that gradual exposure, and systematic desensitization in particular, is preferable if the client can afford to take the time to learn the relaxation skills and progress more gradually. I have found that relaxation training offers clients an invaluable resource that they can utilize in multiple areas of their lives, and I prefer to provide my clients with the least aversive interventions possible. That being said, I have many colleagues who prefer flooding to gradual exposure because they feel their clients benefit most from interventions that alleviate their symptoms in the quickest way possible.

To address Nina's phobia of driving on freeways, I taught her progressive muscle relaxation and autogenics (see Chapter 4 for a detailed description of both techniques) before we developed a desensitization hierarchy for her. Nina immediately began practicing these techniques on a daily basis to prepare for her upcoming exposure trials. It was important for her to have mastered these relaxation techniques so she could use them to diffuse the fear and anxiety she would experience as she went through the steps of her desensitization hierarchy.

Next, Nina and I collaboratively developed the following anxiety hierarchy. Once we had listed all the steps, Nina ordered them according to the degree of anxiety each would provoke. Nina did not find driving independently to be more or less anxiety provoking than driving with a passenger in the car. However, we still chose to include one independent driving task on the hierarchy as the final step to prepare Nina to begin driving on the highway independently again. Nina also expressed the desire to "take it very slowly," so her hierarchy contained eleven steps that increased in intensity at a pace with which she felt comfortable.

The resulting instructions for the hierarchy, going from least to most anxiety-provoking, were:

1. Visualize yourself entering the on-ramp to the freeway.
2. Visualize yourself driving on the highway.
3. As a passenger (with Mom driving), enter the highway during non-peak traffic flow and drive to the next exit.
4. As a passenger (with Mom driving), enter the highway during non-peak traffic flow and remain on the highway for the entire seven miles from home to work.
5. As a driver (with Mom as passenger), enter the highway during non-peak traffic flow and drive for one exit.
6. As a driver (with Mom as passenger), enter the highway during non-peak traffic flow and drive for five exits.
7. As a driver (with Mom as passenger), enter the highway during non-peak traffic flow and drive the entire seven miles from home to work.

Anxiety Disorders

8. As a driver (with Mom as passenger), enter the highway during peak traffic flow and drive to the next exit.

9. As driver (with Mom as passenger), enter the highway during peak traffic flow and drive for five exits.

10. As a driver (with Mom as passenger), enter the highway during peak traffic flow and drive the entire seven miles from home to work.

11. As a driver (with no one else in the car) enter the highway during peak traffic flow and drive the entire seven miles from home to work.

Our goal was for Nina to master one step on the hierarchy each week, practicing the step three to four times during that week. I also met with Nina's mother Linda, once individually before Nina began the desensitization exercises to answer any of Linda's questions and to clarify her role as driver and passenger in Nina's desensitization exercises.

Often the steps of a client's desensitization hierarchy involve the presence of a second, trusted individual. However, if the client is to practice a given step in a hierarchy multiple times in a week, it is simply not feasible for the therapist to be that trusted person. For this reason, relatives, significant others, and close friends can be invaluable resources in the implementation of a client's desensitization protocol.

When other individuals do take part in a client's desensitization hierarchy, however, it is crucial that the individual(s) have a clear understanding of both the protocol itself and their role in it; just as the client needs psychoeducation, so do the other participants.

There are many ways in which participants can receive this psychoeducation. Sometimes a client will prefer to communicate all necessary information to the participant independent of the therapist. At other times the client might desire the individual to accompany him or her to a therapy session, at which time everyone can discuss the implementation of the hierarchy. In Nina's case, both she and her mother preferred that Linda meet with me separately. Regardless of the means by which the dissemination of information occurs, it is paramount that both the client and the participant have a clear understanding of their different roles in facilitating the desensitization procedure. It is also important that both parties—especially the client—feel comfortable with the process through which this information is conveyed.

As with any desensitization hierarchy, I reassured Nina that she would not tackle a new step until she could perform the current one with a low level of anxiety. Each trial consisted of three repetitions of the particular goal, paired with the relaxation techniques. Between and during the repetitions, Nina de-escalated her anxiety using the relaxation techniques and re-evaluated her current level of stress and discomfort. The first trial of all but the eleventh step was conducted with me present (either in my office or in Nina's car).

Nina was also to practice her progressive relaxation and autogenics exercises three times per day without the desensitization exercise in order to enhance her ability to pair the relaxation response with the anxiety-provoking stimuli. Relaxation techniques during the exposure exercises were amended when Nina was the driver of the vehicle. Only those techniques that would not impair her focus on her driving were included.

Applied Muscle Tension for Blood/Injection/Injury Phobias

As mentioned earlier in this chapter, some people with blood/injection/injury phobias experience a decrease in blood pressure upon exposure to their feared object or situation. For some of these people, the significant *decrease* in blood pressure leads not just to dizziness or lightheadedness, but to fainting. This was the case for Ryan, who fainted when he was about to be injected for a TB test.

One of the first steps in treating this subclass of blood/injection/injury phobia is to prevent the decrease in blood pressure through a technique called applied muscle tension. This produces a temporary rise in blood pressure, eliminating the low-blood-pressure response associated with fainting. It takes a bit of practice to master, but with this simple technique under your belt, you can proceed with exposure therapy for your blood/injection/injury phobia without the risk of fainting in the process.

If you suffer from a blood/injection/injury phobia that includes decreases in blood pressure, you can practice the steps of applied muscle tension, which I taught Ryan, below:

1. Sitting in a chair, tense your arms, make fists, and lift your arms away from your body, parallel to the ground, as if lifting free weights.
2. Keep your muscles tense for 15 seconds.
3. Relax your muscles for 20–30 seconds and lower your arms.
4. Tense your muscles again for another 15 seconds.
5. Repeat this cycle 5 times.

Begin applied muscle tension as soon as you feel even the slightest dizziness or lightheadedness at the sight of the needle. Although in time you might encounter your phobic object while standing, it is best to learn and practice this technique while sitting down.

I also taught Ryan to tense his muscles in two alternative ways that are less conspicuous than the arm raising. You can practice these as well. As with the arm-raising technique, these exercises increase your blood pressure. You are likely to feel a slight flush or sense of heat in your cheeks as a result.

- Sitting in a chair, press your heels into the floor while scrunching your toes,
   OR
- Straighten your spine as if you'd been told to "sit up straight," tensing the muscles in your torso.

I suggested that Ryan practice these techniques three to five times daily for a few days, or longer if needed to get the hang of it. Usually you will have no problem developing this skill with only a few days of practice. To Ryan's amazement, this simple exercise helped him elevate his blood pressure enough to counteract his fainting response.

Teaching applied muscle tension is your first step in treating any client who demonstrates decreases in blood pressure upon exposure blood/injection/injury–related fears. Since fainting during treatment does pose a safety concern, it is essential that you not proceed with other interventions until a client has mastered the technique.

Once a client's fainting during treatment is no longer a concern, you can proceed to other interventions, such as desensitization and hypnosis. When planning subsequent treatment interventions, it is essential that you determine the source of the fear and the concomitant avoidance response. My colleague Dr. Ran Anbar, a pediatric pulmonologist, emphasized targeted treatment-planning in a discussion on needle phobia: "When a patient comes in with a complaint of needle phobia I ask [what makes them] afraid. For example, patients have told me the fear relates to pain, a dislike of a foreign object in their body, the sight of blood, a concern about losing too much blood, an association with a previous bad experience, lack of control during the procedure, a part of generalized anxiety, et cetera. . . . My intervention is targeted at the source of the fear." (R. Anbar, personal communication, July 3, 2009).

The New Frontier of Exposure Therapies: Virtual Reality
A cutting-edge form of exposure therapy employs virtual reality. This allows you to experience fully, rather than imagine, your feared scenario or object in the therapy office, with the sights, sounds, feel, and even smells of the actual event. With training and special equipment, you and your therapist can construct an exact virtual reality that mirrors your phobia. In the ther-

apist's office, you then put on a headset with a visor through which you can view the feared scenario. Through built-in headphones, you hear only the sounds in sync with the virtual action, and no sounds in the therapist's office. To simulate the kinesthetic sense of the experience, your chair is placed on a motorized platform that vibrates and moves in tandem with the virtual action. Last but not least, smells associated with the virtual environment are provided by an electronic scent machine. The therapist views the client's visual reality on a video monitor in the office and can talk to him or her at all times by means of a microphone that feeds directly into the client's headset.

The use of virtual reality in the therapy office has two advantages. First, it allows the therapist to be with the client in the feared environment, which normally isn't practical. A therapist is unlikely to trek to the edge of a cliff or the top of a high-rise during a session of exposure therapy, but can do so easily with virtual-reality technology. Second, the virtual-reality technology makes an intermediate level of exposure possible for clients: it is a step above exposure to the feared stimulus through guided imagery, and a step below actual in vivo, or real life, exposure.

As therapies using virtual reality are relatively new, more research needs to be conducted to better assess the effectiveness of these interventions and establish a set of best practices. Fortunately, studies already conducted show promising results, and new studies are forthcoming. For example, researchers Wiederhold, Jang, Kim, and Wiederhold (2002) found that clients who underwent virtual exposure for fear of flying demonstrated decreased levels of physiological arousal and decreased situational avoidance.

The Use of Hypnosis for Unconscious Exploration: Hypnotic Age-Regression and Corrective Memories for Trauma-Based Specific Phobias

In some cases, strictly cognitive behavioral techniques might not completely abate your phobia. When this is the case, I often look for past triggers or traumas or current conflicts or stressors that are maintaining the phobic symptoms and impeding recovery. Sometimes it is difficult to overcome a phobia without working through an event that is associated with it.

If you find that certain clients are not progressing as you and they hoped, you may find that it's time to think outside the box and consider integrating a range of different perspectives and interventions. You also may need to consider the possibility that this phobia has a traumatic origin.

Phobias that originate from traumatic experiences can fall into any of the five phobia categories. Some people are consciously aware that their phobias have a traumatic origin, such as a sustained fear of dogs that immediately followed a dog bite in childhood. However, others are not aware of a traumatic event that might be connected to the onset of their phobia. This might be because there is, indeed, no traumatic origin for the phobia. Conversely, a traumatic origin may exist that the client does not actively remember. I have found hypnotic age regression and EMDR to be extremely helpful tools in my therapeutic arsenal when addressing traumatically-based phobias. If you have not had training in these approaches, it is perfectly reasonable to refer the client to a colleague for specific adjunctive work. I also encourage you to trust your own creativity in developing strategies that are individualized and responsive with your client.

When Allie's fear of vomiting in public did not respond well to exposure approaches, I decided to try a hypnotic intervention called age regression. This approach is based on the understanding that for some people, certain emotions and experiences have been compartmentalized, put on the back shelf of the mind, and forgotten about. But despite being shoved out of sight, they continue to "leak" into everyday life and experience, affecting individuals without their awareness.

It's similar to my experience years ago when my appendix burst without my knowledge. For a week or so, I was in severe pain, but it subsided before I went to a doctor. What had actually happened, I later learned, was that my body had built an inflammatory wall around my perforated appendix. Since this wall was built I was able to function, but I functioned at a slightly diminished capacity. I was tired all the time and felt as if I constantly had a slight case of the flu. I went to four different physicians, including a specialist in gastroenterology, and none correctly diagnosed the condition.

Although the protective wisdom of my body put my burst appendix on the "back shelf," fallout from the initial event kept leaking into my daily life. What's more, my burst appendix was so neatly stored away that none of my doctors were able to identify it as the source of my symptoms. Nearly a year later I finally had exploratory abdominal surgery, and the ruptured appendix was discovered and removed.

My experience with my ruptured appendix parallels that of many clients who have phobias with a traumatic origin. The phobia tends to persist because the source of the problem has neither been discovered nor treated. Fallout from a neatly contained traumatic event may be leaking into your life as phobic symptoms. When the source is correctly identified, however, the right intervention can bring about recovery.

Just like my exploratory surgery, hypnotic age regression allows you access to the back shelves of your mind and the actual source of your suffering. With age regression your therapist helps you return to an earlier experience that may have started the problem. A therapist does this by creating a safe therapeutic environment in which you can observe what is on your emotional back shelf through hypnosis. Once Allie was in a hypnotic trance (see Chapter 3 for detailed explanations of this state), I used age regression to help her enhance her awareness of unfinished business that was connected to her phobia of vomiting.

There are a number of techniques that can be used to induce age regression. With Allie I used an age regression approach called the *affect bridge,* developed by psychoanalyst John Watkins (1992). This technique creates a bridge between the emotions (or affect) that are associated with the symptom and the affect (emotional experience) that accompanied the start of the phobia.

This technique not only helped Allie identify her *experience* of this past event, but also the feelings and images that accompanied it. Once Allie was in touch with this experience, I used hypnotic imagery and suggestion to help her create another story about the event that didn't include the association of vomiting and phobia. I call this second technique *creating a corrective memory.*

It is very important to note that this age-regression exercise seeks to identify a client's specific *experience* of a past event. It is not akin to accessing and playing a videotape of a past occurrence. Rather, it is the *personal experience* that the client has created and stored that is of interest. The "memory" accessed need not even be factually accurate. What is important is that you help the client become conscious of the *experiences and conflicts* from the past that are sustaining the phobia. As John Kilhstrom reported, "age-regressed adults may have the subjectively compelling experience of being children again, and they may appear to behave in a childlike manner, but what we see is an imaginative reconstruction of childhood, not a reversion to the genuine article" (2003, p. 242).

Age Regression: The Affect Bridge
Once Allie was in a light hypnotic trance, I asked her to re-elicit the fearful feelings that accompanied the last time she experienced her phobia: I encouraged her to experience the sensations, emotions, and imagery that accompanied her fear of vomiting. I told her it was safe to bring up all the emotions with intensity. I then counted backward from 5 to 1, and asked

Allie to identify a previous time and situation where she felt that same feeling. I asked her to raise a finger when she re-elicited that early time. We continued to go back in time to earlier experiences until Allie identified the first time she experienced her fear of vomiting. Allie traveled back in her mind to a time when she was six years old.

I next asked Allie to speak in the present tense, as if she were experiencing the event now, and convey her memory to me. Allie began to cough, and said:

"I see my Grandma throwing up. She's staying at our house during her cancer treatment. We share a bathroom and it really smells. It smells so bad that I'm getting nauseated too. I run to my bedroom, and just as I get there, I start to throw up too, and I'm coughing, I think I'm inhaling some of it, too. It's awful. The throw-up is all over my bedroom carpet. Mom comes in. She looks upset. She has tears in her eyes when she's cleaning it up. She says something like, 'Oh, Allie, I can't take it anymore. I can't deal with my mother and you at the same time. You can't be throwing up every time your grandma gets sick. She's sick, you're not!'"

Creating a Corrective Memory

Now that we had identified an experience that linked Allie's current fear of vomiting to an aversive experience from the past, we could use this information to alter her associations with vomiting in the present. To do this we used hypnotic imagery to create a corrective scene—in effect, to write another story. While a new story does not erase the past, it can provide the sense of resolution and comfort that is needed but absent.

To accomplish this I asked Allie to travel back to her childhood bedroom. We replayed the scene she described, but when her mother came in, Allie offered this new ending:

"When mom comes into my room, she's not mad at all. She says, 'It's OK, honey. Everyone gets sick sometimes.' Then she brings me into her bedroom, away from all the bad smells and sounds, and she wipes my face with a cool washcloth. Then she tucks me into her bed."

As soon as Allie stopped, I added, "Yes. And she disappears to the kitchen for just a moment, coming back with some cold Coca-Cola to settle your stomach. The sweet drink does the trick, and you fall asleep soon, in the middle of your favorite story, which your mother is reading to you. And perhaps you can also imagine that your mom is getting help for your grandma. Maybe a nurse or a relative comes in to take care of her, too. "

We can't change the past. We can, however, revivify past experiences and experience the nurturance, support, and reassurance that we missed way back when. Through the creation of a corrective memory, Allie experienced comfort and reassurance in response to throwing up. In the future she accessed this same sense of comfort and reassurance when fears of vomiting would pop into her mind. With this added resource, she tried exposure therapy again. This time, her efforts were successful.

Corrective approaches like the one I used above stem from the work of psychiatrist and physician Franz Alexander (Alexander & French, 1946), on the importance of fostering *corrective emotional experiences*. There are many techniques for creating corrective emotional experiences. I particularly want to acknowledge the work of psychiatrist Claire Frederick (1993, 1999), and psychologists Shirley

Medication

Unlike other anxiety disorders, there exists little to no evidence in research that medications are helpful in diminishing phobic fears. Thus, medications are rarely used to treat specific phobias. If anything, a doctor might prescribe a fast-acting anti-anxiety medication, a benzodiazepine (for a more detailed discussion of benzodiazepines, see Chapter 10). A benzodiazepine may help calm your nerves when you experience your phobic object or situation, or when you know you are about to be exposed to it.

However, this medication is a temporary anti-anxiety aid not intended for habitual use. In fact, use of benzodiazepines is even thought to interfere with some exposure therapies. Thus most of my clients who have specific phobias do not also see a psychiatrist as a part of their treatment. For specific phobias, therapy alone is a very powerful tool and often all clients need.

Recovery: Tom, Nina, Ryan, Allie, and Jackie's Stories

Working in a one-story office building throughout his career as a tax attorney, and avoiding work that involved ladders, Tom didn't let his fear of heights interfere with his functioning. With the exception of the debacle in the tour bus in the Hollywood Hills, he and his wife took vacations on flat land. Thus Tom chose to structure his life so that he avoided exposure to his phobia rather than seeking treatment.

In contrast, Nina, Ryan, Allie, and Jackie had specific phobias that did indeed interfere with their functioning or the demands of a job. They received comprehensive treatment that included cognitive therapy, exposure therapy, and hypnosis. Relaxation training was emphasized in three of the cases. As is typical for the treatment of specific phobias, medication was not a component of their treatment plans.

Nina's Story

Treatment for Nina (fear of freeway driving) was relatively straightforward. Early in treatment Nina asked whether medication might decrease the anxiety she was experiencing and help her therapy progress. While I remained open to this possibility, I let her know that medications were usually not used to treat phobias. Rather, I assured her that the many techniques she would learn in therapy would provide her with the resources to successfully complete her desensitization hierarchy and master her anxiety.

Indeed, Nina mastered relaxation techniques early in her therapy and adhered to a daily practice of meditation, which increased her resilience to stress in general. But Nina still felt she needed some extra resources before she began exposure treatment. "I'm more relaxed now in general," Nina stated, "but I'm still scared to start the exposure. I don't think I'm ready." In response I taught Nina self-hypnosis, which she used prior to each exposure exercise. With that, Nina felt ready to begin exposure and progressed through all 11 desensitization steps in only six weeks. After only two months of therapy, Nina was driving to work on the highway again.

Nina continued in therapy with me for about a year after recovering from her phobia in order to work on her trust issues with her boyfriend. She takes the expressway whenever she visits him.

Ryan's Story
Treatment for Ryan's needle phobia was a particular challenge because of its time urgency. The technician doing the employee medical assessment was to return to the restaurant in just two weeks. Since Ryan would faint when exposed to his feared stimulus (the needle), I taught him applied muscle tension. Then we focused on exposure therapy using graded exposure. Ryan's last step on his desensitization hierarchy was getting the injection at the restaurant. By the time the technician returned two weeks later, Ryan was ready. After his successful exposure to the TB test, Ryan had a hypnosis session during which he was able to honor the courageous part of himself that mastered his fear. Soon afterward he agreed to a trip out of the country with friends, as vaccination shots weren't a deterrent for him any longer.

Allie's Story
Allie's treatment for her vomiting phobia incorporated a variety of therapeutic tools. Initially, treatment incorporated relaxation techniques, gradual exposure to restaurants, and expanded food choices. However, it wasn't until the exploratory hypnosis, when Allie discovered the incident that triggered her fear, that Allie's progress accelerated.

After the hypnosis Allie moved on to gradual exposure. She began to accept invitations from her boyfriend's parents and her friends. We set up a gradual exposure to foods, so she could broaden her food choices. Soon Allie and her boyfriend were going out to dinner once a week; Allie was even OK with letting her boyfriend pick the restaurant.

Jackie's Story

Three years after I'd finished working with Jackie, she called me. "Remember me, Dr. Daitch?" I assured her that I did and asked how she was doing. She responded: "Well, I have an issue I want to see you about, but first I have to tell you I have absolutely no fear of spiders anymore. It's totally gone. *Gone.* It went away when I saw you and it never came back! I love summer now, I garden every day, and I join my husband on the boat every weekend. The never-ending spider passengers don't even bother me." She went on to tell me about a family issue she wanted help with.

It's always a pleasure to hear from former clients, and it is particularly satisfying to get feedback, as in Jackie's case, that the gains in therapy have been sustained.

CHAPTER 8

Social Anxiety Disorder

*B*en,
This letter is to inform you that as of mid-semester, you are cur-rently failing my class. While your written critiques have been well articulated and excellently researched, 45% of your grade depends upon in-class participation and quizzes. You simply cannot pass this course if you do not attend our class meetings, and my attendance records show that you have missed 8 out of 10 classes. Your written work demonstrates you are a gifted student. I hope that you can turn your grade around in the second half of the semester by regularly attending my classes.

Ben brought and read this letter to me at our first session, a full year after he had failed the above class and dropped out of college altogether. What Ben's professor did not know was that Ben had, indeed, tried to make it to all eight of his missed classes. He had even gotten within 50 feet of the classroom door. But Ben never made it in.

"I could handle the parking lot well enough," Ben began. "It was huge, so big that I could always manage to find a parking spot that wasn't close to anyone who was walking in the parking lot. But once I got closer to the building, I would get really agitated, and walking down the hallway toward the class was unbearable. It was so crowded that everyone was practically stacked up on top of each other. Anyone who glanced my way for a second could see how red my face was, and that I was all slouched over, and in the fluorescent light the sweat on my face showed even more. I usually just gave in, turned around, and drove back home. My parents both work during the day, so they didn't know I was skipping my classes.

"The two times I did make it to class, the professor arranged all the desks in a semi-circle so we could see each other's faces. *Everyone* could see me, all the time! I'm OK with just me and you talking by ourselves. And I'm fine with my closest friends and my parents. But there were nearly 20 kids in that class. It was all I could think about the entire class. I kept trying to hide my face without being too noticeable, keeping my arms at my sides so no one could see the huge sweat stains that kept getting bigger and bigger. I wouldn't have passed the in-class participation grade even if I had shown up because I was so embarrassed just to be seen.

"I'm just better off not being in that kind of school. I'm thinking about getting my degree online."

While Ben's condition interfered with his academic success, similar problems can challenge relationships. Take Andrew, a 32-year-old accountant who came to see me with an anxiety issue. When I asked him why he wanted therapy now, he said that his girlfriend's sister was getting married at the end of the summer, and that he was dreading the event. He said that typically he was able to avoid social situations.

"I'm lucky that Erica, my girlfriend, doesn't mind going out with her friends without me and doesn't pressure me to go to parties. But she said that missing her sister's wedding was not acceptable. In fact, she said that if I backed out like I often do when we are invited out, it would be a deal-breaker for her. I really don't want to lose this relationship, but the idea of going to this wedding and interacting with her family, having to dance with her out on the dance floor—I can't see myself doing it. Do you think you can help me?"

Pieces of the Puzzle

Ben and Andrew suffered from social anxiety disorder (SAD), which is characterized by extreme anxiety about being judged by others or about doing something that might cause embarrassment or ridicule. This intense anxiety then triggers the body's autonomic nervous system to rev up into fight/flight mode (see Chapter 6 for a detailed description of the fight/flight response). So if you have SAD, when you are in a social situation that you fear, your nervous system might cause a variety of physical reactions, including blushing, sweating, stammering, dizziness or disorientation, shaking hands, or heart palpitations.

Unfortunately, these reactions add to your embarrassment and apprehension of being judged by others; not only do you feel physically uncomfortable, you worry that your fear—announced by your blushing, sweating, trembling—will be obvious to others. You become preoccupied with the concern that others are observing your fear, which increases your embarrassment and anxiety as long as you remain in the dreaded social situation. In many cases, embarrassment and anxiety morph into shame and then shame becomes a compounding feature to this already taxing disorder.

If you have SAD, you probably avoid social events that you think will cause this snowballing cycle of anxiety, fear response, and embarrassment. When you have to endure them, these dreaded situations exact a heavy toll physically, emotionally, and psychologically. You have to make an exhaustive effort to bear them. Afterward you might ruminate for days, going over a blow-by-blow analysis of all the ways you humiliated yourself.

The fear of judgment and embarrassment and its accompanying cycle of anxiety are common to all who have SAD. However, the disorder has been divided into two sub-categories—generalized SAD and specific SAD—based on the type of social situation an individual fears.

Generalized SAD

If you, like Ben and Andrew, feel comfortable when you are alone or with a trusted friend or family member but get very anxious in any larger social situation, you may suffer from generalized SAD. For both Ben and Andrew, an innocuous glance from a passerby or another guest at a party provoked intense anxiety. Both avoided social settings in which they had to interact with a large group of people.

Psychiatrist and psychotherapist David Veale notes that in clients with SAD, "eye gaze is commonly averted. . . . These behaviours might be linked to the submissive defensive behaviours used to reduce aggression in another person in response to the threat of rejection"(2003, p. 259). While this is true, when assessing for SAD it is essential to take a client's cultural background into consideration. For example, in many non-Western cultures the aversion of gaze is a common practice and sign of respect when one is addressing an authority figure. Thus a client's lack of eye contact may not be indicative of SAD at all, but rather may be due to a client's display of respect for a therapist. To avoid misdiagnosis, it is important that you take cultural variables into account.

Specific SAD

If you have specific SAD, you experience intense social anxiety in very specific situations. Consider the case of Lilly:

Lilly, a 32-year-old attorney in a small law firm, was referred to me because of her fear of speaking in public. During the initial consultation, she told me that while she was successful in her work, when she had to go to court, she suffered terribly. "I worry about it for weeks in advance. I can't even sleep at all the night before. I lie awake afraid that no matter how well prepared I am, I'll forget what to say. And I stammer, so I worry that everyone will think that I'm stupid, and I'll disappoint my client and lose the case." Lilly picked at her cuticle and sighed. "I'm not stupid—I made law review at Michigan, for goodness sakes—but my confidence goes out the window when I have to speak in front of groups of people. I even have a hard time at our staff meetings at the firm."

"How often do you go to court?" I asked.

"Actually, not that often; maybe six times a year or so, but I'm constantly worried about it. In fact, even though I love my job, I've thought of looking for a position in a big firm where I could specialize in something that didn't involve litigation."

Many of us have some fear of public speaking and worry that we'll perform poorly when we are in the spotlight. What distinguishes normal worry and specific SAD is the degree of suffering and the extent to which it interferes with our functioning. Lilly's fear of going to court caused her prolonged distress and affected her functioning in her profession. If you are comfortable in most social situations but suffer from intense anxiety in one or two specific situations, you may have a specific social phobia.

Another common type of Specific SAD is paruresis, also called bashful bladder. If you suffer from bashful bladder, you have a fear of urinating in public restrooms (particularly in urinals, where there is very little privacy). This fear can also apply to urinating in bathrooms at others' homes. You may even find that in these situations you cannot urinate at all.

Some people suffer from a fear of eating or drinking in public, others from a fear of writing on a blackboard or signing documents in front of others. In the former, you may be afraid that others will see you spilling your food or criticize your table manners. If you have a fear of writing in front of others, your chief concern might be that your hands will shake and others will notice. In both types of specific SAD, your intense anxiety causes the physiological fear response, and indeed, your hands do begin to shake or you do spill your food. By then the vicious cycle of anxiety, fear response, and shame is well underway, and your dread of this specific situation is reinforced.

The Differences Between the Disorders

Both generalized and specific SAD share similarities with specific phobias and panic disorders (PD) with and without agoraphobia. What is important to keep in mind is that although some of the symptoms of these disorders might look the same, the *reasons* that the symptoms occur are different.

For example, people with any of the disorders mentioned above might experience panic attacks. However, with SAD, the panic attacks do not come out of nowhere, as they often do in PD, but are elicited by uncomfortable social situations. Also, the primary fear that people with SAD have is not that they'll have a panic attack or the physical sensations of anxiety, as do those with PD. Rather, the chief fear is of others' judgment, which secondarily spurs a fear response. In this sense, SAD is more like specific phobias.

People who suffer from specific phobia disorder are most concerned about avoiding whatever elicits their fear, such as spiders, choking, or not being judged critically by others. Individuals with SAD do not fear people; they fear people's scrutiny.

Generalized SAD can also appear similar to panic disorder with agoraphobia (See Chapter 6 for a description). People with both disorders often avoid crowded or public places, but for different reasons. A person with PD with agoraphobia is afraid that she or he will have a panic attack in public. Someone with generalized SAD will avoid the same situation due to a fear of being seen.

Notably, people with PD with agoraphobia often find it helpful to venture out with a trusted companion who can help in the event of a panic attack. This can decrease their anxiety. For a person with generalized SAD, the presence of a friend usually does not alleviate the anxiety of being scrutinized. In fact, it might add to the anxiety, as the friend might represent just another set of judging eyes.

Many people experience a fear of being seen by others because they suffer from body dysmorphia, which is an extreme self-consciousness and even self-hatred about how they think their faces and bodies appear. Body dysmorphia is a distinct diagnosis from generalized SAD, but it often co-exists with SAD. If you become intensely preoccupied with some aspect of your appearance that most people would not give a second thought to, you might also have body dysmorphia. It is easy to see how the fear of one's physical appearance being judged by others could lead to or worsen social anxiety disorder.

Who Develops Social Anxiety Disorder?

SAD is the most common anxiety disorder and the third most common psychological disorder after depression and alcohol dependence, and about 5% of the population will suffer from this disorder at some point in their lifetime (Veale, 2003). People are most likely to first exhibit symptoms of SAD in adolescence, but some develop it in childhood. As is true with most of the anxiety disorders, people with SAD tend to be anxious as children, before the disorder presents. Youngsters who go on to develop SAD also tend to be shier than their peers. Genetic (familial) factors are particularly strong for people with this disorder: if you have SAD, it's likely that one of your immediate family members does as well (Barlow, 2002). Once you develop SAD, the disorder tends to persist unless you seek out treatment, although the severity of your symptoms can fluctuate depending on the stress you are under at different points in your life.

Although it often first occurs in adolescence, SAD can occur at any point in one's life. For example, a specific SAD can begin when someone faces an unexpected task or pressure in a social situation, and has a strong fear response. For example, a man in his mid-40s who is put on the spot in a television interview and freezes may, from then on, be afraid of public speaking. He would be accurately diagnosed with specific SAD with adult onset.

A range of other presenting problems might actually be components of SAD. You might want to consider SAD as an underlying condition when clients present with issues such as sexual performance anxiety, alcohol abuse, and excessive concern about their appearance. Likewise, SAD has been found to precede the onset of some disorders, such as mood, substance abuse, bulimia, and other anxiety disorders (APA, 2000). One study found that generalized SAD is the *only* anxiety disorder associated with major depression for children and adolescents (Chavira, Stein, Bailey, & Stein, 2004).

There is also debate as to whether SAD occurs equally among men and women. Some studies have found that men are treated for SAD more frequently than women. However, other studies based on the general population have found that more women have SAD than men (APA, 2000).

The Good News

Social anxiety disorder can impact all aspects of your life: success at work or school; relationships with family, friends, and coworkers. However, whether your anxiety over speaking in public keeps you from participating in board meetings at work, or your partner is about to leave you because you will not accompany her to family gatherings, there is hope for you. No matter how greatly SAD rules your life today, with the right treatments, your quality of life can markedly improve.

The Goals and Gains of Therapy
- Develop skills to calm an overreactive nervous system
- Identify and challenge negative self-statements
- Replace negative self-statements with supportive statements

- Develop an external focus in social situations
- Develop a strategy of exposure to a range of social situations
- Develop distress tolerance

How to Get There: Therapeutic Techniques and Interventions

Minding the Mind with Cognitive Therapy: Self-Statements

As you've already read, Cognitive Therapy (CT) is based on the premise that identifying and changing your thoughts changes your resulting beliefs and behaviors. The majority of people who have phobias admit that their fears are blown far out of proportion. In cognitive therapies, you take an in-depth look at the thoughts that accompany your fears. Then you and your therapist brainstorm to come up with new thoughts that you feel are more appropriate responses to the situations you fear.

In each of the social anxiety cases introduced in this chapter, I helped my clients create supportive self-statements.

Self-statements for Ben:
- "I look perfectly normal."
- "It is safe for me to be seen."
- "I can smile and make eye contact."
- "When I ask a question of someone they respond."

Self-Statements for Lilly:
- "I am well prepared."
- "I am intelligent."
- "I am doing my best for my client."

Self-statements for Andrew:
- "I am curious to learn about this other person."
- "I am a likeable, kind person."
- "I have a good sense of humor."

I then directed them to write down these statements on 3 x 5 cards and keep them close at hand. Next, Ben, Lilly and Andrew were to repeat their self-statements and incorporate saying them into their daily routines. While self-statements or cognitive therapy alone are not powerful enough to totally eliminate your symptoms of SAD, this simple and practical intervention can help when coupled with exposure therapy.

Exposure Therapy for Generalized SAD

Exposure therapy has been found to be a very effective treatment for social anxiety disorder. Unlike the specific phobias discussed in the previous chapter, people with generalized SAD do not have one specific, fearful situation or object that they avoid. Rather, their fear of a range of social situations and interactions needs to be addressed in therapy. So rather than making a single desensitization hierarchy for one feared situation or object, as we do for specific phobias, people with generalized SAD need to progress through multiple desensitization hierarchies.

This being the case, the exposure process for SAD begins by compiling a list of all the aspects of social situations that are fearful to the client. Once the list is complete, we organize it by general categories, and list each situation in each category from least to most distressing.

Let's return to Ben, the young man who quit college because of his SAD. His social-anxiety hierarchy was divided into two categories—his re-entry into college and what we labeled "other concerns." Ben had chosen a class at a local community college that would not be academically challenging for him, so he could keep up easily while he focused much of his attention on working through his anxiety hierarchy.

In the school-related category we included:

1. Going online and signing up for classes, which began in one month, at a community college
2. Walking through the parking lot at the community college
3. Walking through the halls on the way to class
4. Sitting down in class
5. Contributing to class discussion

In the category labeled "other concerns," we included:

1. Going through a checkout line at the grocery store (rather than the self-checkout)
2. Going for a walk in the neighborhood
3. Going to a party with his girlfriend
4. Answering the phone
5. Going to the gym

While some researchers and clinicians favor flooding, as I have mentioned repeatedly, I prefer a more integrative approach that combines relaxation training, gradually facing one's fears, challenging one's negative thinking, and refocusing. Veale noted that one significant shortcoming of exposure therapy pertains to the substantial rate of client refusal or dropout associated with it; some clients will not be willing to initiate an exposure treatment, and many discontinue the treatment before its completion (2003). I have found that the integrative approach I use helps to abate the rates of attrition often associated with flooding techniques. This more integrative, gradated exposure will be detailed in Ben's treatment below.

Each exposure session with Ben included instruction and practice in a relaxation technique. I taught him four-square breathing, safe-place imagery, and self-hypnosis. (See Chapter 4 for detailed instructions on these approaches).

Next, we proceeded through each item on our hierarchy of SAD-related challenges. We began with the list of school-related fears, as re-entry into school was his most pressing concern. In each session, Ben confronted a new item on his hierarchy.

Below, we follow Ben's process of working through Step 3 of his school-related hierarchy, having successfully confronted his discomfort with Steps 1 and 2.

Step 3, walking through the college hallways on his way to class, was particularly daunting because Ben, like others with social phobia, dreaded being seen. "I just can't stand all those people coming out of their classes, merging into the hall. I know they're not really interested in me but I *feel* like they are all staring at me," Ben told me.

With systematic desensitization, however, Ben did not have to immerse himself fully in this dreaded situation immediately; rather, we worked up to it by following the desensitization hierarchy steps below. We planned for him to go through one step on the hierarchy per week, but we were open to accomplishing more or less depending upon Ben's comfort level with each step.

1. Imagine walking through an uncrowded hallway at school.
2. Imagine walking through a crowded hallway at school.
3. Walk the halls for 15 minutes early one morning well before the first classes begin, when only a few students will be in the halls.
4. Walk the halls for 10 minutes, just before classes begin, when the halls are more crowded.
5. Walk the halls for 15 minutes, just before classes begin.
6. Walk the halls for 20 minutes, just before classes begin.

Ben was able to go school and walk the hallways during the month before the semester began, so by the time he arrived on campus for his first day of classes he was already acclimated to walking the hallways in both low and peak levels of foot traffic. Before and after each exposure, Ben used the relaxation techniques he had learned. Our goal was that Ben would repeat each step on the hierarchy at least three times, and would not progress to the next step until he could endure the previous one with a greatly diminished amount of anxiety. For example, he got to the point where he experienced no anxiety whatsoever walking the uncrowded hallways before he moved on to walking the crowded hallways.

Since the first two steps of the hierarchy involved only imagery, Ben did one per week in my office. He accomplished the last four steps at the college between our sessions and we discussed his experience in each following session. As is common, Ben needed more time to progress through some steps than others. Indeed, Ben needed two weeks of exposure to walking in the crowded hallways before he significantly reduced his anxiety and could comfortably walk the busy halls for 10 minutes. Once he overcame that hurdle, he progressed through the two remaining steps, which lengthened his time in the busy hallway, in only two weeks.

While some clients perform their community-based exposure trials independent of the therapist, some therapists choose to accompany their clients during these in-vivo trials. Thus for a given session the therapist and client might meet at the site of the exposure trial, rather that at the therapist's office. For example, I've taken clients with SAD to restaurants, grocery stores, or the local coffee shop. While taking the session out into the community posses an added challenge to maintaining client boundaries and confidentiality, Zur (2006) noted that out-of-office experiences are often an integral part of cognitive behavioral treatment plans. As long as your client feels comfortable with the possibility of encountering acquaintances and you have established how you each will respond in such an instance, I feel that out-of-office experiences can be well worth your while.

Exposure Therapy for Specific SAD

Like exposure therapies for specific phobias, exposure for specific SAD need not have the breadth seen in exposure therapies for generalized SAD. Rather, it need only address the social anxiety the individual experiences in limited environments, and often necessitates the use of only one desensitization hierarchy. This was the case for Lilly, the lawyer, when she sought to resolve her social anxiety around speaking in the courtroom.

When I asked Lilly what aspect of courtroom speaking was particularly challenging to her, without hesitation she replied, "The opening statement. I've been told that in the eyes of jurors, the opening statement really establishes my credibility—or lack of it—and could make or break my case. It doesn't matter how compelling the case is. When I get nervous, I have a hard time remembering what I planned to say and sticking to that. To top that off, I've been told that when I get nervous I seem cold and detached, which is the absolute last thing I need when I'm arguing a case. And I can't stop thinking that my clients are paying top dollar for me, and I'm letting them down."

For Lilly's desensitization hierarchy, we came up with the following list of actions she would take:

1. Go to court and observe a variety of experienced lawyers whom she respects giving their opening arguments.
2. Practice an opening argument in front of her husband.
3. Practice an opening argument in front of an assistant.
4. Practice an opening argument in front of a small group of lawyers in the firm.
5. Practice an opening argument in front of a small group of lawyers and allow them to offer constructive criticism through out the argument.
6. Volunteer to sit as second chair in a case (sitting behind the counsel's table, assisting the lawyer handling the case, often by passing critical documents to her as needed, but not speaking to the courtroom).
7. Volunteer to do pro-bono work in a case and present the opening statement.
8. Accept and present a case for her firm.

Lilly progressed through all eight steps of her hierarchy over a three-month period. For all but the final three steps, she did each step three times before she felt comfortable enough to go on to the next.

You can expect to feel some distress when you are practicing exposure. Embrace it, as it is a part of your recovery. Anyone who has practiced weight-training knows that for a muscle to get stronger there must be some pain. In the same way, some mild pain in your emotional muscles during your recovery will make you stronger.

A number of my clients with anxiety disorders are concerned that a component of their anxiety is negatively affecting their job performance. As is evident with Lilly, these concerns are often reality-based. When this is the case, it is essential that we not only actively work through their job-related challenges, but also identify any underlying conflicts that may be worsening their symptoms. In Lilly's case, I needed to address her guilt about charging the high fees that were standard at her law firm as well as the concern that her anxiety was interfering with her performance. As with many female professionals I see, there was an impostor syndrome factor at play in this case. As my work with Lilly demonstrates, you sometimes have to peel the onion a bit to discover if there are conflicts underlying or exacerbating the presenting symptoms.

Changing Maladaptive Thoughts with the Use of Imagery

The therapeutic use of imagery can be a helpful adjunct to both cognitive and behavioral interventions. In Ben's case, I employed the use of computer imagery to aid him as he progressed through a desensitization hierarchy that we constructed to decrease his anxiety surrounding going to the gym. Like many people his age, Ben is quite computer savvy. As he began his exposure trials by imagining himself at the gym, we used computer imagery to help Ben "reprogram" his SAD-related thoughts as they popped up.

> *CD: Now imagine that you are on the treadmill in the gym and you begin to feel self-conscious. Type in your computer the self-statements that you might say to yourself.*
>
> *B: Everyone is looking at me. I look out of shape. I hardly look athletic. They can tell I don't work out.*
>
> *CD: Now delete those statements and type in a self-supportive statement.*
>
> *B (typing): No one is really looking at me. No one really cares what I look like. I don't have to have a perfect body to work out. I certainly know how to walk on a treadmill. I'm enjoying the music on my iPod.*

I suggested Ben spend part of each day at his computer entering any negative self-statements that emerged during his exposure treatment, then deleting them and typing self-supportive statements to replace them.

Ben was very comfortable with this assignment, as it made use of his interest and comfort with computer work. The incorporation of Ben's interests and strengths into a therapeutic intervention is an example of *individualization*. Individualization broadly consists of integrating a client's abilities, personal attributes, interests, and behaviors into therapeutic interventions. When you individualize a client's interests in crafting an intervention, it is more likely that your client will comply with that intervention and have an experience of success. Emphasis on the significance of individualization comes largely from the work of Milton Erickson (1958).

Social Skills Training

Most people with specific SAD have and use well-developed social skills when they are with trusted friends and family. Thus, if you have SAD, part of your difficulty is that you have not learned how to apply social skills that you already possess in situations involving people you don't know well. That's why social-skills training is commonly included in treatment. This was the case with Ben, too.

Once Ben had mastered his discomfort in navigating the walk from the parking lot and through the halls to his class, I encouraged him to think of questions to ask people in his class. Then he progressed to asking a classmate a question each time he went to class. We rehearsed the questions in the office and he wrote them down before going home.

If you, like Ben, feel shy in groups outside your safety net, you might first practice establishing and maintaining eye contact with the people you encounter. You can begin with someone who is not threatening, such as your mail carrier, the barista at Starbucks, your neighbor, or the cashier at the drug store. Then you could advance your training by smiling at someone in a class or at a store.

Writing down conversation openers, which is all the questions are, is a technique you can try on your own. The easiest way to get a conversation started is by asking an open-ended question, one that requires more than a yes/no response. Andrew wrote down a list of conversation starters that he could use at his girlfriend's sister's wedding. For example, he planned to ask different guests how they knew the bride or groom and how they were enjoying the food being served. Most people like to talk about themselves. If you are armed with a few open-ended questions, the other person may take the social ball and run with it. Then your role is simply to relax and listen. This is a simple but very useful social skill that takes the pressure off of you to do all the talking.

Group Therapy

Although participating in group therapy might seem daunting, it is a supportive place to practice new skills because other participants understand your fears and share them. Members of the group support each other's efforts to recover and to role-play anticipated social interactions. Some groups have field trips during which the members practice social skills together in a variety of situations.

To help him to prepare for the wedding he would attend, I encouraged Andrew to join a group for SAD. As one of his chief concerns was having to sit at a round, ten-person table during the reception, he agreed that getting some support in the company of others with SAD would be a good place to start.

Many studies have demonstrated the effectiveness of Cognitive Behavioral Group Therapy in addressing SAD, both alone (Heimberg, Salzman, Holt, & Blendell, 1993) and in conjunction with medication (Barlow, 2002). Online forums, such as the one at SocialAnxietySupport.com, can be valuable for finding group therapy for sufferers. The techniques for this can be obtained through the Social Phobia Program at Temple University, if no groups nearby are available. However, there are several subgroups of people for whom CBGT may be counterproductive, including those with very severe SAD, depression, or other concurrent anxiety disorders (Heimberg & Becker, 2002).

Countering Negative Self-Appraisal

If you have SAD, you most likely focus on how inadequate you think you appear, and you assume that your negative self-appraisal is shared by others. A group is a perfect setting to challenge this belief by getting others' feedback. If you are not in a group, you can still seek more objective feedback from a trusted friend.

Andrew role-played with another group member as if talking to a guest at the upcoming wedding he would attend. I occasionally asked them to freeze, and then asked the group members to write down their perceptions of Andrew's emotional state, physical appearance, and demeanor. The member playing the guest reported that he was comfortable in Andrew's presence and thought Andrew was well groomed and intelligent. "Really?!" an incredulous Andrew responded. "I felt boring, I'm sweating, and I can't believe you didn't notice how hard it was for me to come up with words."

The other group members corroborated the partner's feedback and added that they didn't think he was boring. One person said, "Now that you mention it, I can see that there is some sweat on your forehead, but I wouldn't have noticed it if you hadn't mentioned it."

External Focus

People with SAD, like others with anxiety disorders, are excessively self-focused. This does not mean that if you have SAD you are selfish; it means that your fear and self-consciousness pull your attention from others to your physical responses and negative self-appraisal. In the SAD group, members practiced focusing their attention on the group member who was speaking. They learned mirroring, a form of active listening. Mirroring involves listening to the person speaking and paraphrasing what was said back to the speaker. The key is to accurately reflect the content and feeling of the speaker's message. Knowing that they might be called on to mirror someone's comments encouraged the group members to focus on the speaker rather than themselves. They learned to notice when they had stopped listening, and then interrupt their own thoughts with a self-statement like "external focus now." You might try this exercise yourself any time you find yourself in a challenging social situation.

Hypnosis

Just as with the treatment of specific phobias, hypnosis combined with cognitive behavioral techniques can be a powerful adjunctive treatment for SAD. Hypnosis complements cognitive therapies in enhancing your ability to change maladaptive thoughts. Utilizing hypnotic imagery of future success in social situations also effectively complements exposure treatments. As the client, you could, with hypnotic imagery, not only see yourself successfully navigating situations you'd typically avoid, but also feel the satisfaction of mastery. Likewise, you can also access memories of successfully overcoming challenges that you have faced in the past. This can embed the belief that you can indeed proceed through your treatment with success and face social challenges in the future.

Medication

There are a host of medications that have been found to be helpful in the treatment of SAD. Two different types of antidepressants that have been found to be particularly helpful are selective serotonin reuptake inhibitors (SSRIs) and serotonin norepinephrine reuptake inhibitors (SNRIs; for a more detailed discussion of these medications, see Chapter 10). While I would never recommend medication treatment in the absence of therapy, some of my clients have found going on these daily medications for a short period of time (ranging from months to one or two years) to be beneficial in their recovery process.

Another family of medications that can be helpful in the treatment of SAD is benzodiazepines. These are fast-acting anti-anxiety medications that can be taken just before you know you are going to enter into a socially stressful situation, or when you are in the midst of a stressful situation already and are feeling extremely overwhelmed by the anxiety that the situation triggers. This family of medication is not intended for indefinite use, as a long-term solution. I have found that some psychiatrists occasionally prescribe benzodiazepines during the initial phases of treatment. Benzos can provide clients with an added resource with which to combat their anxiety and decrease their avoidance of possibly triggering social situations. Indeed, there is research that supports this practice (Davidson et al., 1993; Munjack, Baltazar, Bohn, Cabe, & Appleton, 1990). However, I have found that therapeutic interventions can be particularly powerful in de-escalating the acute anxiety that can arise with SAD. Thus for the majority of my clients I have not felt that the use of benzodiazepines is typically necessary.

If you, like Lilly, have a specific social phobia that manifests as "performance anxiety," such as the fear of speaking, beta blockers might be particularly helpful for you. Beta blockers reduce the physiological manifestations of anxiety, such as a rapid heartbeat or nervous sweating. Although beta blockers are capable of this *physical* type of anxiety reduction, they are not especially powerful. That is why they are not usually prescribed for generalized social anxiety disorder or panic disorder. However, if your social anxiety centers around fears of performing in front of others, such as public speaking, beta blockers just might do the trick. They can literally help your nerves to calm down and enhance your ability to combat your anxiety as you undergo therapy.

Recovery: Ben, Andrew, and Lilly's Stories

To overcome social anxiety disorder, it's important to not only face, but embrace distress as part of the recovery process. At times throughout their respective therapies, Ben, Andrew, and Lilly were willing to face and push through their discomfort regarding their aversions to being seen. Their commitment and perseverance were important factors in their recovery.

Ben's Story

During the summer that he attended community college, Ben was able to conquer his fears of going to university in the fall. In preparation for the start of classes Ben progressed through his entire systematic desensitization hierarchy regarding school. After some discussion with me, Ben also chose to see a psychiatrist. He began by taking the SSRI Paxil, but switched to the SSRI Lexapro because he felt the Paxil was making him too drowsy. With the combination of medications and therapeutic preparation, Ben did well enough in his summer community college coursework that in the fall he was re-accepted into the university from which he had previously withdrawn. He remained on a daily antidepressant medication to help with his SAD until his final semester of college, when Ben, his psychiatrist, and I all felt that he had progressed significantly and was ready to begin to wean off his medication.

Ben has broadened his horizons considerably since the start of treatment. He is able to walk comfortably in his neighborhood and strike up casual conversations with neighbors, classmates, and store clerks. Although Ben remains shy and prefers spending free time with his girlfriend or one other friend, he is now quite willing to attend social functions and frequently double-dates with friends. While Ben feels he will always remain a "homebody," his self-described shyness no longer inhibits his quality of life.

Andrew's Story

Andrew did make it to his girlfriend's sister's wedding, thanks to his persistence with the exposure hierarchy and regular attendance at his therapy group. He also chose to consult with a psychiatrist before the wedding and had been prescribed a benzodiazepine, Ativan, to have on hand just in case his anxiety escalated during the wedding reception. He was pleased to report that the wedding was far from the painful undertaking it once would have been. He and his girlfriend had originally agreed to stay at the dinner reception for three hours, but wound up staying until the end of the party. Andrew stated that he successfully employed some of the conversation starters he had previously prepared, and effectively interrupted his self-focused thoughts when he noticed them popping up. Although he had his Ativan with him, Andrew found that his therapeutic tools were all he needed to help him negotiate the social interaction. After the wedding he never renewed his prescription.

While Andrew still needs an arsenal of therapeutic strategies and techniques to navigate social gatherings, he no longer avoids them. He reports that with each successful encounter, his anxiety lessens. He recently told me, with a Cheshire-Cat grin, that his girlfriend offered to help him devise a desensitization hierarchy for saying his wedding vows—"just in case" the occasion might arise one of these days.

Lilly's Story

Lilly made rapid progress in therapy. Although her specific phobia around making opening statements in court was distressing to her, the fact that her symptoms were more limited and less complex than Ben and Andrew's made recovery less challenging. In addition to the desensitization and exposure therapy, Lilly took several other steps to fortify her recovery. She enrolled in a training program with the National Institute for Trial Advocacy, where her courtroom skills were strengthened. Repeatedly presenting in front of her peers and faculty further desensitized her. The program was a good adjunct to her therapy. I also recorded a series of audio CDs for Lilly in which she imagined herself performing with confidence and composure. She was directed to listen to the CDs daily. Although we discussed the possibility of going on beta blockers, Lilly felt that she wanted to give psychotherapy a try first. As Lilly quickly began to experience success in her psychotherapy treatment, it became clear that a consultation with a psychiatrist was not necessary.

Lilly's drive and self-discipline were used to her advantage in the treatment, as she brought the same commitment to therapy as she did to her career. She now reports that she views her court appearances as exciting challenges, and experiences little accompanying distress.

CHAPTER 9

Obsessive–Compulsive Disorder

"They have absolutely no right to tell me how I have to keep my house," Henry stated adamantly as soon as he sat down in my office. "They say my home is a fire hazard. *Any* home is a fire hazard! Every home is combustible—they're made of wood! How dare they threaten to take action against me if I don't comply with that inspector. I think this is all ridiculous. The only reason I'm here is because my lawyer said that seeing you might somehow help in my dealings with the city."

Henry, a 49-year-old high-school chemistry teacher, was recently forced to call in paramedics when he slipped on the tile floor in his kitchen and broke his ankle. Unable to drive himself to the emergency room, Henry called 911. Upon their arrival, the unwitting paramedics had to navigate through a maze of magazines, newspapers, receipts, bank statements, and other various papers—spread throughout about 90% of the floor space in each room. In fact, *every* horizontal space, including the bathtub and furniture, was covered. Because there was such little room to maneuver, the paramedics had a considerable amount of trouble getting Henry from his kitchen, which was in the back of the house, to his front door. The report filed by the emergency responders to the city, which Henry had given me a copy of, stated that from Henry's front door to his kitchen there existed only a two foot–wide path that was free of paper debris. They had pronounced Henry's home a serious health and fire hazard, and the local fire department ordered that the clutter be removed from doorways and hallways to establish safer walkways and means of egress.

When I asked Henry if others had responded with similar trepidation upon seeing his home, he sighed. "Well, I don't really invite anyone over. The last person in my house . . . well, I guess that would have been Penny. But we broke up, oh, a little over 10 years ago now. When Penny started spending time at my house—that's when it fell apart between us. She said she couldn't live in all my 'clutter.' But there are just some things that you shouldn't throw out. You never know when you might need them again later.

"It's just as well the relationship ended, though," Henry continued. "We weren't really a good match. Since Penny didn't want to be at my place, I would usually go over to her place for dinner. But Penny just couldn't understand the importance of my making sure I was leaving my house safe: checking to make sure the stove was off, the faucets weren't running or leaking, the lights were off, and the window latches were all locked. Sometimes I would be 15 or 30 minutes late, but that time was necessary to make sure I had left everything safe. Penny was always getting angry at me for being late. I find it's better for me just to be single, and to keep my home as my own private space."

Colleen, a 52-year-old administrative assistant on a college campus, came to see me because, according to her boss, her habit of wearing gloves at work in the summer was causing a stir among her student workers. He suggested she simply stop wearing them, which she wouldn't consider. Rather, she came to see me for help with her problem.

"I can't *just not wear them*!" Colleen told me. "There are germs *everywhere*—on door handles, railings, faucet knobs, on other people's hands, circulating in the air and cascading down onto any uncovered surface . . . everywhere. When I'm at my desk I have my hand sanitizer and antibacterial spray, so I don't need the gloves. And I'm able to use paper towels to handle the faucets and door knobs when I use public restrooms, but in general it's just safer that I wear leather gloves when I'm out and about—walking the campus, walking to my car, grocery shopping, you know. It's usually cold here, so I don't look too conspicuous in the fall, winter, and spring. In the summer I sometimes do get stares, but frankly, I just don't care what other people think. The gloves are a very effective shield from the germs, and that's far more important than blending in. My boss and the people at my job don't seem to agree."

As Colleen spoke she rifled through her purse and removed a travel-size bottle of hand sanitizer sealed in a plastic, zippered baggie. She placed this in her lap before gingerly removing her gloves. As soon as the gloves were off she placed them in a separate air-tight baggie in her purse, and then immediately squirted the sanitizer onto her hands, rubbing them together briskly. "The more friction you use when rubbing your hands, the more germs you kill," she said. I noticed scabs where Colleen's knuckles had cracked from overexposure to the sanitizing chemicals, and red splotches where her palms had become raw from the frequent sanitizer applications.

Patricia, a 47-year-old librarian, had not seen a doctor for well over a decade, despite her husband's pleas. Unlike someone with a specific phobia who might avoid seeing doctors out of a fear of contracting an illness, seeing others who are injured, or getting a shot, Patricia was obsessed with the fear of being diagnosed with a catastrophic disease, which she thought about constantly. She also spent lots of time imagining in detail the course and consequences of an illness. She was particularly afraid of cancer.

"I'd have to go through chemo or radiation—or both—lose my hair, my job, be sick and throw up all the time . . . maybe Ronnie would even leave me over it. Or I'd die and he'd be devastated without me," Patricia said in our first session. "I could have something—there's a chance—and I couldn't bear having a doctor confirm my suspicions. I know I'm getting older, and Ronnie wants me to start having the precautionary screenings they give women my age. But I *can't* do it."

Pieces of the Puzzle

When we think of obsessive–compulsive disorder (OCD), popular characterizations from television and movies often come to mind: the man who is so afraid of contamination from germs that he washes his hands well over 100 times a day and will not shake anyone's hand in greeting; the woman who, like Henry, switches each light in her house on and off eight times before leaving and after coming home in order to feel that she is averting some unnamed catastrophe. But OCD has many different forms. Henry's hoarding—his compulsion to hold onto magazines and papers of all sorts out of the fear that he will need them if they are discarded—is also a manifestation of OCD, just as is Patricia's consuming fear of being diagnosed with a catastrophic illness.

There are many different ways OCD can manifest. The seven most common types of OCD, categorized by psychologists Edna Foa and Reid Wilson (2001) are:

- Washers and cleaners
- Checkers
- Repeaters
- Orderers
- Hoarders
- Thinking ritualizers
- Worriers and pure obsessionals

Washers and Cleaners

Washers and cleaners' obsessions and compulsions, like Colleen's, center on fears of germs and becoming contaminated. If you are a washer and cleaner you might insist that your house and work space be extremely clean. You might avoid places in which you are likely to be around people with illnesses. Or you may wash your hands repeatedly throughout the day or take several lengthy showers each day. It is possible to experience obsessions revolving around cleanliness without developing compulsive rituals to calm the anxiety triggered by such thoughts, but it is not common. More often than not, washers and cleaners will have developed a set of rituals like Colleen's that will help to lessen anxieties over contamination.

Checkers

If you are a checker you may feel compelled to check the alarm clock several times before you go to sleep, check to see if the stove is off, perhaps repeatedly check that the front door is locked and the garage door is closed before you go to bed at night. Just as the name suggests, checkers need to check and then re-check various objects to ensure a sense of safety and well-being. For example, you might have to get up early in the morning to repeatedly check everything in the house that could potentially lead to a problem (e.g., leaving the iron on could lead to a house fire). Foa and Wilson have pointed out that some checkers are also doubters. "Usually these people will check an object once, then immediately doubt whether they completed the check properly, and have to check again" (2001, p. 9).

Repeaters

Repeaters engage in an action over and over again, often subscribing to the belief that the repeated action will prevent harm of some sort. If you are a repeater, the action may not be logically connected to the specific feared occurrence. For instance, re-setting the table with different cutlery is not logically related to preventing your son from getting hurt in a car accident. To a repeater, however, performing a certain ritual such as re-setting the table provides a sense of being able to prevent a feared event: for example, one's son getting into an accident.

Orderers

If you are an orderer, you are likely to demand that everything be in a prescribed place. It may be hard for you to share a work space with a coworker who leaves papers on your desk. You may get upset when someone rearranges your things. And you could very well spend an inordinate amount of time organizing your belongings according to self-imposed rules. For example, you might arrange your clothes in a gradation of colors, alphabetize your spices, or spend hours arranging your books into categories by color or size.

While orderliness can be admirable and enhance efficiency, it can become problematic if you must adhere to a rigid ordering system to maintain a sense of calm. If you spend too much of your time organizing your things, organization no longer enhances your efficiency; it detracts from your ability to attend to the other tasks in your daily life. Likewise, if your sense of well-being is dependent on the maintenance of your organizational system, living or working in an environment that you share with others can be a great challenge. Other people will inadvertently disrupt your system of order and this disruption can cause you a significant amount of distress.

Hoarders

Hoarders are obsessed with holding onto possessions, papers, materials. Like Henry, you might have trouble throwing things out because you think that someday you might need them, becoming angry or anxious if anyone insists that you have to go through your stuff and get rid of much of it. In fact, you might be embarrassed to have company over because whole rooms in your house are filled with possessions and there may be few uncovered horizontal spaces. Perhaps you collect things (theater stubs, old magazines, etc.) that others find useless. You might buy things in quantity, say greeting cards, or several copies of the same book. Most importantly, it's not what you buy or save, but why you save it: if you are a hoarder, giving away or throwing away your hoarded possessions will bring about significant anxiety and distress.

Thinking Ritualizers

If you use repetitive thoughts to calm your obsessions rather than repetitive behaviors, then you might be a thinking ritualizer. While a repeater may flick a light switch eight times, you might a say a prayer eight times or repeat a series of thoughts eight times to counteract unsettling thoughts or imagined catastrophes.

Some people with OCD exhibit *hyper-religiosity*. It is important that you become familiar with your clients' religious and cultural practices, so that you can distinguish religious from OCD rituals. For example, the Jewish tradition of keeping Kosher or the Catholic ritual of praying the rosary could, to someone unfamiliar with either religion, seem like compulsive rituals. Rather, hyper-religiosity occurs when an individual takes religious principles and practices to extreme expressions. For example, many religions employ fasting. The individual who not only abstains from food or drink but also attempts to avoid swallowing his or her own saliva in fear that it is a sacrilegious act would be demonstrating hyper-religiosity associated with OCD.

When working with clients who demonstrate hyper-religiosity, it is important to remember that religious beliefs and adherence to religious practices do not cause OCD. As Hyman and Pedrick aptly state, "strong religious beliefs . . . are only the grist for the OCD mill in a person who is biologically disposed to it" (1999, p. 125).

Worriers and Pure Obsessionals

If you are an obsessional worrier, your mind gets stuck on a particular, rigid and repetitive focus. Unlike individuals with GAD, whose worries fluctuate depending on what is happening in their lives, your worry about one thing may just repeat over and over, regardless of what is happening in your life. This was the case for Patricia, whose obsessions centered on the persistent fear that she might be diagnosed with a catastrophic illness. She was sure that if she saw a doctor, this fear would be confirmed.

Another common obsession in this category is the fear that you will inadvertently bring harm to another by some action or inaction. For instance, as illogical as it sounds, someone may believe that if she wears black while her husband is traveling, he'll die in an accident. Similarly, you might experience repetitive, intrusive urges to harm yourself or others, and greatly fear acting on these impulses.

What is common to all these different categories are the obsessive, repetitive, intrusive thoughts about one theme (germs or contamination for the washers and cleaners; the possibility that a stove is on or a door unlocked for the checkers). These obsessions are unwanted and anxiety provoking for the individuals who experience them. They also have a strong biological base: OCD has been linked to very specific neurological malfunctioning. Psychiatrist Jeffrey Schwartz noted that "OCD is associated with a biochemical problem that causes the underside of the front part of the brain to overheat" (1996, p. 7). While some people attempt to ignore their obsessions, because they are biologically based they are often too powerful and repetitive to ignore for long. So many individuals with OCD develop activities or rituals to ease the distress brought about by the obsessions.

Functional brain imaging studies have produced a model for the pathophysiology of OCD, which involves hyperactivity in certain subcortical and cortical regions. In particular, a neuronal feedback loop involving the orbitofrontal cortex, cingulated gyrus, striatum, globus pallidus, and thalamus appears to demonstrate dysregulation in individuals with OCD. Some of the interventions discussed within this chapter, such as Schwartz's four-step self-treatment method, make use of this information, emphasizing that OCD-related thoughts are simply the result of some faulty wiring that, with psychotherapeutic intervention, can become better regulated.

Therefore, in all but the "pure obsessionals" category from above, obsessions are generally accompanied by compulsions: repetitive, often ritualized behaviors that serve to help the person appease the threat he or she has been obsessing over (excessive hand washing to avoid contamination; elaborate routines of locking and unlocking doors; turning the stove off and on and off again). The compulsive rituals are not performed because they are innately rewarding or gratifying, but because they help ease the distress caused by the obsessions.

These compulsive rituals can become very elaborate. For example, Henry's checking ritual took him 20 minutes every time he left his house. In Henry's ritual, he turned the stove and each switch in his house on and off a set number of times in response to his obsession that the stove or a light might be left on. Logically, he need not have turned the stove or light on and off even once: he could have simply visually confirmed that the knob or switch was in the "off" position. But this would not have alleviated his anxiety.

The person with OCD might not be able to explain why the rituals are helpful. Rather, she or he just believes that they *are* helpful, somehow, and feels compelled to complete them.

Studies have found that the revving, sympathetic nervous system often kicks into gear when an obsessive thought arises and calms with the activation of the parasympathetic nervous system when the compulsive response has been completed (recall our discussion of the autonomic nervous system and fight/flight in Chapter 6 on panic disorder). Thus it makes sense that, in the face of heightened anxiety, the enactment of the compulsion that serves to calm one's system is hard to resist. It is important to remain cognizant of these physiological reactions when planning treatment interventions.

To successfully treat OCD, powerful interventions are needed. But before we discuss them, we will first get a better understanding of what OCD is not.

Of course, to successfully treat OCD we, the therapists, need to know that our clients are experiencing OCD symptomatology. While this sounds obvious, I have found that OCD is often a hidden disorder; many clients who present initially with other disorders may not be forthcoming in disclosing their obsessions and compulsions. Therefore, I find it is especially important to screen for OCD, regardless of a client's stated presenting problem.

The Difference Between the Disorders

OCD bears similarity to generalized anxiety disorder (GAD), panic disorder (PD), and social anxiety disorder (SAD) in that individuals with those disorders are beset with intrusive, anxious thoughts. However, for people with GAD, the intrusive, worrying thoughts generally occur in response to events in everyday life. For people with PD, these thoughts revolve around the fear of having a panic attack, and for people with SAD, the fears revolve around being seen and judged in social situations. In OCD, the intrusive thoughts cluster around specific, recurring themes of obsessive concerns. The intensity or frequency of the intrusive thoughts might increase in response to life stressors, but the content of the thoughts remains consistently centered on particular obsessive themes, as described above in Foa and Wilson's categories.

Additionally, individuals with GAD, PD, and SAD do not engage in ritualized compulsions to neutralize their anxiety as most individuals with OCD do. For example, someone with a specific phobia of germs might avoid doctors' offices or eating food prepared in restaurants, but would not initiate extensive rituals such as Colleen's washing protocols in response to this fear.

People with body dysmorphic disorder (BDD) and trichitillomania (repeated urge to pull out body hair) *do* exhibit both obsessions and compulsions, but the contents of the obsessive thoughts and the compulsive behaviors are more narrowly ascribed: for example, in BDD, the obsessions and compulsions relate to the individual's perception of his or her body and appearance. Even more narrowly, obsessions and compulsions in trichitillomania center around plucking body hair.

When discussing OCD, it is also important to distinguish between OCD and addiction. Some people with addictions refer to their substance-seeking and using behavior as a compulsion. The two disorders are similar in that both the individual with OCD and the addict feel compelled to perform a compulsive behavior or compulsively ingest a substance, and for both this act can initially provide both an emotional and a physical sense of relief. However, the compulsions in OCD differ because the ritualized behaviors are not innately pleasurable or craved, as in an addiction. While both OCD rituals and substance use can be sought out for their anxiety-reducing effects, the OCD rituals are initiated for that reason *only*.

A final similarity among the disorders is the decision of the individuals to remain largely homebound as a means of coping with the anxiety disorder. People with PD with agoraphobia, generalized SAD, and OCD all might confine themselves mainly to their homes, but each for a different reason. Individuals with OCD might do so because of excessive fear of contamination, or because their rituals might make it challenging to spend much time out of the house. Someone with PD with agoraphobia might stay home to avoid having a panic attack in public, and someone with an extreme case of generalized SAD might do so to avoid being seen and judged by others.

Who Develops OCD

OCD is usually diagnosed in adolescence or early adulthood, but can also begin in childhood. Typically, males develop OCD between the ages of 6 and 15, while females develop OCD between 20 and 29 years of age. The rates of OCD diagnosis between men and women are about equal, although when the disorder begins in childhood, boys are more likely to receive diagnoses than girls. For both genders, the severity of the obsessions and compulsions usually intensifies gradually from onset. Likewise, over the course of the disorder the severity of the OCD symptoms varies, often increasing with heightened life stress. About 15% of individuals with OCD have worsening symptoms that lead to trouble functioning at work and at home. A smaller percentage, about 5%, have time-limited episodes of OCD with periods in between during which they are completely symptom free. Typically, however, the obsessions and compulsions remain consistently present, and a person's ability to function does not worsen over time.

Interestingly, a small subset of OCD cases in children is correlated to the occurrence of a particular strain of strep throat, the Group A beta-hemolytic streptococcal (GABHS) infection. Although GABHS can present in adults and adolescents, only children appear to be vulnerable to GABHS-related OCD. When it does present in children, the OCD has a swift onset in association with the strep infection, and OCD symptoms can worsen at times when the child experiences recurrences of the strep infection. Thus you should advise parents of children who have already acquired this type of OCD to get their child to the doctor right away at the onset of a sore throat in order to minimize the worsening OCD symptomatology. Likewise, they need to be sure their child completes the full course of each antibiotic treatment and follows all treatment protocols precisely.

OCD *has* been shown to have a genetic component. You are more likely to develop the disorder than the general population if you have a biological parent or sibling who has the disorder. Identical twins are more likely to both have OCD than are fraternal twins.

People with OCD are also more likely to have major depressive disorder. Of the anxiety disorders, they are more likely to also have a specific phobia, social anxiety disorder, panic disorder, or generalized anxiety disorder. Eating disorders also commonly co-occur with OCD, as do three personality disorders: avoidant, dependent, and, not surprisingly, obsessive–compulsive personality disorder.

Researchers have observed a link between OCD and Tourette's disorder. Not only are you more likely to develop OCD if a parent or sibling has Tourette's, but surveys have found that between 35% and 50% of individuals with Tourette's *also* have OCD. Conversely, only 5% to 7% of individuals who have been diagnosed with OCD have also been diagnosed with Tourette's. Research also indicates that between 20% and 30% of people with OCD have reported experiencing *tics*, an uncontrolled, involuntary movement common in Tourette's, at some point in the course of their OCD (APA, 2000).

People with OCD also have a higher incidence of excessively using alcohol or sedative, hypnotic, or anxiolytic (anxiety-reducing) medications. The use of these substances could well be an attempt to diminish the distress brought about by the intrusive obsessions and resulting compulsions. If you have OCD and self-medicate, know that your desire to do so is understandable due to your distress, but there exist far better options to help you deal with and even overcome your symptoms.

It is also important to distinguish between OCD and obsessive–compulsive personality disorder. Most of us have at least one acquaintance who is rigid, perfectionistic, and excessively concerned with order and control. For example, my friend Julie can't start working at her computer if there is one paper on her desk, and she gets angry with her husband if he leaves mail in her work space. But unlike someone with OCD, the individual with the obsessive–compulsive *personality disorder* does not feel that this way of being causes him or her any anxiety, or is problematic. People with obsessive–compulsive personality disorder are generally comfortable with their ordered, albeit rigid, way of being. They also do not experience the intrusive thoughts and enact the compulsive rituals that are the hallmarks of OCD.

In contrast, people with OCD do have obsessions and compulsions and find that their obsessive thoughts and compulsive behaviors are at odds with their idea of the way they would like to function. Indeed, the obsessions and compulsions are often experienced as a burden. Luckily, this is a burden that can be lifted.

The Good News

If you are overwhelmed by your obsessions and compulsions, there are many therapeutic avenues through which you can alleviate your symptoms and improve the quality of your life. You have used great creativity to create rituals that temporarily negate the distress caused by your obsessive thoughts. But many therapeutic techniques provide more adaptive ways to cope with and eventually recover from your obsessions and break free from your compulsive rituals—a freedom that you more than deserve.

The Goals and Gains of Therapy

- Gain an understanding of the causes and treatment of your OCD.
- Master relaxation techniques.
- Develop a hierarchy of anxiety-provoking situations related to your compulsions.
- Establish a plan of exposure and response treatment to meet each challenge on your hierarchy.
- Develop the ability to postpone thinking about your obsessions until a later, set time.
- Develop the ability to practice mindful awareness of your obsessive thoughts and the resulting compulsive behaviors.
- Cultivate a sense of hope about recovery.

How to Get There: Therapeutic Techniques and Interventions

Exposure and Response Prevention

Exposure and Response Prevention (ERP) is considered, hands-down, to be the most efficacious treatment approach for OCD. ERP therapy has two parts, the first pertaining to your obsessions and the second to your resulting compulsions. First, with the help of a therapist, you activate the distress you experience when an obsessive thought pops into your mind. This distress will most likely trigger your desire to engage in one of your compulsive rituals.

Second, you need to *refrain* from engaging in the compulsive rituals that were triggered by your distress. Through this technique, you are, in effect, deviating from your typical response to your obsessions and not using your compulsion to neutralize the distress brought about by your obsession. This two-part process allows you to confront your distress and discover that your anxiety can lessen *whether or not you engage in your compulsion.*

This process habituates or acclimates you to your distress, and you discover that in time your distress begins to diminish. Eventually you won't need to engage in a compulsive behavior to neutralize the distress brought about by your obsessions. Some research suggests that with ERP techniques, you actually retrain and alter the pathways in your brain. Essentially, you are rewiring your brain!

How does it work? For example, if you are a washer and cleaner who fears contamination, you might be given the assignment of shaking hands with someone and then refraining from applying the hand sanitizer you always carry for such an occasion. Or if you are an orderer, you might place something "out of order" when putting groceries away in the refrigerator, and then not rearrange this item. If you are a repeater and you snap your fingers two times every time you see the number 13 or hear it spoken, you would encounter this number and then refrain from snapping your fingers.

When using this treatment strategy, your therapist will take you through the three-step process below. Through this process, you will recognize your obsessive thoughts and identify the situations that your exposure therapy will then incorporate.

1. Make three lists labeled "obsessions," "compulsions," and "avoidance." For the obsessions list, write out all of your obsessive thoughts, images, and impulses, and the situations with which they are associated. For the compulsions list, write out your compulsive rituals, and for the avoidance list, write out the things, places, or situations you avoid entirely (if there are any) as a result of your OCD.

2. Next, go through your compulsions and avoidance lists, imagining your response if you were asked to refrain from engaging in the compulsive behavior or asked to expose yourself to the avoided situation. You might find it helpful to rate each item on a scale from 1 to 10, in which 1 is mildly distressing and 10 is so distressing that you think you might have a panic attack. This scale is commonly used in treatments; the ratings are called Subjective Units of Distress, or SUDs. Using your SUDs ratings, you can order the items on your compulsions and avoidance lists from least distressful to most distressful.

3. Combine the items on the two lists, starting with the lowest SUDs rating and going to the highest. This is the fear hierarchy you and your therapists will use in your ERP trials.

Here is an example of the hierarchical lists of compulsions, avoidances, and fears that Colleen made to address her rituals and avoidances surrounding germ contamination:

COMPULSIONS (ORDERED BY SUD RATING)	
COMPULSION	**SUDs RATING**
Washing all canned goods and bottles with disinfectant before putting them in the cupboard	2
Washing canned goods and bottles again before using them	2
Taking showers three times a day	4
Leaving work station to wash hands repeatedly	4
Insisting on using own pen	6
Sanitizing hands after handling money	7
Sanitizing hands repeatedly throughout the workday	7
Using paper towels to open doors in public places	8
Using paper towels to turn on the faucets in public bathrooms	9
Wearing gloves outside	9

AVOIDANCE (ORDERED BY SUD RATING)	
AVOIDED OBJECT/SITUATION/ACTIVITY	**SUDs RATING**
Loaning or borrowing items to or from friends	2
Checking out books from the library	2
Touching light switches at work	4
Touching the AC knob at work	4
Purchasing and eating foods from street vendors	5
Borrowing friends' cell phones	6
Going to a gym	7
Going to the doctor for yearly physicals	8
Visiting friends in hospitals	8
Being around friends and coworkers who have cold or flu symptoms	9

FEAR HIERARCHY (THE COMBINED RANKING OF THE TWO LISTS ABOVE)	
TASK	SUDs RATING
Washing all canned goods and bottles with disinfectant before putting them in the cupboard	2
Washing canned goods and bottles again before using them	2
Loaning or borrowing items to or from friends	2
Checking out books from the library	2
Taking showers three times a day	4
Leaving work station to wash hands repeatedly	4
Touching light switches at work	4
Touching the AC knob at work	4
Purchasing and eating foods from street vendors	5
Insisting on using own pen	6
Borrowing friends' cell phones	6
Sanitizing hands after handling money	7
Sanitizing hands repeatedly throughout the workday	7
Going to a gym	7
Using paper towels to open doors in public places	8
Going to the doctor for yearly physicals	8
Visiting friends in hospitals	8
Being around friends and coworkers who have cold or flu symptoms	9
Using paper towels to turn on the faucets in public bathrooms	9
Wearing gloves outside	9

Once you've prepared your exposure hierarchy, you are ready to begin your exposure and response trials using the SUDs scale to rate the level of distress you experience during each trial. As you work through the hierarchy with your therapist, there are a few important things to keep in mind. First, tackle only one item at a time. Do not move on to the next item in your list until you are comfortable refraining from the ritual you just targeted. Using the SUDs rating system, wait until your SUDs level is at a 1 or 2 before you move on.

It is important to pace yourself as you proceed through your list. If your SUDs get up to a 9 or 10 when you refrain from a particular ritual, engage in this ERP trial *only once* a day. Remember, your rituals are firmly ingrained behavior patterns that you have engaged in for a long time. Be gentle and understanding with yourself. Your desire to use your rituals will be strong. They have provided you with relief for a long time. Do not expect them to go away overnight. With time and sustained effort, however, they will decrease, and some will disappear altogether.

If you are on a daily medication regimen to help you with your OCD, you can maintain it while doing ERP. However, it is important that you *not* take any fast-acting anti-anxiety medication while you are progressing through your fear hierarchy, even when you become anxious. When you make an effort to refrain from enacting a compulsion, it is important that you be able to attribute your decreasing levels of distress to your toleration of and resilience to the changes you are making, *not* to the effects of a fast-acting drug.

Likewise, most therapists who use ERP suggest that you *not* use relaxation techniques to help you cope with the distress that will arise during the actual ERP trial. Relaxation techniques and exercises are great tools to calm your nerves and enhance your sense of well-being. Incorporating them into your day, especially on the days you do ERP, is suggested. But the purpose of ERP is to show you that you will be OK in the absence of your compulsive rituals. Initiating a relaxation procedure *during* an exposure trial is analogous to taking a fast-acting anxiety-reducing drug. You need to see that your distress will diminish on its own, without the help of any other drugs or anxiety-reducing techniques.

Finally, while you are doing ERP, schedule activities that are enjoyable to you into your day. Treat yourself to something special that you like (other than engaging in one of the rituals you are trying to negate). As ERP can be challenging, you need to step up your self-care activities and congratulate yourself on the effort you are sustaining and the progress that results.

The fast-acting anxiety-reducing drugs referred to largely fall into the family of benzodiazepines. Medication regimens such as the use of antidepressants are not thought to interfere with the ERP trials, as they do not work to decrease anxiety symptoms in the moment, but rather bring about a more global change in an individual's functioning. For more information on the difference between these two types of medications, see Chapter 10.

Schwartz's Four-Step Self-Treatment Method

This easy-to-learn and effective technique was designed by Jeffrey Schwartz, a psychiatrist and author of the book *Brain Lock: Free Yourself from Obsessive-Compulsive Behavior* (1996). Schwartz's technique is the first presented in this chapter that specifically makes use of the knowledge that OCD is based on a biochemical imbalance. I have added a few techniques to broaden the application of Schwartz's steps, but first we will examine this four-part technique to reframe your OCD-based thoughts and urges as Schwartz presented it. The four steps are as follows:

1. Relabel: Recognize your unwanted thoughts and compulsions for what they are: obsessions and compulsions caused by your OCD.
2. Reattribute: Reconceptualize your symptoms by recognizing that the OCD itself is related to a biochemical imbalance.
3. Refocus: When an obsessive thought or urge comes up, immediately shift your attention by busying yourself with another activity for several minutes.
4. Revalue: The result of your actively going through the first three steps—a reevaluation and reconceptualization of your obsessive thoughts and compulsive behaviors.

1. Relabel

The relabeling process involves identifying obsessive thoughts and distinguishing them from other, more adaptive thoughts that go through your mind. Schwartz wrote that you first need to "call an obsessive thought or compulsive urge what it really is. Assertively relabel it so you can begin to understand that the feeling is just a false alarm, with little or no basis in reality" (1996, p. 207). To do this, Schwartz suggested you work to develop an observing self he termed the *impartial spectator*. Schwartz defined this impartial spectator as "the observing power within us that gives each person the capacity to recognize what's real and what's just a symptom and to fend off the pathological urge until it begins to fade and recede" (1996, p. 207). The emphasis is that these urges come from an imbalance in your brain.

2. Reattribute

When you are using Schwartz's four steps and an obsessive thought pops up, you say to yourself: "this is not *me*, this is just my OCD." These are not reasonable thoughts; rather, they are faulty thoughts that keep getting triggered by a biological imbalance in the brain. By saying "this is not *me*," you separate yourself from the condition you have. Your obsessive thoughts are like static from a weak radio station. Although you can't turn off the radio, you can alter how you respond to it. By identifying where the thought comes from—an imbalance in the brain—you are in effect reconceptualizing your symptoms. Having done this you are ready to diminish the power of the obsessive thoughts by learning to shift your attention when they occur.

Schwartz's second step provides an excellent example of the apt utilization of psychoeducation within a treatment protocol. Once clients can understand the brain, or get their head around it, so to speak, clients can recognize that they are dealing with hardwired glitches, and that their disorder is not merely the result of a weakness of will on their part. I usually keep a model of the brain on my desk, so I can help delineate different structures of the brain and concretely point out the sections in the brain that are implicated in a given disorder. For example, the orbitofrontal cortex, which Schwartz call the "hot spot" in OCD, is a structure that is involved in the misattributions present in OCD.

---

3. Refocus
When an obsessive thought or urge comes up, immediately shift your attention by busying yourself with another activity for several minutes. Ask yourself, "What can I do to refocus myself?" My clients have found that practicing different deep breathing techniques, going for a walk or jog or engaging in some other physical activity, or doing work can be successful distracters. Schwartz suggests you engage in your chosen enjoyable activity for about 15 minutes.

4. Revalue
A reevaluation of your obsessive thoughts and urges occurs as the result of sustained practice of the above three steps. Once you become skilled at relabeling, reattributing, and refocusing, your obsessions will not have as much power over you. You will discover that you have the power to change the way you think about your obsessions and urges: reconceptualization can result in *revaluation*.

Adjuncts to Schwartz's Steps
As many of my clients remark to me, obsessive thoughts often occur at times when you cannot take a 15-minute break to refocus, as in Schwartz's Step Three. The following techniques are useful for these situations.

External Focusing
The external focusing technique that was discussed in Chapter 8 can be helpful to use if you are in a meeting or classroom, carrying on a conversa-

tion, or at another social gathering. If your obsessive thoughts occur when listening to another person speaking, try to cultivate a curiosity about what the other person is communicating, and focus all your attention on this.

5,4,3,2,1 Technique

Developed by Milton Erickson, M.D., a renowned practitioner of clinical hypnosis, this quick interruption and refocusing technique is useful when you are alone or in social situations (B. Erickson, personal communication, April 3, 2007). If you are alone, select a spot to gaze at and note five things you see. Say the five things out loud. For example, "I see the lamp, I see the picture on the wall, I see the window, I see the tree outside the window, I see the leaves moving in the wind." Then you state five things you hear: "I hear the ticking of the clock, I hear the heater going on, I hear the traffic, I hear myself taking a breath, I hear someone walking in the hallway." And then five things you physically feel: "I feel my feet in my shoes, I feel the chair against my body, I feel my hair against my cheek, I feel the fingers of my right hand touching my left hand, I feel my right foot on the floor."

Then you proceed to say four things you see, hear, and feel, and then three, two, and one progressively. If you are in a social situation, you can think these things rather than saying them aloud. In work or school settings, the technique may impede your abilty to concentrate on what is being said to some degree, but you can stop the exercise at any point once your intrusive thoughts are under control. You needn't repeat the same list of sights, sounds, and feelings as you cycle through the number regression, although listing the same sight, sound, or feeling multiple times is perfectly OK. The point of the exercise is to shift your focus, not to test your short-term memory. You are simply to note the sensory phenomena that are in your awareness at each moment, shifting your attention from your obsessive thoughts to the world around you.

As the process performed during the 5,4,3,2,1 exercise has some characteristics that are similar to the repeating and counting that can be a component of OCD, I use caution when using this exercise with clients who are checkers or repeaters. While this exercise can adeptly help a client to shift attentional focus, it is important that you monitor checkers and repeaters to ensure that this exercise does not mimic the feel of their chosen compulsive rituals. This technique is also very helpful for people with panic disorder and social anxiety disorder.

Tight Fist

I have also suggested that clients use the tight fist intervention described in

Chapter 4 while they are driving or in other situations when they cannot easily step away. In this technique, imagine that your urge or thought is going into one of your hands. Make a fist with that hand, squeeze it tightly, and focus on feeling the tension in your fist. Next, magnify or increase this tension by tightening that fist even more. Once your fist is considerably tighter, imagine the tension becoming a liquid in a color of your choice. This liquid represents the thought, compulsion, or worry that had just popped into your mind. Imagine that your fist is absorbing all of the colored liquid that contains the worry and discomfort. Once you have done this, relax your fingers, wave your hand, and pretend that all the feelings have been sent out the window.

Mindfulness

Rather than discouraging your obsessive thoughts, mindfulness techniques cultivate a non-judgmental perspective toward intrusive thoughts. In mindfulness, the goal is to welcome all your experiences with this neutral attitude.

A quick appreciation of the basic premise underlying mindfulness can be gained from the following exercise: for the next 60 seconds, try not to think of chocolate. If you are like most people, the first thing you will think of is the very thing you are trying to avoid: chocolate. So trying to *not* think about the obsessive thought—that is, the chocolate—will likely make you think about it even more.

Mindfulness approaches are useful for all the anxiety disorders, but are particularly helpful for OCD because they directly counter the instinctual yet counterproductive desire to push away obsessive thoughts or compulsive urges. Rather than push away thoughts and feelings, mindfulness brings your focus to whatever is happening to you in the moment, both externally and internally in your thoughts, sensations, and urges.

Drawn from Eastern philosophy, mindfulness is gaining increasing popularity among Western psychotherapists. In the previous section we were introduced to Dr. Schwartz's four-step approach, which incorporates mindfulness in its first two steps. Psychologist Steven Hayes also incorporates mindfulness in his Acceptance and Commitment Therapy (ACT), which we will examine later in this chapter. And no discussion of mindfulness would be complete without mention of Jon Kabat-Zinn, a physician and researcher who founded the Mindfulness-Based Stress Reduction Clinic at the University of Massachusetts. Many clinicians have since incorporated mindfulness practices into their treatment interventions for various disorders.

Describing mindfulness, Kabat-Zinn wrote, "It is about allowing things to be as they are, resting in awareness, and then, taking appropriate action when called for" (para. 3, n.d.). Thus mindfulness is a frame of mind in which you observe thoughts and sensations with a detached, neutral perspective. With practice, you learn to view thoughts as simply transient occurrences that come and go and that do not reflect the entire reality of who you are.

The mindfulness training Henry learned as a component of his therapy with me had several components: mindful attention in an action; self-statements and mental imagery to reinforce the mindful action; detached awareness of urges; compassion for self; and mindful attention to the breath. In his first mindfulness exercise at home, Henry used mindfulness to help curtail his checking ritual. He progressed through the components of the mindfulness intervention as follows.

Mindful Attention in an Action

After Henry cooked his dinner, he was to walk to the stove slowly and push the knob on the electric stove to the off position. As he was doing this, he was to say aloud, "I am lifting the forefinger of my right hand and pushing the white rectangular button to the off position. My finger has pushed the off button. The stove is off."

Self-Statements and Mental Imagery to Reinforce the Mindful Action

After mindfully attending to his actions, Henry was to say, "I feel my finger pushing the button down. I move my hand to the side of my right pant leg, and I look at the button in the off position. I see the rectangular button in the off position. The stove is off." Then he was to sit in a chair at the kitchen table, and before beginning dinner, Henry was to close his eyes, remember the image of the stove knob in the off position, and repeat to himself, "The stove is off."

After finishing dinner, Henry was to get ready to leave the house. If, when leaving the house, he got the urge to check the stove again, he would sit down and go through the following actions and statements:

Detached awareness of urges

"I am aware of my brain's compulsive urge to check."

Compassion for self

"I notice this urge with compassion and without judgment. I observe the urge, but I do not judge it."

Mindfulness of breath

"I focus my attention on my breath, and take four slow, deep breaths. I am staying very focused on my breathing.

Self-statements and mental imagery to reinforce the mindful action
"I see the rectangular button of the stove in the off position. I remember the feeling of my finger as I touched it. The stove is off, and I am OK."

Mindfulness and Acceptance Practices

People who suffer from anxiety disorders are critical of themselves. This is particularly true of those who have obsessions and compulsions; they not only suffer from the distress of their thoughts and urges but secondarily from self-recrimination and shame. The acceptance practiced in mindfulness provides a much-needed reprieve from self-contempt. When you practice mindfulness, you bring an attitude of loving kindness to yourself as well as to others. You bring an accepting, non-judgmental stance to your ever-transient experience. Kerry Moran, psychotherapist and author, noted: "[This] is where the 'Big No' (your basic rejection of experience) meets the 'Big Yes' (your compassionate awareness)" (para. 1, 2003). You notice a thought, a sensation, or an urge and are a silent witness to it. You notice it without judgment, embrace it and yourself with compassion, and then notice what changes occur, if any. And even if judgment comes, you don't judge yourself, but simply let that judgment "be," as well.

Auditory Exposure: The Loop Tape

Another technique to help decrease the power of obsessive thoughts, used by Edna Foa and Reid Wilson (2001), is auditory exposure. A typical auditory exposure intervention involves recording an obsessive thought that pops into your mind onto a loop audio recorder that repeats brief audio input (about 10 seconds to 3 minutes) over and over. With this, you can listen to your obsessive thought over and over again in one 30- or 45-minute sitting. While you listen to the recording, rather than trying to block the thought or minimize your distress, you focus on the anxiety and fear the thought brings up; you allow yourself to become as distressed as possible. No matter how distressed you initially become, the theory behind this exercise is that with repeated exposure, your distress will naturally subside. Your therapist will suggest that you listen to the recording once a day until the thought on the tape no longer distresses you. By the end of the lengthy listening sessions, the thought will likely have lost the alarm and sense of urgency that it once held for you.

In my office, Patricia created an audio recording of the thought "Somewhere inside me I have the start of a horrible disease—maybe the first few cells of a cancer. It's too soon for me to feel sick now, but if I go to a doctor, he'll do some tests and tell me that it's there. I'd rather someone just shoot me than tell me that." I instructed Patricia to listen to the audio recording for 45 minutes every day during the week. The next week, Patricia reported she had only listened to the recording twice and each time for only 15 minutes. "It takes up too much time—I'm really busy with work and when I get home I make dinner for me and Ronnie, clean up, and go to bed. Besides, listening to that tape is annoying. I listen to those thoughts all day already. By the time I get home at night, I don't want to listen to them anymore."

After hearing Patricia's concerns, we discussed her waking an hour early each morning so she could play the tape for 45 minutes before starting her day. I reassured her that after listening to the tape for 45 minutes in the morning she might find that her obsessive thoughts did not bother her as much when they popped into her head for the remainder of that day.

Patricia's initial response to this protocol highlights the importance of collaboratively and creatively addressing non-compliance. For this to occur, a strong therapeutic alliance needs to be present. It is very important that you be able to validate the client's concerns, acknowledge the practical roadblocks present in the client's life, and brainstorm ways your client can work around this. Likewise, it is important to empathize with your client's concerns and convey your commitment to and investment in his or her progress. As is evident with Patricia, it is very helpful to discuss and even anticipate difficulties in following through with practice.

We also estimated the total amount of time per day that Patricia spent thinking about her obsessions. Patricia guessed it totaled over two hours. When she realized that 45 minutes in the morning might decrease the amount of time she spent on and distress she encountered in response to her obsessions, she was ready to give the recording another try. I also reminded her that she only needed to listen to the recording daily for two or three weeks, a short time compared to the years she could look forward to living free from her obsessions.

After two weeks of listening to the tape daily in the mornings, Patricia noticed that the number of times her obsessive thoughts intruded during her day did decrease, although with this intervention alone they did not go away completely. However, she reported with a smile, "When I do have a thought about having an undetected disease, I don't stress out about it nearly as much. I can usually let it go after less than a minute and go on with my day."

Postponement
This deceptively simple technique, which involves postponing thinking about your obsessions until a certain time each day, is helpful for many

people with OCD, including Colleen. I suggested this technique when Colleen said she was worried about how much time she was spending at work each day thinking about germs. "My boss has no idea how much time I spend thinking about all the germs floating around in the air," she told me. "Of course, I still get all my work done and my boss is happy with my output, but I could increase my productivity if I weren't spending so much time thinking about germs. Each time I start thinking about it, it takes me at least three or four minutes to get back to the work I was doing."

I adapted the postponement technique described by Foa and Wilson (2001) to fit Colleen's need to let go of her obsessive thoughts during her work day. Any time she had an obtrusive thought relating to her fear of contamination from germs while at her desk, she was to take out a sticky note and write, "Fear of contamination. I'll think about it at 7:30." She was then to put the sticky note in an envelope and return to her work.

At 7:30 in the evening, after getting home from work and having dinner, Colleen was to sit down in a comfortable chair and play her audio recording. We began with the goal of listening for 45 minutes. During this time she was to let her obsessive thoughts run free without trying to curtail them or redirect her attention. As in imaginal exposure, Colleen's relatively lengthy exposure to her loop tape also served another purpose: it helped her to become less distressed by her obsessional thoughts. With the use of the audio recording and her postponement activity, Colleen was able to both postpone her obsessive rumination and decrease the extent to which her obsessional thoughts distressed her when they did pop into her mind throughout the day.

Protocols to Address Hoarding

Henry, like many hoarders, was ambivalent about giving up this behavior. It was only his fear that he would get in trouble if he didn't clear out his house that drove him to action. Once in therapy, however, he admitted how lonely he was and that he no longer could deny that his hoarding was preventing him from opening his home to anyone. This admission helped open the door so that Henry became willing to embark upon the process of decluttering his home and discontinuing his hoarding.

The first step in this process involves ceasing the accumulation of unnecessary items. Henry learned to make and *stick to* a list when he went grocery shopping. If he wanted other items, such as clothes, books, or music, he was to postpone the purchase for 48 hours, and ask himself the following questions:

1. Do I already have this at home?
2. Do I really need this?

3. Will my life be better if I have it?
4. Do I have the space for it?

If he answered the first question yes and the second no, he was to refrain from the purchase. Even if the item passed the test, he was not to buy it until he got rid of four *similar* items he already owned.

Ceasing the accumulation of hoarded materials is a huge step, but it is only half of the battle. Henry also needed to dispose of much of the stuff that he had already stowed in his house, and he had to do so promptly to avoid sanction by the city. For this treatment, I adapted Bruce Hyman and Cherry Pedrick's procedure from their book *The OCD Workbook: Your Guide to Breaking Free from Obsessive–Compulsive Disorder* (1999).

It can also be helpful to recommend that your clients hire a professional organizer to help facilitate the sorting and organizing process. While getting clients to a point of willingness to initiate and follow through with the decluttering process is your area of expertise, having a professional whose strength lies in organization can help facilitate the in-home process itself. I have also found that clients have benefitted from joining support networks such as Clutterers Anonymous.

I gave Henry the following instructions:

1. Create an inventory of the possessions in each room of your home. For each room on the inventory, rate the percentage of space in the room your clutter takes up. Then note how you would like to use that room in the future, and set a percentage for how much clutter can acceptably remain in the room.

2. Make some ground rules. Establish a few simple rules to govern what you will keep and what you will throw away, and how you will organize what you keep. Henry donated all of the magazines he had been saving to a local arts and crafts center, where they could be used for craft projects. He planned to shred and recycle receipts and bills that were more than seven years old. For those receipts that he needed to keep, he purchased two four-drawer filing cabinets, designating one drawer for each year. Once a new year began, he agreed to shred all the bills from the least recent year, and replace bills that would accumulate throughout the next year in the empty drawer.

3. Review your inventory, decide which room you want to start with, and begin!

After consulting his inventory, Henry chose to start with the family room and work his way through the downstairs first. He chose to begin by the doorway and proceed through the clutter in a clockwise direction. To remain in compliance with his ground rules, Henry also obtained three boxes: one labeled "keep," one labeled "throw out," and one labeled "give away." While going through each room he kept his inventory and ground rule lists handy to help keep himself on track and to refrain from holding onto items that he had planned to dispose of or give away.

Medication

Medications can be very helpful in the treatment of OCD (for a more thorough discussion of medication, see Chapter 10). As I have mentioned in previous chapters, I would never recommend going on any psychotropic medications in the absence of therapy. However, a number of my clients have found that medications have helped enhance their recovery process. Selective serotonin reuptake inhibitors (SSRIs) are a type of antidepressant that have been found to be particularly effective in treating OCD. Clomipramine (Anafranil) is reportedly the most effective of these, with some research showing that approximately 80% of people who take clomipramine report significant relief of their OCD symptoms. The downside of this medication is that it has a higher side effect profile. People sometimes get off this medication due to drowsiness, dryness of mouth, increased appetite, and weight gain. Other SSRIs commonly used for OCD are fluvoxamine (Luvox), fluoxetine (Prozac), sertraline (Zoloft) and paroxetine (Paxil).

While SSRIs are some of the most commonly used medications, there is also a host of other medication combinations available to treat OCD (for a more detailed list, see the table in Chapter 10, page 187). I highly recommend that you and your therapist at least discuss the possibility of consulting with a psychiatrist to see if a medication regimen might be a good choice for you.

Recovery: Henry, Colleen, and Patricia's Stories

While their presenting symptoms and course of treatment varied, Henry, Colleen, and Patricia all found relief from their obsessions and compulsions in therapy. No matter how different the type of obsession or compulsion, there is a constellation of therapeutic interventions that can work for you. The outcomes of Henry, Colleen, and Patricia's different treatments are described below.

Henry's Story

Henry's treatment was divided into two goals: eliminating his checking behaviors and working on his hoarding behaviors. Early in his therapy I referred him to a psychiatrist for an evaluation for medication. She prescribed Prozac, starting him on 10 mg a day and then increasing his dosage to 80 mg per day. The combination of medication and behavioral interventions worked well for Henry, as the medication helped to address the compromised neurological functioning associated with OCD.

Henry also responded well to Dr. Schwartz's four-part protocol. Because he was motivated to do the at-home practice, he was able to extinguish his checking behaviors within two months. He also ordered Jon Kabat-Zinn's mindfulness meditation CDs, which helped him develop a daily practice of mindfulness meditation. This diminished his overall anxiety. The mindfulness reinforced Dr. Schwartz's fourth step: Revaluing.

Henry had one relapse when his mother had a stroke. In response to his heightened stress, he began to compulsively check to see if the garage door was closed after he left his house. After only the second day of his relapse, however, he re-started the Schwartz protocol and was able to stop the behavior within a week.

Henry's hoarding behavior was a greater challenge for him. He selected one room at a time to de-clutter, and he hired a sensitive, psychologically-oriented organizer to help him. He also joined Clutterers Anonymous, a 12-step group patterned after Alcoholics Anonymous. The group was a powerful adjunct to his treatment and diminished Henry's isolation. He now has a social network and regularly goes out for coffee with other group members after the meetings.

Colleen's Story

Colleen continues to use her postponement techniques on a daily basis as she progresses through her fear hierarchy in the exposure and response prevention treatment method. Early in her treatment she, like Henry, was prescribed Prozac. Despite some initial skepticism, Colleen discovered that it helped her tolerate the exposure component of the treatment. After five months, she was able to progress through the first eight items on her fear hierarchy. Colleen also applied Schwartz's four-step self-treatment method effectively to her ritual of cleansing her hands with her hand sanitizer. Within ten months she was weaned off the medication, under the consulting psychiatrist's supervision.

While she continues to carry the sanitizer with her and uses it frequently throughout the day, she has significantly decreased the number of times she does so. Colleen also practices mindful awareness as she washes her hands, which has helped her rub her hands less vigorously. Thus Colleen no longer has the scabs and sores that used to cover her hands.

While she has not yet worked up to discontinuing the use of her hand sanitizer or gloves, Colleen is committed to remaining in therapy and continuing to progress through her fear hierarchy.

Patricia's Story

One month into therapy, after only two weeks of exposure to her audio recording and using thought postponement on a daily basis whenever her obsessions arose, Patricia reported a remarkable increase in her quality of life. "I enjoy my days so much more now," she remarked to me. "I had no idea that I could really spend less time thinking about having an illness. Before, it wasn't an option for me. A thought popped up, and I chewed it over again and again. It's great to be able to let go."

This change, while significant, was not enough to help Patricia overcome her fear of getting routine screenings at the doctor's office. At this point I recommended that she consider a trial of medication. However, Patricia was insistent on overcoming this problem without the use of pharmaceuticals. As medication for the treatment of OCD is not a necessity, I honored her decision and recommended that she initiate a mindfulness awareness and meditation practice.

To address her fear of doctors' screenings, we next created an exposure plan using ERP in which Patricia set up appointments for all her routine screenings—internist, gynecologist, and mammogram—in the same week. Despite her intentions, she cancelled all three of her appointments and rated the testing processes as a 9 on her SUDs scale. I encouraged Patricia not to view this as a setback, however. It simply meant that we needed to continue to search for interventions that *would* provide Patricia with the tools she needed to proceed with the doctors' appointments.

In this light, I worked with Patricia for a month on Schwartz's four-step process, using mindfulness and imagery techniques. These techniques proved a turning point in Patricia's treatment. Bolstered by her new skill set, Patricia rescheduled her three appointments and successfully went through with all of them. She now sees me yearly in preparation for her annual screenings, and reports that her husband is thrilled and relieved that she now is getting the preventive medical care she needs.

CHAPTER 10

Medications and Neutraceuticals

"Hi, Carolyn, this is Natalie, Marilyn's daughter-in-law. I wanted to thank you for helping me find such a great therapist."

You may remember Natalie, whom I introduced in Chapter 3. Marilyn, my neighbor, had asked me for advice explaining to Natalie the treatment options for her anxiety disorder.

"Dr. Sorkin is terrific," Natalie continued. "But I'd like a second opinion about her suggestion that I consult with a psychiatrist. She thinks that some medication might be helpful. I don't want to be rigid, but I'm a little nervous about taking medications, and my husband is really uncomfortable with the idea. I've explored some more natural approaches, like plant extracts, but I don't know which ones are best or if they really work at all. I was hoping Dr. Sorkin could cure my anxiety just with psychotherapy. What do you think? Should I make the appointment with the psychiatrist?"

If you, like Natalie, have an anxiety disorder and face this decision, I feel compassion for your dilemma. For starters, the information available is often conflicting, biased, or unreliable. If you have difficulty making decisions in general (as many people with anxiety do), the abundance of information becomes even more difficult to sort through.

Rather than add to the information overload, this chapter will provide you with basic information about the medications and neutraceuticals that can be helpful in the treatment of an anxiety disorder (neutraceuticals are natural food substances, herbs included, that have a medicinal effect on the body and mind). This is not a comprehensive discussion of every pharmaceutical and neutraceutical that can be helpful for anxiety. You needn't become an expert, but it is important that you become an informed consumer.

Medications

As I have mentioned throughout this book, I do not recommend the use of anti-anxiety medications in the absence of therapy. However, medications, when combined with therapy, can play a crucial role in your recovery from an anxiety disorder. Some people hope they can just take a pill and their anxiety will disappear, but it's not that simple. It is the integration of a variety of approaches that leads to recovery. As scientist and author Candace Pert asserted, we are "Body/Mind" (1997). All of our systems—chemical, hormonal, electrical, and psychological—are inextricably linked. The goal of treatment is to regain the optimal functioning of all of these components of your being. In some cases medications can facilitate that process, but medication alone may not create the change you want.

Many of my clients are reluctant to consider medication as part of their treatment. They say some version of, "I don't even like to take an aspirin. I don't want to take anything that could affect my brain!" Cautious and somewhat pessimistic, they also worry about possible side effects. These are valid concerns.

All medications have their pros and cons: all have some side effects, although they are often minimal and easily tolerated. No medication suits everyone, and because each person responds differently, it often takes some trial and error to find the medication or combination of medications and dosages that works best for you. Nevertheless, I encourage my clients to keep an open mind about meds. Even if you are apprehensive about incorporating medication into your treatment plan, I suggest that you and your therapist have a conversation about it. Your therapist can help you explore the ways medication might or might not enhance your treatment.

The first step in considering whether to include meds in treatment is to understand what meds can and cannot do. Medications *can* help your system by altering the way that your brain processes certain neurochemicals, which can help you be less prone to heightened anxiety. In the short term, some of the fast-acting meds can also lessen immediate feelings of panic. Medications *cannot* teach the coping strategies and skills that will help you overcome your anxiety in the long run. When used wisely, medications can help enhance your treatment, but they are not, in and of themselves, a cure.

Types of Medications

Today many types of medications are used both individually and in combination with one another to help treat anxiety disorders. Of course, some types of medications treat a disorder better than other types. Because of this, some medications are lumped into a "first choice" (first-line) category, and others into a "second choice" (second-line) category for the treatment of each disorder. First-line medications can be used in combination with one another or independently. Often if a particular first-line medication doesn't work adequately for you, your doctor will try either replacing it with another first-line medication or adding another medication from the same category. If the first-line medications still do not yield adequate results, your doctor will then often switch you to a second-line medication, or add a second-line medication to enhance, or augment, the first-line med.

Although first-line and second-line medications differ with each particular anxiety disorder, first-line medications for anxiety disorders are generally antidepressants, benzodiazepines, and buspirone (Buspar). Second-line medications for anxiety disorders include anticonvulsants, beta blockers, and second-generation antipsychotics. For a more detailed list of the types of medications used to treat each disorder, you can reference the chart presented later in this chapter (see page 187), but for now we will begin with a broader explanation of the types of medications used.

First-Line Medications

Antidepressants

Don't let the name fool you: antidepressants can treat anxiety as well as depression. In fact, only 50% of the antidepressants prescribed in the U.S. are prescribed for depression. The rest are used to treat a variety of symptoms. Antidepressants are thought to reduce various symptoms of anxiety by altering the way specific neurotransmitters, or chemical messengers, work in the brain.

Antidepressants work slowly over time to make your system less likely to fall into heightened states of anxiety. The length of your medication treatment will vary, but usually antidepressant treatment lasts anywhere from a few months to a few years.

The antidepressants commonly used to treat anxiety include SSRIs (selective serotonin reuptake inhibitors), SNRIs (serotonin and norepinephrine reuptake inhibitors), NaSSAs (noradrenergic/specific serotonergic antidepressants), and tricyclics. Less commonly prescribed are MAOIs (monoamine oxidase inhibitors) due to negative interactions with certain other medications and foods. Not all antidepressants are considered first-line treatments for anxiety disorders. For example, trazodone, an antidepressant that does not fall into any of the abovementioned categories, is used as a second-line treatment for panic disorder and generalized anxiety disorder. Later in this chapter I'll delineate which types of antidepressants work for which disorders. First, I'll explain each of the five types of antide-pressants.

1. SSRIs

Some of the most widely known and prescribed antidepressants on the market today are called selective serotonin reuptake inhibitors, or SSRIs. You are probably familiar with the brand names Prozac (fluoxetine), Zoloft (sertraline), Lexapro (escitalopram), Paxil (paroxetine), and Celexa (citalopram), just to name a few.

SSRIs work by increasing the amount of serotonin (a neurotransmitter) that is available for your brain to use. This is helpful because chronic anxiety has been linked to a deficiency in the brain's ability to utilize serotonin. Common side effects associated with SSRIs include weight gain, diminished sexual drive, drowsiness, and nausea or other gastrointestinal upsets. However, sometimes side effects such as nausea and gastrointestinal upsets will diminish after several weeks of treatment.

2. SNRIs

Serotonin and norepinephrine reuptake inhibitors (SNRIs) not only increase levels of serotonin in your brain (like SSRIs), but also increase levels of norepinephrine. Both of these neurotransmitters are believed to be out of balance when symptoms of either depression or anxiety occur. Three of the most common SNRIs are: venlafaxine (Effexor), duloxetine hydrochloride (Cymbalta), and the new kid on the block, desvenlafaxine (Pristiq), a version of Effexor. All of these have been effective in the treatment of generalized anxiety disorder. There are also reports that they may be helpful in the treatment of panic disorder and social anxiety disorder. Side effects typically associated with SNRIs include nausea, weight loss, headaches, drowsiness, dizziness, nervousness, and insomnia.

3. NaSSAs

NaSSAs, or noradrenergic and selective serotonergic antidepressants, also work on two neurotransmitters. Mirtazapine (Remeron) is a NaSSA that, like the other antidepressants discussed in this section, is helpful with anxiety disorders as well as depression—in fact, mirtazapine is the only NaSSA that is typically used in the treatment of both anxiety and depression. It reduces insomnia, a complaint that often goes with being anxious, but the downside to that benefit is that it might make you feel tired during the day. In addition, some clients on Remeron complain that they are hungrier on the medication (a side effect of several of the other antidepressants as well). Despite the side effects, I have seen Remeron help people when other meds were unsuccessful.

4. Tricyclics

Formerly the gold standard for the treatment of anxiety disorders, tricyclics, such as imipramine (Tofranil), are now prescribed less frequently than the newer SSRIs and SNRIs. This decreased use of tricyclics has more to do with side effects than with effectiveness. Dry mouth, urinary retention, constipation, and increased sweating are common with tricyclics, so they are tolerated less easily than newer drugs. On the plus side, however, the tricyclics generally have fewer sexual side effects than do SSRIs.

Tricyclic drugs effective for panic disorder include nortriptyline (Pamelor), desipramine (Norpramin), and clomipramine hydrochloride (Anafranil). Anafranil is also effective in treating obsessive–compulsive disorder.

5. MAOIs

MAOIs, or monoamine oxidase inhibitors, are seldom used due to their tendency to interact negatively with some other drugs and with certain foods that contain the naturally occurring compound *tyramine*. If you are taking a MAOI, you cannot eat most fermented or aged foods such as some cheeses, wines, or vinegars, and some aged, smoked, or marinated meats. A handful of medications (including other antidepressants, antihistamines, asthma medications, and some pain killers) interact negatively with MAOIs as well. Because antidepressants without those side effects have been recently developed, MAOIs are often prescribed only after the newer types of antidepressants have been tried without success. Side effects often associated with MAOIs include dizziness, orthostatic hypotension (dizziness due to a drop in blood pressure when going from sitting to standing), dry mouth, and constipation.

Antidepressants: Pros and Cons

Antidepressants can be very helpful in stabilizing your nervous system on a long-term basis, which reduces some of the chronic symptoms of anxiety. Most people are able to find at least one type of antidepressant that they can take without notable side effects.

While antidepressants usually bring about comprehensive change, you won't notice the benefits, on average, for two to four weeks after you start taking it. For some people it can take as long as eight weeks. Of course, the time between beginning the medication and experiencing its benefits varies by medication and individual. For example, the SSRI Lexapro and the SNRI Cymbalta can take as little as two weeks to begin working, while the full benefit of Paxil (an SSRI) may take up to six weeks to be felt. Due to this often-significant time lag, some doctors prescribe benzodiazepines (discussed below) to ease panic attacks or sudden heightened anxiety in the short-term.

What is more, while the beneficial effects of antidepressants take several weeks or more to kick in, the side effects (if any) may crop up more quickly. Some common side-effects include an increase in appetite and sleepiness and a decrease in concentration and sex drive. Increased levels of anxiety occasionally result, strange as it sounds. If this occurs, your doctor will probably switch you to a different antidepressant or a different type of medication altogether.

Antidepressants may also leave you feeling a little apathetic. One of my colleagues calls them "dimmer switches." While you are less likely to have spikes of anxiety, you are also less likely to feel excited about events in your life, such as a loved one's birthday party or a romantic evening with your partner. If needed, the "dimming" effect can often be reduced by lowering the dosage of the antidepressant.

Each medication affects everyone differently, so the side effects you experience and your ability to tolerate them can't be predictable. This is why finding the right antidepressant may take some time and adjustments. Unless the immediate side effects significantly impact your quality of life, I suggest that you give a medication time to take effect before you decide whether to discontinue it. I often tell my clients not to give up one minute before the miracle.

Benzodiazepines

Unlike antidepressants, benzodiazepines are fast acting, reducing your anxiety symptoms almost immediately after you take them. They help to relieve anxiety by slowing down the central nervous system. This makes them ideal to have on hand if you experience panic attacks or if you know your anxiety will spike in a specific situation. They include alprazolam (Xanax), lorazepam (Ativan), diazepam (Valium), chlordiazepoxide (Librium), and clonazepam (Klonapin). Benzodiazepines are especially helpful in the initial stages of your treatment, before you've learned how to control your anxiety symptoms. This can reduce your anticipatory anxieties and decrease your avoidance of certain situations and environments. Think of them as a Band-Aid rather than a preventative. Antidepressants and therapy are far more comprehensive treatment options, with longer-term effects.

Benzodiazepines: Pros and Cons

Benzodiazepines are ideal if you have just begun taking an antidepressant for your anxiety and are still waiting for the anxiety-reducing effects of the antidepressant to kick in. Remember, the antidepressants that you take on a daily basis often take two to four weeks to begin to reduce your levels of anxiety. Even if you would rather avoid using benzodiazepines, you might want to consider their use initially and then taper off of them when your antidepressant begins to take effect.

No medication is perfect. Benzodiazepines might make you feel drowsy and can be dangerous when combined with alcohol. More importantly, they are habit forming to varying degrees. You are more likely to become dependent on the short-acting, quickly metabolized benzos, such as Xanax, which stays in your body six hours, and Ativan, than the slower-acting ones, such as Klonopin and Valium, which stay in your body between 18 and 20 hours. Possibly for this very reason, an extended-release form of Xanax, called Xanax XR, is now available. It takes about 12 hours to metabolize, so your body will not go through as rapid a withdrawal as with the original Xanax.

If you have struggled with addiction in the past or currently struggle with addiction, be sure to tell your doctor, as you should avoid taking benzodiazepines. If addiction is not a problem for you, you may benefit greatly from the fast-acting effects of benzodiazepines. However, it's always wise for you and your therapist to monitor their effects to guard against overuse.

It is important to inform your clients that, as with alcohol, they need to be aware of the effect that benzodiazepines can have on their ability to safely drive. Studies have shown that the use of benzodiazepines has been linked to an increase in the risk of causing a traffic accident (Barbone et al., 1998). Barbone and colleagues also noted that elderly individuals taking benzodiazepines with long half-lives are particularly at risk.

Buspirone

Buspirone (BuSpar) is used as a first-line medication only for generalized anxiety disorder, while the other two first-line meds mentioned above are prescribed far more broadly. Buspirone is an anti-anxiety medication like the benzodiazepines, but with important differences. The chief advantage of buspirone is that there are reports that it can work as well as some benzodiazepines in calming anxiety but without the risk of dependence. However, unlike the benzodiazepines, buspirone is not fast-acting. Like the antidepressants, buspirone is taken daily rather than as needed and can take several weeks to take effect. A first-line treatment for GAD, it can also be used as a second-line treatment for obsessive–compulsive disorder.

Second-Line Medications

Trazodone: A Different Class of Antidepressant
Trazodone is an antidepressant in the phenylpiperazine family. It is used as a second-line treatment for generalized anxiety disorder and panic disorder. Particularly sedating, it can be especially helpful if insomnia accompanies your anxiety disorder.

Anticonvulsants
In recent years, anticonvulsants, which are typically used to prevent seizures, have been discovered to be useful in treating anxiety disorders. There are many ways that anticonvulsants work, but in general they reduce the activation of the neurons in your brain. In *The Anti-Anxiety Workbook*, psychologists Martin Antony and Peter Norton reported that the anticonvulsant gabapentin (Neurontin) has been found to be particularly helpful in the treatment of social anxiety disorder and panic disorder (2009).Likewise, pregabalin (Lyrica) has been effective in the treatment of generalized anxiety disorder.

Beta Blockers
Beta blockers work to block the body's responses to anxiety, seemingly calming the body. They help to stop the fight / flight response of the sympathetic nervous system from revving into action. This reduces sensations such as shakiness, sweating, and increased heart rate, which are associated with excessive nervous-system arousal.

Beta blockers are often given to individuals who do not have an anxiety disorder but experience performance anxiety: public speaking, performing in a concert, or taking tests. However, they are not effective as stand-alone drugs for the treatment of anxiety disorders, and thus are occasionally used in conjunction with antidepressants to enhance treatment. This is particularly the case when performance anxiety presents along with panic disorder or social anxiety disorder. The most common beta blocker used for this purpose is propranolol (Inderol).

Second-Generation Antipsychotics
Don't be scared by the name: if you are prescribed an antipsychotic for an anxiety disorder, it does not mean that you demonstrate any symptoms of

MEDICATION	GENERALIZED ANXIETY DISORDER	PANIC DISORDER	SPECIFIC DISORDERS	SOCIAL ANXIETY DISORDER	OBSESSSIVE COMPULSIVE DISORDER
MEDICATION TREATMENTS BY DISORDER					
SSRIs	1	1		1	1
SNRIs	1	1		1	2
NaSSAs	2	2			
Tricyclics	2	2			2
MAOIs		2		2	2
Benzodiazepines	1	1		1	1
Buspirone	1				1
Trazodone	2	2			
Anticonvulsants	2	2		2	
Beta Blockers				2	
Second-Generation Antipsychotics	+	+		+	+

KEY
1: used as a first-line treatment
2: used as a second-line treatment independently OR in combination with other medications
+: used as a second-line treatment ONLY in combination with other first- or second-line medications

psychosis. Second-generation antipsychotics are a broad category of medications that work to enhance brain functioning by affecting the neurotransmitters serotonin, dopamine, or both in a variety of ways. These medications are very potent and are often used in relatively small doses in combination with first-line meds. They can be used as such for the treatment of generalized anxiety disorder, panic disorder, and social anxiety disorder. Quetiapine (Seroquel) and risperidone (Risperdal) are two second-generation antipsychotics that are frequently used.

Tardive dyskinesia (TD), a serious muscular disorder, can develop with continued use of second-generation antipsychotics. Clients who develop TD experience repetitive, uncontrollable muscle movements, especially in the facial or neck and shoulder muscles. Once developed, the condition is irreversible. The risk increases the longer a client continues to take these meds. The prescribing physician will monitor your clients closely for signs that TD is developing, but it is important that you do not mistake TD symptoms for tics, especially in clients who are on antipsychotics for the treatment of OCD.

Medications for Each Anxiety Disorder

Now that you are familiar with the types of medications prescribed for anxiety disorders, the chart below illustrates the types of medication therapies that are currently used to treat the five anxiety disorders this book addresses. Just as each anxiety disorder differs, so too do medication regimens. For example, you will note that medications are not typically used to treat specific phobias. In contrast, many different possible combinations of medications are used to treat the other four anxiety disorders. With more time and research, more information about the brain mechanisms involved in each disorder will come to light, and more medications will be developed. Given the current understanding of each disorder and the current medications that exist, the following treatments are commonly used.

Do's and Don'ts When Using Medication

- Do make sure you have selected a prescribing physician with whom you can communicate easily.
- Do consider the pros and cons of seeing a general practitioner versus a psychiatrist for anti-anxiety medications. While you might already have a good working relationship with your general practitioner, psychiatrists have special training and experience in treating anxiety disorders.
- Don't be afraid to ask your psychiatrist or prescribing physician where he or she was trained, if he or she is board certified, and what his or her sub-specialty is.
- Do switch from a general practitioner to a psychiatrist for your psychotropic medications if you are not getting better.
- Do seek out recommendations for psychiatrists from trusted friends, your physician, or your therapist.
- Do let your other physicians and your pharmacist know that you are taking psychotropic medications.
- Do ask your psychotherapist and psychiatrist or prescribing physician to communicate with one another (you'll need to sign a release-of-information form for this).
- Do switch psychiatrists (or prescribing physicians) if you feel like you are not being listened to carefully. Likewise, it *is* OK to get a second opinion.

- Do be patient. It often takes several weeks before medications are effective, and up to 50% of the time, the first medication prescribed isn't the best one for you.
- Don't be too patient. Let your physician know if the drug prescribed is not working.
- Do be mindful of when you need to refill your prescription in sufficient time to avoid problems. (Some people run out of meds at times when they can't reach their doctors, so they attempt to stretch their supply by cutting back on the dosage or stop taking the medication completely for a short period of time. Not a good idea.)
- Do take the medications at the same time each day.
- Do inquire about the best time of day to take your meds in order to minimize side effects.
- Do recognize that each person is unique in their dosage needs for optimal benefits.
- Don't be afraid to call your physician between appointments if you have side effects or if the medication is not alleviating your symptoms.
- Don't stop taking your medication abruptly.
- Don't stop your meds just because you feel better and think you don't need them.
- Don't stop your medications without the guidance of your physician.
- Don't think that similar-sized dosages of different drugs are equivalent. For example, it would be easy to think that 0.5 mg of Xanax is not as strong as 10 mg of Valium. However, these two dosages have similar effects.
- Don't assume the size of the tablet is related to its potency. Some of my clients remark, "It's just a teeny little pill; it can't be very strong," or "The pill is pretty big; maybe I should just take a quarter of it." Remember, size doesn't matter.
- Do ask your psychiatrist or prescribing physician about using alcohol while you are taking your medications.
- Do tell your psychiatrist or prescribing physician about other prescribed or over-the-counter medications and supplements you are currently taking.
- Finally, in case I forgot to mention it, take your medications consistently and don't stop abruptly!

Neutraceuticals

Neutraceuticals, or natural food substances including herbs, have a medicinal effect on the body and mind. These products are purported to have benefits that can help release muscle tension, induce calmness, and relieve anxiety. Many of my clients have found that they have a significant and positive effect on their symptoms and are helpful as a complementary treatment to psychotherapy.

Neutraceuticals are found in foods, vitamins, minerals, herbs, and other food supplements, and are available in grocery stores, pharmacies, and health- and natural-food stores. They come in measured doses in the form of capsules, tablets, tinctures, oils and teas, or powders.

Neutraceuticals can be purchased without a physician's prescription. However, I strongly suggest that you consult your primary-care physician or an integrative medical or holistic physician before beginning a neutraceutical regimen. Although neutraceuticals can be highly effective, it can be challenging to determine which neutraceuticals will be of benefit to you, at what dosage, and for what length of time. Unfortunately, many primary physicians who are trained in *allopathic*, or traditional Western medicine, may not be aware of the benefits of neutraceuticals or their interactions with other medications. If you think your primary-care physician does not have sufficient expertise in this area, I advise you to work with a holistic or integrative physician. Integrative and holistic physicians combine allopathic medical approaches with complementary and alternative approaches. Ask your internist or family doctor to communicate with the integrative practitioner you consult for supplements. It is quite possible they may hold diametrically opposed viewpoints, but you have every right to ask them to consult with one another on your behalf.

In order to expand your awareness of treatment options, the following section provides a brief discussion of neutraceutical products that can be used in the treatment of anxiety. For simplicity's sake, the neutraceuticals discussed are presented in five categories: omega-3 fatty acids, amino acids, vitamins, minerals, and medicinal plants.

Omega-3 Fatty Acids

Omega-3 fatty acids have been shown to play an important role in brain functioning and normal growth and development of human beings. Although researchers haven't discovered exactly how they reduce symptoms of anxiety, research does suggest a link between a deficiency of certain fatty acids and anxiety (Ross, 2009).

One way to get omega-3 fatty acids is to eat plenty of fish, especially cold-water salmon, halibut, mackerel, tuna, sardines, and other deep-sea fish. Flax seeds, soybeans, pumpkin seeds, and walnuts are also a rich source, as are avocados. However, because most people don't eat enough fish, it's considered wise to take fish oil supplements.

Fish Oil

Fish oil is an excellent source of fatty acids. The health benefits of fish oil supplements are well documented in numerous studies throughout the world. Pure fish oil contains the omega-3 fatty acid eicosapentaenoic acid (EPA). This essential fatty acid helps to reduce the risk of cardiovascular disease and lower triglycerides (a type of fat found in the blood). Fish oil has also been found to help stabilize mood and alleviate some symptoms of depression. Because many of the medications that help treat depression have also been found to help alleviate anxiety, researchers are now hypothesizing that fish oil might have considerable benefits for individuals with anxiety disorders as well (Ross, 2009). Research is currently underway to further investigate this hypothesis.

As the benefits of fish oil appear promising, I recommend that my clients discuss with their physician the possibility of adding fish oil to their diets. Fortunately, most people tolerate fish oil well. However, if you are taking blood thinners or high dosages of aspirin, you should ask your doctor if it is safe for you to take fish oil, as omega-3 fatty acids can interfere with platelet clotting.

Amino Acids

5-HTP (5-hydroxytryptophan) and L-tryptophan
Some amino acids are the building blocks of neurotransmitters, the chemicals in your brain that play a large role in regulating your overall levels of anxiety. In order to have enough of these neurotransmitters, your body needs to have the materials necessary to synthesize them. The amino acids 5-HTP and L-tryptophan are involved in the synthesis of serotonin, one of the neurotransmitters targeted in many pharmaceutical treatments for anxiety disorders. A simple blood test can determine whether your levels of these amino acids are low. If this is the case, these two amino acids can help to bolster your body's ability to manufacture serotonin.

Theanine (Also Called L-theanine)
Theanine, an amino acid present in green tea leaves, has been found to diminish the effects of stress by increasing levels of GABA, a neurotransmitter that inhibits excitability. One study found that subjects who took theanine produced more alpha (relaxing) brain waves. The researchers speculate that theanine inhibits the excitability of some nerve cells in your brain that occurs under stress (Kimura, Ozeki, Juneja, & Ohira, 2007). A chief advantage of theanine is that, for some, it creates a calm feeling without the drowsiness associated with other anti-anxiety remedies or pharmaceuticals. It promotes relaxation in the absence of sedation. Many of my clients report that when taking theanine they feel both calm and alert.

I am sometimes asked if you can get enough theanine from green tea itself. It would be difficult. You would need to drink around four or five cups of tea a day, and even then it would be difficult to know the exact amount of theanine you were consuming. To get sufficient, consistent amounts of theanine, it is better to take theanine supplements. Another problem with attempting to obtain enough theanine through green tea is the caffeine in green tea. As we noted earlier, because caffeine exacerbates anxiety symptoms I recommend consuming as little caffeine as possible. If you do intend to obtain theanine through green tea, I suggest you make sure the tea is decaffeinated.

GABA

Another common amino acid neutraceutical is GABA (gamma amino-butyric acid). GABA reduces stress and produces relaxation. There is, however, some debate as to whether GABA, when taken orally as a neutraceutical, actually makes it to the brain to produce its anxiety-reducing effects. Proponents of GABA supplements claim it is beneficial and effective for people with an anxiety or panic disorder or some types of depression. GABA supplements are also reported to help regulate one's attention span, improve cognition, produce and enhance pleasure-activity chemicals, and help proper hormone production in the human body. The jury is still out as to the validity of these claims, however. I recommend exercising healthy skepticism regarding this particular neutraceutical.

If you do choose to try GABA, it is important to note that it can cause drowsiness. GABA can also cause an annoying tickly and itchy sensation on the face. Other reports have noted that GABA's ingestion can cause a change in one's breathing, either too fast or too slow. If you experience these side effects, GABA might not be the right neutraceutical for you.

Once again, you should recommend that your clients consult a physician when deciding whether or not to take any neutraceutical, including GABA. This is especially important if the client has a chronic medical condition, such as chronic pain; if the client is using prescribed drugs for this condition or for a mood or anxiety disorder; or if the client is pregnant, planning a pregnancy, or breastfeeding.

Vitamins

Vitamin D

Vitamin D has long been recognized as essential to calcium absorption and strong bones, overall good health, and prevention of osteoporosis in adults and rickets in children. Recent studies have discovered that Vitamin D, particularly D_3, is critically important in brain function as well. Studies have also shown that low levels of the different forms of Vitamin D are associated with a wide range of psychological disorders, including anxiety (Armstrong, Meenagh, Bickle, Lee, Curran, & Finch, 2007).

If you have an anxiety disorder it is a good idea to ask your doctor to check your vitamin D levels, particularly if you live a northern climate where exposure to sunshine, our natural source of Vitamin D, is limited.

One should know that because Vitamin D is fat soluble it is possible that using Vitamin D in high daily doses over several months' time could cause toxicity and *hypercalcemia*, high calcium level in the blood. While hypercalcemia can cause vomiting and fatigue, it is also associated with more serious conditions such as pancreatitis and kidney stones. Thus if your clients are taking Vitamin D, it is a good idea to have them inform their regular care physicians of their usage so that the physician can routinely monitor blood levels.

Vitamin B

The B vitamins are widely recognized to help fortify your body's response to stress. Vitamin B_6 and B_{12} are particularly helpful, as they are essential nutrients for maintaining a balanced nervous system. If you suffer from anxiety, taking a vitamin B complex on a daily basis is a good idea. B vitamins are necessary for the smooth functioning of your neurotransmitters. Because these vitamins work best in combination with other nutrients, I recommend that you also take a multivitamin and mineral supplement. They are best taken with food.

Inosito

Inositol, which is one of the B vitamins, has shown promising impact on the treatment of obsessive–compulsive disorders. Since OCD can be particularly challenging to treat, both with therapy and medications, this is good news. One study, conducted by Dr. Mendel Fux and his colleagues (1996), reported that not only was inositol effective in diminishing the symptoms of OCD, but that it was effective for some clients who were unable to tolerate the side effects of traditional medications (the SSRIs). Researchers have also found that inositol was effective in the treatment of panic disorder (Palatnik, Frolov, Fux, & Benjamin, 2001).

Minerals

Magnesium

Research has found that people who are chronically stressed often show deficient levels of magnesium. A study conducted by Dr. M. S. Seelig at the

University of North Carolina School of Public Health found that when magnesium levels are low, the body may produce increased amounts of adrenaline. As adrenaline is a major stress hormone, low levels of magnesium are linked to feelings of anxiety (Seelig, 1994). Thus it could be well worth your while to ask your physician to assess your magnesium levels.

Medicinal plants

Kava (also known as kava kava and piper methysticum)

Kava, a plant indigenous to the South Pacific Islands, is commonly used in supplements as a neutraceutical to treat anxiety. Since the 1950s, studies have suggested that kava is an effective anti-anxiety remedy. It is thought to affect specific neurotransmitters that mediate anxiety. Many researchers are currently investigating the use of kava for various anxiety disorders. For example, a study by the medical school at Duke University found that kava can be used effectively to control the heart rate of clients with GAD (Watkins, Connor, & Davidson, 2001). Another study, conducted by German researchers, found that subjects taking kava had a significant reduction in their anxiety levels within one week (Kinzler, Krömer, & Lehmann, 1991).

Safety Concerns About Kava

Although kava had been evidenced to work well, there is a downside: In 2002, the US Food and Drug Administration announced that there may be a risk of liver damage associated with kava. This warning was strongly contested by some manufacturers of kava who conducted independent research in the hopes of refuting these findings. Despite contradictory claims, it is wise to be conservative. If you have liver disease or are taking other drugs that could affect your liver, kava supplements are not a good choice for you.

Valerian

Valerian, another herb, is commonly used as a treatment for insomnia and sometimes for its calming effects. You can take it in pill, capsule, or drop form; it is generally available at most health stores. Although valerian has been used to promote sleep since the second century, research currently shows that evidence for the effectiveness of valerian in treating insomnia is inconclusive. Many of my clients who have severe insomnia have stated that the use of valerian alone wasn't particularly helpful for them. However, when my clients took valerian *and* listened to an audio CD to induce sleep, they generally reported more success than when trying either sleep-induction method on its own. It is also important to note that valerian can significantly increase the sedating effects of opiates and barbiturates, so I would not recommend taking both simultaneously.

Bach Flower Remedies (Rescue Remedy)

Rescue Remedy is the best known of the popular Bach Flower Remedies. These infusions of wild plants and flowers were developed in the 1930s by Dr. Edmund Bach, an English physician and homeopath. His remedies, available at health food stores, are used today to treat anxiety, depression, insomnia, and other emotional conditions. The remedies are said to restore the disharmony of the "spirit" by restoring the emotional, mental, and physical imbalances.

Bach Flower Remedies are natural extracts of flowers commonly considered effective for a variety of emotional difficulties, including anxiety and panic. A few drops of an extract can be put directly on the tongue or mixed with a cup of water and sipped. The remedies have no known negative side effects and cannot lead to over-dosing. My clients have often used Bach Flower Remedies as they would a benzodiazepine, because they are fast acting and keep one alert and calm. This neutraceutical can be easily carried in a purse or pocket and dropped onto the tongue as needed.

Passionflower (Passiflora incarnata)

Passionflower is another plant-based neutraceutical commonly used for its anti-anxiety effects. The ancient Aztecs reportedly used passionflower as a sedative (a tranquilizing relaxant) and pain reliever. Today, herbalists continue to recommend its use to counter feelings of restlessness, heart palpitations, and muscular tension. It can also help if your restlessness causes you to have difficulty falling asleep. It is especially helpful for use as a relaxant because it calms without also affecting rates of respiration or clouding mental functioning the way many prescription sedatives do.

Cautions and Concerns

It is important to remember that although neutraceuticals are natural, they need to be taken with care. I have found that many of my clients are less reluctant to take neutraceuticals than pharmaceuticals because they are "natural" and perceived as less invasive. However, just because neutraceuticals are "natural," it does not mean that they are necessarily benign. If something is powerful enough to have a positive effect on your body, it is also powerful enough to cause some unwanted reactions. As you have now learned, many of the neutraceuticals have side effects. In addition, some neutraceuticals do not mix with prescribed or even over-the-counter drugs. An adverse reaction can cause illness or in some cases a medical emergency.

Reportedly, between 60% and 70% of clients do not mention the supplements they are taking to their physicians (National Center for Health Statistics, 2003). It is important that you take the initiative in inquiring as to the various neutraceuti-cals your clients might be consuming, as this can be a factor that influences an accurate assessment of a client's symptomatology. Specifically, some neutraceuti-cals can actually generate physiological symptoms of anxiety that you might oth-erwise mistake as organic. For example, common herbs such as guarana, yohimbine, and ginseng can be stimulants and increase anxiety, causing nervous-ness and even insomnia. Valerian, kava, and St. John's wort will increase sedation when combined with alcohol. Other herbs can lower glucose levels (which can lead to a release of cortisol), including bilberry and garlic. Ginkgo biloba can cause racing heart and restlessness.

Since many of your clients are already taking neutraceuticals or might express interest in taking this route, you might consider further educating yourself about the benefits and risks of neutraceuticals. I also recommend that you establish working relationships with integrative and complementary medical physicians and naturopathic and holistic health practitioners. For suggestions of further resources, you can consult the Appendix of this book.

Neutraceuticals are not tested or approved by the Food and Drug Admin-istration (FDA) because they are classified as a food or food substance. Therefore they are not subject to rigorous testing as are "approved drugs" for human use. The FDA demands exhaustive testing and clinical trials for drugs and issues strict controls on quality for purity. Because there isn't any regulation for neutraceuticals, the ingredients and quality of ingredients in different brands of the same supplement can vary quite a bit, despite what is stated on the bottles.

Advertisers also make unscrupulous claims about the power of particu-lar neutraceuticals to relieve pain, boost energy—even to avert cancer. Although these are seductive and alluring, they are not easily verified. Some studies of some supplements indicate that little is known about their effec-tiveness, optimal dosage, side effects, or interactions with medications.

I cannot emphasize enough the importance of obtaining sound and trusted advice and guidance from credible practitioners. Many neutraceu-ticals are highly effective and safe—*when they are taken as directed*. Make sure you do your homework to educate yourself about anything that you are thinking of taking. It is up to you to learn about neutraceuticals and consult with your physician and pharmacist regarding their appropriate use (especially if you are also taking other medications). And remember that information on the Internet can be inaccurate or slanted. Just as you shouldn't be swept away by advertisements for every antidepressant or acid-reflux medication, don't be misled by all the hype about some neu-traceuticals. Look for credible articles by professionals. If the people writing the articles are also selling the supplement, be wary. Further, check out the up-to-date research that is available on the National Institute of Health and Federal Drug Administration Web sites. (See Appendix for a listing of additional resources).

Final Thoughts

This chapter has presented a vast array of information on the medication and neutraceutical options that can be incorporated into the treatment of your anxiety disorder. Just as there are many different ways to treat an anxiety disorder with psychotherapy, there are many different treatment regimens with medications and neutraceuticals. The good news is that you and your treatment team of therapist, doctor, and pharmacist have a lot of choices and can work together to find the options that are best suited to you.

The jury is still out as to what treatment methods work the "best" for any given anxiety disorder. Because research will always come up with new findings, I doubt there will ever be a definitive answer to this question. But scientific research continues, and clinicians in the field also continue to customize combinations of therapy, medications, and neutraceuticals every day. My hope for you is that you are willing to explore the many different possibilities recommended to you by your therapist and other doctors, and that this process can become an empowering element of your recovery from your anxiety disorder.

CHAPTER 11

A Healthy Lifestyle:
Exercise and Diet

Embracing a healthy exercise regimen and diet is important for everyone, but it is especially vital if you have an anxiety disorder. Exercise and good nutrition provide a solid foundation upon which you can begin to recover from your anxiety. Although much of Western medicine has long operated on the assumption that the mind and the body function as two largely separate entities, research findings in the fields of holistic health and neuroscience have long since confirmed that the mind and the body function synergistically, as one. What happens in the mind, such as extreme worry, cannot be divorced from the body; what happens in the body, such as low blood sugar, cannot be divorced from the mind. If you want to recover from an anxiety disorder, don't just treat your thoughts—treat your entire *self*.

Many of my former clients have told me that the self-care they learned during treatment for their anxiety disorders developed into a healthy lifestyle that they maintained even after their recovery. They discovered the payoff of regular exercise, a healthy diet, regulating stress, and a good night's sleep. For example, one of my clients began to take yoga classes on my recommendation. A busy mother of three little girls, she said it was the first time in 10 years that she regularly took any time out for herself. She found it so relaxing that she was soon practicing yoga and meditation daily and enthusiastically. She discovered that the yoga worked synergistically with many of the treatment exercises she learned in therapy with me. Her generalized anxiety disorder was soon under control, to her great delight. And within a year of starting yoga, she became certified as a yoga instructor.

You don't have to become a yoga or aerobics teacher to recover from an anxiety disorder. Simply making small changes to your lifestyle can speed your recovery. The following suggestions about exercise and diet are geared toward optimizing your functioning if you have an anxiety disorder. You'll be surprised at the unexpected benefits you experience.

The Value of Exercise

I have seen such startling benefits of exercise for my clients that I strongly encourage all people with anxiety disorders to include exercise as part of their treatment plans. Extensive research has found that aerobic exercise can help people become more resilient to stress and thus less anxious (Salmon, 2001). Pierce Howard (2000), director of research for the Center for Applied Cognitive Studies in North Carolina and author of *The Owner's Manual for the Brain,* described this effect of exercise on stress by explaining that exercise helps the body get rid of the excess cortisol (a stress hormone) that builds up in the body in response to stress. Studies have also shown that the increase in body temperature that occurs during exercise is linked to increased calmness.

Studies have also found that aerobic exercise regimens can help decrease levels of depression in individuals suffering from depressive disorders (Dunn, Trivedi, Kampert, Clark, & Chambliss, 2005). It is hypothesized that this research could apply to people with anxiety as well since depression and anxiety are closely connected, involving similar imbalances in neurotransmission and disruptions in neural circuitry.

An article published by the Academy of Psychosomatic Medicine warned that some people with anxiety disorders experience greatly increased anxiety due to exercise. The authors write, "Many people with anxiety disorders are somaticizers and hypervigilant to any physiological changes observed. Exercise can be particularly challenging for some who misinterpret physiological by-products of exercise, such as sweating and quickened breath, as signs that a panic response is underway. Particularly, some research has found that up to 30% of test subjects who had Panic Disorder displayed exercise sensitivity" (Cameron & Hudson, 1986, p. 720).

More recent research has not supported these findings, however. A joint study at the Universities of Georgia and Wisconsin (Smith & O'Connor, 2003) found that even when done intensely, exercise did not initiate panic attacks among people diagnosed with panic disorders. Other studies have found that aerobic exercise is more effective in the treatment of panic disorder than a placebo (Broocks et al., 1998).

While the jury is still out regarding exercise sensitivity and especially its association with panic disorder, it is important that clinicians be aware that it is a possibility. If exercise does heighten a client's anxiety, you can work with the client to understand the physical sensations caused by exercise and the possible misinterpretations informing the panic response. Likewise, as your own understanding of exercise sensitivity increases, you will both be able to address the fear response and identify types of aerobic exertion that might be less antagonistic and more suitable.

Exercise Compliance

Knowing exercise is good for us and actually exercising are two different things. I've heard all the excuses for not exercising: "I'm just too busy." "I have to be at work at 7:00 A.M. and I just can't get up any earlier." "I'm too tired to exercise when I get home." "I'm just not an exerciser, never have been." It's true that most people are so busy with competing work and family demands that many non-essentials fall by the wayside. However, you *can* get in a workout that can help decrease your anxiety levels in 30 minutes or less.

Sometimes your anxiety disorder itself might appear to be a roadblock to committing to daily exercise. Common concerns include: having a panic attack while you are exercising, being exposed to too many germs on public exercise equipment or in public exercise facilities, and exercising where people might see you. For all of these concerns, there are solutions. I encourage you to address them with your therapist and to begin viewing exercise as an essential component of your anxiety treatment. To help my clients develop an exercise plan, I walk them through the process below.

Exercise Plan for Beginners

1. Check with your doctor to make sure that you can start an exercise program.

2. Find a type of exercise that you enjoy, such as walking briskly, jogging, climbing stairs, bike riding, or swimming laps. Many people find it more convenient to purchase an exercise machine and exercise at home or to exercise at home using an exercise DVD. This can be an especially good initial solution for you if you have social anxiety disorder, obsessions, compulsions, or specific phobias. On the other hand, you might discover that the camaraderie that you can develop at a gym reinforces your commitment to exercise.

3. Find a time that you can devote to daily exercise, one you are most likely to stick with faithfully. I recommend exercising in the morning, if possible, because it's less likely you'll be distracted by other demands at that time of day. However, if you know that an exer-

cise time slot in the afternoon or evening will work best for you, by all means plan that into your schedule instead.

4. Try interval training. This approach to exercise alternates short spurts of moderate-intensity aerobic exercise with periods of high-intensity exercise. There is increasing evidence that interval training provides an effective and efficient mode of exercise. Research conducted at the University of Missouri, Columbia, found that high-intensity exercise is more beneficial than low- or moderate-intensity activity for reducing anxiety levels (Thomas, Hinton, Donahue, & Cox, 2004). Subjects who engaged in high-intensity exercise felt a significantly higher reduction in anxiety between 30 and 90 minutes after they finished exercising. After consulting your physician to make sure that a workout incorporating high-intensity exercise is appropriate for you, you can begin with the following simple routine (using indoor aerobic exercise equipment or outdoor equivalent).

Step 1: *Warm-up* (4–5 minutes). Start your exercise session at the intensity of a casual walk. For example, when I exercise on the treadmill, I usually start by walking at 2.7 or 2.8 miles per hour. Increase the intensity slightly toward the end of the warm-up, getting up to the pace of a brisk walk. At this pace you'd still be able to carry on a conversation without needing to interrupt your speech to catch or regulate your breath.

Step 2: *Interval exercise* (7–8 minutes, increasing to 15 as you acclimate to the workout). Alternate one minute of high-intensity exercise (equivalent to a brisk run) with one minute of low-intensity exercise (equivalent to a brisk walk). Once you are comfortable with that, increase each interval to two minutes and eventually to four minutes, alternating intense pushes with slower movement. For the high-intensity exercise, think about the pace you'd choose if you were trying to catch a bus that was pulling away from the curb. You want to push yourself hard enough to break a sweat.

Step 3: *Cool-down* (3–5 minutes). Exercise at the same intensity as the warm-up (casual walk) and gradually decrease the intensity toward the end of the cool-down.

5. Exercise for 30 minutes, 6 days a week. Although it is optimal to exercise at least 30 minutes, on those days when you just can't get it in, don't skip your workout altogether. Instead, commit to doing a partial workout. Even seven minutes on the treadmill or running up and down the stairs will be beneficial and will reinforce your exercise habit.

The following are strategies that can help you stay in the habit of daily exercise:

- Before you go to sleep at night, visualize yourself doing your daily workout the following day. You can also incorporate self-hypnosis (see Chapter 4) to enhance the visualization.
- Having an exercise partner helps you stick with your exercise routine. See if you can get a friend or your spouse to join you on a brisk morning walk or at the gym.
- Books on tape prevent boredom as you work out; lively music on a headset helps you keep up your exercise intensity.
- There are excellent, free exercise programs on cable TV, as well as some online in audio format that you can down load to an MP3 player and take with you. Simply search online or go to iTunes.com to find interval-training exercise routines. In addition, YouTube.com offers exercise routines, as do a variety of exercise "apps" available on smart phones.
- If you have the time and money, a personal trainer can also get you motivated and committed to maintaining a consist ent exercise regimen.
- Write down your exercise appointment with yourself in your calendar.
- Set an alarm on your cell phone or PDA to remind you when it is time to exercise.
- Log your progress in a notebook.

6. When possible, also exercise following stressful incidents or anxiety reactions. The exercise helps deplete the excessive levels of cortisol released during the stress.

While aerobic exercise is important to health and a quick way to decrease your levels of anxiety, it is not for everyone. Some of my clients also find much benefit from attending yoga classes or doing yoga independently or with a group of friends. Like yoga in many ways, Tai Chi and Qi Gong also provide slow, focused, meditative movement that calms the body and mind.

Yoga
People often think of yoga as the physical postures that are part of traditional Hatha Yoga. However, yoga also includes training in breathing, meditation,

and mindfulness, all of which help you relax, focus, and release tension.

Some of my clients have found a regular practice of yoga to be the perfect complement to psychotherapy treatment of their anxiety disorders. They report that they feel less anxious and more resilient to stress. Research has also shown the positive effect of a yoga practice on anxiety, particularly obsessive–compulsive disorder (Kirkwood, Rampes, Tuffrey, Richardson, & Pilkington, 2005). There is also evidence that yoga helps increase heart rate variability, an indicator of the body's ability to respond to stress more flexibly.

Sleep!

Amidst all this talk of *action,* it is important not to overlook the role of sleep in relieving anxiety. As you sleep, your body is carrying out important restorative functions. Getting enough sleep and maintaining a consistent sleep cycle or regimen is vital for your physical and psychological health. When you have an anxiety disorder, it is even more important to get sufficient sleep every night.

Unfortunately, as we discussed in Chapter 3, anxiety can make it hard to sleep, and insufficient sleep can bring about anxiety. The average person needs about 8 hours of sleep each night in order to function optimally. Even if you don't have an anxiety disorder, insufficient sleep can leave you irritable and emotionally reactive. If you have an anxiety disorder, your system is already taxed by your worries and fears. The last thing you need is the irritability and heightened emotional reactivity that comes with sleep deprivation. Sleep deprivation simply fans the flames of an already-burning fire—in this case, your anxiety.

If you are anxious, your system is running on high alert. It can be very hard to gear down at night and calm your system to the point that you can easily fall asleep. Thus many people with anxiety disorders also experience primary insomnia: extreme difficulty falling asleep. For others, falling asleep is not a problem, but staying asleep is. This is called secondary insomnia, when you wake frequently during the night or wake early in the morning and cannot fall back into sleep. In all of these instances, you are losing the precious sleep that your system needs to function optimally.

Many of us carry a great deal of sleep debt because our hectic lives lead to stress and insomnia. Fortunately, there are many things that can be done to better our sleep hygiene and get the sleep we need. Adhering to the following suggestions can help us all sleep better:

- *Keep to a sleep schedule.* Your body's circadian rhythm helps regulate your sleep cycle. However, it can only work if you maintain a more or less consistent sleep schedule. Depriving yourself of a steady sleep schedule is akin to depriving an international traveler of a permanent home. Your body is consistently searching for a "time zone" so that it can regulate itself, and you are constantly experiencing the fatigue, irritability, and higher levels of emotional reactivity that come along with this exhaustion.

- *Avoid lengthy naps.* Long naps during the day can also disrupt your circadian rhythm, especially if you are trying to make up for lost sleep the night before. Do not nap for longer than 25–30 minutes.
- *Avoid alcohol before going to bed.* While alcohol is a depressant and can induce sleep when first consumed, it has a stimulative effect while it metabolizes. In the next section, on diet, I recommend that you rarely drink alcohol at all if you have an anxiety disorder. If you do, however, I strongly suggest that you do not drink during the 4–6 hours before you plan to go to sleep.
- *Avoid late-night caffeine.* I recommend that you significantly curtail your caffeine intake if you have an anxiety disorder. Caffeine is a stimulant that can increase anxiety. It also takes about 6 hours for half of the caffeine you ingest to leave your system. Thus even a mid-afternoon coffee can interfere with your sleep.
- *Avoid heavy, spicy, or sugary foods at or after dinner.* All of these foods can have strong physical effects that disrupt sleep.
- *Exercise, but not before bed.* Afternoon exercise greatly aids sleep. However, exercising 2 hours before bedtime can make falling asleep more difficult.
- *Create a bedtime ritual.* Bedtime rituals, like a bit of reading or doing a relaxation technique each night, help reinforce your circadian rhythm. They also can help you relax and quiet your mind for sleep. You might also find that a white-noise machine or a relaxation audio CD can do wonders in helping you fall asleep (see the Appendix for some additional audio resources such as *The Insomnia Solution*).
- *Create a sleep-friendly environment.* Temperature: keep the temperature in your bedroom between 55 and 70 degrees Fahrenheit. Optimal temperatures for sleep vary considerably with each person's comfort level and metabolism: if your metabolism burns energy more quickly, you tend to be more sensitive to heat. In general, however, simply comply with the Goldie-Locks rule: not too hot, not too cold, but just right for you.
- *Lighting:* the presence of light is a natural cue that you should be awake, so when you're going to sleep, the room should be predominately dark. If you need to have a nightlight or a bathroom light on, try to find as a dull a light as possible. Also, try to block out all light coming into your room from outside.

- **Associations:** make sure that you associate your bed with sleep and rest. Sleep experts are in agreement that beds should be used only for sleep or sex. That eliminates many other activities that are often brought into the bed, such as eating, working, talking on the phone, and checking e-mail.

Although we know that anxiety disorders often go hand-in-hand with insomnia, don't assume that anxiety is the only factor at play when an anxious client presents with insomnia. It can be helpful to ascertain whether the client is suffering from chronic pain, gastrointestinal disorders, sleep apnea, restless leg syndrome, depression, or hyperthyroidism, just to name a few. You might consider referring your client to a sleep disorders clinic. Then your client can undergo a sleep study so that his or her sleep patterns can be more accurately monitored and possible sleep disorders can be investigated.

It is also important to consider any medications, over-the-counter or prescribed, that the client is taking, as many cold medications, asthma medications, and even some antidepressants can contribute to sleep difficulties.

The Value of a Healthy Diet

No matter how much you exercise, your system will still be stressed if your body isn't getting healthy food. Despite all the fad diets and warnings, good nutrition doesn't need to be complicated. My basic suggestions are very much like your grandmother's: eat a balanced diet, drink lots of water, don't skip meals, and eat three regular-sized or four to six smaller meals a day. If you have an anxiety disorder, this advice is especially important to follow.

As you learned in previous chapters, if you have an anxiety disorder your body is usually overly stressed. You do not want to add the additional stressor of a poor diet. In fact, eating a healthy diet is a concrete way to bolster your resilience to stress. The following discussion provides a list of tips that will help you optimize your diet. First, you need to consider the importance of stable blood-sugar levels.

Regulating Your Blood Sugar

Blood sugar provides fuel to the brain and nervous system. Maintaining a healthy level of blood sugar is essential to every person for optimal functioning. Low blood sugar can cause nervousness, shakiness, irritability, and other symptoms that mimic an anxiety or panic attack. Edmund Bourne and Lorna Garano, authors of *Coping with Anxiety* (2003), explained that when your blood-sugar levels drop, your body releases extra adrenaline and cortisol, stress hormones. The physical sensations caused by these hormones can be misinterpreted as anxiety, when, in fact, they are simply signaling that your body needs fuel in the form of a meal or a snack.

To stabilize your blood-sugar level, doctors and nutritionists recommend eliminating simple carbohydrates from your diet—what Dr. Robert Greene and Leah Feldon (2005) aptly called *hormone chaos carbs*. Simple carbohydrates are so rapidly broken down by your body that they have a roller-coaster effect on your blood-sugar levels.

Common foods that are considered simple carbohydrates include white bread, white pasta, white rice, pastries, fruit juices, sodas, processed food that contains high-fructose corn syrup, sugars (glucose, fructose, galactose, maltose, sucrose, lactose, etc.), and white flour. Be observant of your body's reaction to eating these foods: if you experience fatigue or heightened anxiety, it is likely that your sense of unease is caused by the "sugar rush," rather than an anxiety reaction. Once you know you are sensitive to "hormone chaos carbs," you can begin to replace them with vegetables and complex carbohydrates, such as whole wheat, brown rice, and nuts. Eating protein is crucial to avoiding drops in blood-sugar levels. Regular exercise also helps to maintain a healthy blood-sugar level.

Foods That Enhance Your Resilience to Anxiety

Most doctors and nutritionists recommend that people who tend toward anxiety eat foods that contain the amino acid tryptophan, such as eggs, tofu, peanuts, beans, turkey, cottage cheese, and whole grains. It's possible, although not yet proven, that foods containing tryptophan have a calming effect on the nervous system.

Complex carbohydrates can also increase levels of serotonin in the brain. Since low serotonin levels are associated with anxiety, eating balanced meals containing complex carbohydrates not only maintains blood-sugar levels, it also can help strengthen your resilience to stress. Again, eating protein is important to maintaining ideal levels of serotonin. Edmund Bourne and Lorna Garano pointed out that "the body has no way to make neurotransmitters (and serotonin in particular) without a steady supply of amino acids, which are derived from protein" (2003, p. 96).

CATS: Substances to Cut Out

Every day we hear alarms about foods that are bad for us, and these alerts change frequently. However, there is no doubt that some substances exacerbate anxiety. In her book *The 10 Best-Ever Anxiety Management Techniques* (2008), psychologist and author Margaret Wehrenberg used the acronym C.A.T.S to remind her readers to avoid caffeine, alcohol, tobacco and sweeteners.

Caffeine

Like Dr. Wehrenberg and other anxiety specialists, I encourage my clients to avoid caffeine. In our first session I always ask new clients how much caffeine they use. Some come to therapy as caffeine abstainers, often having discovered that an anxiety attack can follow on the heels of drinking coffee or tea. Others, however, are surprised to learn that their daily latte plays into their anxiety disorder.

Caffeine stimulates the central nervous system to release the stress hormone cortisol. When you ingest caffeine (in the form of coffee, tea, sodas, energy drinks, or chocolate), many physical changes occur, including increased heartbeat, rapid breathing, increased muscle tension, and heightened blood pressure. If you have an anxiety disorder (and especially if you have panic disorder), you are likely to be particularly caffeine sensitive.

Caffeine is also linked to insomnia, because it stays in your body for more than 10 hours. For the average adult, caffeine has a half-life of about 6 hours, which means that it takes about 6 hours for half of the caffeine you ingested to leave your body. So 12 hours after you've finished a cup of coffee, 25% of the caffeine is still in your body and affecting your nervous system. One cup goes a long way. Insufficient sleep increases your vulnerability to panic attacks.

While I do recommend you eliminate from your diet foods and beverages that are high in caffeine, I suggest you do so gradually to avoid unpleasant withdrawal symptoms. Wean yourself off caffeine slowly by cutting back on your intake for a few weeks. You might reduce your coffee, tea, and soft drink intake by a half-cup each day, or switch to half-caffeinated and half-decaffeinated coffee, gradually fading to decaf only. Remember, decaffeinated beverages do contain some caffeine. If you are especially sensitive, cut those out over time. You might also consider decreasing your intake of chocolate.

One explanation for caffeine's stimulant effect is that it tricks receptors in the brain into thinking it is the neurotransmitter adenosine, which helps calm the central nervous system. When caffeine takes the place of adenosine by binding to the adenosine receptors, it stops adenosine from having its calming effect on the brain and central nervous system. Thus caffeine revs the system chiefly by interfering with its ability to slow down and calm down.

Alcohol

Regardless of the specific diagnosis, people with anxiety disorders often use alcohol for its initial calming and sedating effects (I have found this particularly true with those who have social anxiety disorder, who drink alcohol to cope with social situations). What people don't realize is that as alcohol is metabolized, their anxiety is often heightened. This rebound effect often results in feelings of shakiness, agitation, and excitability, which are also symptoms of anxiety disorders. Studies suggest that the nervous system, in an attempt to maintain balance, reacts to the sedative effects of alcohol by creating a state of psychophysical arousal. In addition, the negative impact of alcohol is compounded by its high sugar content, which can create an imbalance in blood sugar. So, alcohol actually *brings about* the very symptoms of anxiety that one might be trying to counter. It can also start an insidious cycle in which you drink alcohol to calm your anxiety, which causes hyperarousal, which you then try to avoid by drinking more alcohol, and so on.

Tobacco

If you're a smoker, you do something that we all need to do: you take regular breaks throughout each day during which you take deep, long breaths, inhaling slowly. This is just what the doctor ordered to combat the stress of daily life. Regrettably, in addition to the well-known detriments to health, smoking is especially harmful to people with anxiety disorders. As with alcohol, nicotine initially provides a pleasant, calming sensation, which is why many anxious people smoke. And, just like alcohol, nicotine has a backlash effect. In fact, it takes nicotine only seconds from the moment you inhale to reach your brain. Nicotine levels peak in your blood stream within about five minutes of smoking and then rapidly decline. By the time you've stubbed out your cigarette, you're already plummeting into withdrawal. Each time you smoke a cigarette, you repeat this roller-coaster-like spike and withdrawal.

If you have an anxiety disorder, these frequent ups and downs are likely to exacerbate your symptoms. The momentary relief you get from a cigarette exacts its toll by contributing to a greater sense of being on edge whenever you aren't smoking. Evidence also suggests that smoking tobacco can actually reduce the effectiveness of the prescription medications you take for anxiety (Yoshimura, Ueda, Nakamura, Eto, & Matsushita, 2002). While kicking the habit of smoking can be challenging, having an anxiety disorder gives you one more reason to quit.

Preliminary research suggests that smoking tobacco might interfere with the efficacy of treating anxiety with fluvoxamine (Luvox) and propranolol (Inderal), two commonly used SSRIs and beta blockers (Yoshimura et al., 2002). In particular, smoking increases the metabolism of Luvox and other drugs, decreasing the concentration of drugs in the blood stream and thus decreasing their effectiveness (Spigset, Carleborg, Hedenmalm, & Dahlqvist, 1995).

Sweeteners

Earlier in this chapter's discussion of maintaining optimal levels of blood sugar, I advised avoiding simple carbohydrates, which include refined sugars. Your first thought might have been to substitute sugar with artificial sweeteners. Sorry, but there's more bad news: it may be wise to stay away from artificial sweeteners, for a number of reasons. First, using artificial sweeteners may make it harder to get off the real stuff (sugar), because you are essentially tricking your brain into thinking that you are eating sweets, which bolsters your craving for sweets. Second, numerous studies show that many artificial sweeteners are harmful to nerve cells and nerve tissue (Blaylock, 1997). In his book *Excitotoxins: The Taste That Kills* (1997), neuroscientist Dr. Russell Blaylock listed the numerous detrimental effects of aspartame alone. He noted that Aspartame (in Nutrasweet, diet sodas, sugar-free chewing gum, and many other sugar-free products) has been the subject of a number of studies that link its use to dizziness, numbness, muscle spasms, insomnia, heart palpitations, breathing difficulties, and anxiety. All of these are symptoms of anxiety disorders that you may already experience and certainly don't want to worsen. Better choices for sugar-free sweeteners include stevia, xylitol, and blue agave nectar. Increasingly, these products are available at your local grocery store or health-food store.

While treatments for anxiety vary by disorder and by individual, the importance of exercise and good nutrition is universal. Creating an exercise routine and maintaining a healthful diet will help you across the board. One of my clients, a chronic worrier with generalized anxiety disorder, once told me, "Some days my morning walk is the only thing I know I'm not going to stress over. It's like that 40 minutes is a beacon for me, an anchor that sets the foundation for any harsh waters that come my way later. And for that I'm grateful." Another client who had panic disorder told me, "Once I cut down my caffeine and tried to make sure I took my lunch break on time so my blood sugar didn't plummet mid-day, I didn't notice my heart racing as much . . . and in therapy I learned that the sensation of my heart racing was what triggered most of my panic attacks. It was such a relief to see that there were some concrete things I could put into place immediately to help me get my anxiety under control." You deserve to care for your body wisely, and in doing so you can reap the benefits of exercise and diet in the forms of stress reduction and improved outlook. Even if the last thing you feel like doing is getting off the couch or eating brown rice, it's well worth putting in the effort.

Anxiety Disorders

CHAPTER 12

Practice Makes Permanent

As he sat down at the start of his session, Jerry began, "I got here early today and started flipping through the magazines you had out there in the waiting room. I get so tired of reading about celebrities. Anyway, in my quest to find something to read, I took a look at one of your therapy magazines and saw you had an article in it."

I knew Jerry was referring to the piece I had written for the *Psychotherapy Networker* called "Practice Makes Perfect: There's No Shortcut to Lasting Change" (Daitch, 2008). In the article, I talked about the importance of clients' practicing what they learn in therapy between sessions, and the need for therapists to help them stick to their practice so their treatment will be successful.

"What you wrote in that article is really true," Jerry continued. "You've gotta practice. I know I wouldn't be so much better today if I hadn't been doing the practice sessions that you gave me to do in between our meetings. I'm glad you insisted that I practice, even when I whined and complained that I was too busy. And the audio CDs you made were really helpful.

"But I think the title of the article should have been 'Practice Makes *Permanent*.' I've been practicing my fearful thinking for years, to the point that I thought my anxiety was set in stone. I think my old behaviors would have been permanent if you hadn't given me new behaviors and responses to practice *over and over and over again*. Now my new way of responding actually does feel pretty permanent. But I know that what you say is true: the gains won't stick unless I continue to practice them."

Jerry's alternative title was absolutely right. With repeated practice, just about any response or reaction, negative or positive, can seem permanent. That is how anxiety disorders become rigid and engrained.

Conversely, this explains how new, healthier patterns of response learned in therapy can bring about and solidify change. Therapists are learning from our colleagues in neuroscience that the human brain has the remarkable ability to change and rewire itself throughout life. In response to repetition, neurons can create new pathways in the brain for neural communication or rearrange existing ones, making it possible for us to continue to learn and change at any age. With repeated practice, we can retrain our brains to respond differently.

In therapy for anxiety disorders, we do this by challenging the old patterns of behavior that reinforce experiences of fear and anxiety. But successfully overriding the ingrained behaviors and reactive styles underlying anxiety disorders requires practice, and lots of it. It is my job as a therapist to guide clients through the specific steps that help make this a lasting change over the long haul. It is your job as the client to engage in this process of change in your therapist's office and between sessions. I cannot speak strongly enough about the importance of being an active participant in your therapy *every* day. Many clients think that therapeutic growth happens only in the therapy room. In fact the greatest amount of growth often happens between sessions.

We have discussed in this book many ingredients crucial to a successful integrative treatment plan: finding a therapist who is a good fit for you; communicating your needs so that your therapist can choose techniques that are best suited for you; working collaboratively as a treatment team and incorporating psychiatrists, holistic physicians, and other service-providers as your individual needs dictate; and complementing your treatment with lifestyle changes, such as altering your diet and initiating an exercise regimen. However, even the best set of therapeutic interventions and the finest integrative treatment plan will be ineffective if you view yourself as a passive recipient of therapy. It is vital that you actively pursue growth and change rather than sitting back and waiting for your therapist to change you.

One of the most fundamental ways to actively pursue therapeutic growth is by bridging the gap between your therapist's office and your everyday life. To do this, remember to follow this commandment: practice, practice, practice. Before you know it, the techniques you are practicing will become a habit and that habit will become a way of being. Lasting change begins in the therapy room, but it only takes root when you take your therapeutic techniques home with you.

Tips for Applying What You Learn

As a client, you can take many steps to hold onto the insights and changes created by therapy and apply them to daily life. Practice, as you know by now, is essential. Take advantage of your therapist's suggestions about things to do outside the session to continue your progress. What follows are strategies for therapists (and clients) taken from methods I use to ensure my clients apply what they are learning.

Tips for Therapists

Psychoeducation and the Homework Contract

In the first psychotherapy therapy session, I teach clients about the importance of homework. I explain that studies have demonstrated that a client's adherence to therapeutic homework is directly related to the success of therapy (Burns & Spangler, 2000; Coon & Thompson, 2003; and Kazantzis & Lampropoulos, 2002). For this reason I have a homework contract that I include as a condition of therapy. In fact, I tell my clients that I won't take them on if they are not willing to make an earnest attempt to follow through with assignments. Of course, with each client the type of homework will vary. For example, for a client with obsessive–compulsive disorder, the homework assignment might be to listen daily to a loop tape that we have made of her obsessive thoughts. That assignment would continue until the thoughts no longer plagued her. For a person who suffers from phobias or social anxiety disorder, an assignment might involve proceeding with the next set of trials for systematic desensitization. Or it might be committing to an exercise schedule that is maintained daily.

I give all my clients a series of soothing hypnotic/relaxation CDs such as *Dialing Down Anxiety* (see Appendix) and instruct them to listen to one daily, regardless of other assignments. Consistent daily relaxation is a key element in reversing anxiety and even in re-training the nervous system.

As therapy progresses, I often have multiple assignments for clients to practice between sessions. For example, a typical client with GAD might start the day listening to *Dialing Down Anxiety*, then exercise for 30 minutes on the treadmill, and take four mini-breaks throughout the day to practice four square breathing. If worry crops up, the client also records worried thoughts, and next to them writes more adaptive thoughts. Does all this practice take time? Yes, but not as much time as clients might think. Does it lead to mastery? Yes!

In an examination of 16 empirical studies, Scheel, Hanson, and Razzhavaikina (2004) found that homework compliance was significantly correlated with positive treatment-outcome. Even more interestingly, they also noted a positive linear correlation between a client's degree of therapeutic improvement and the amount of homework a client engaged in during the treatment process. For specific strategies to increase homework compliance, see my article "Practice Makes Perfect: There's No Shortcut To Lasting Change" (Daitch, 2008).

Modeling Persistence and Commitment

As I stated above, given each client's needs and individualized treatment plan, the types of practice, and thus homework needed, will vary considerably. What is consistent is the insistence that the practice occur. Communicate that you are committed to their success and that you will support them in following through with their homework. Not only will you individualize their homework, you will also agree upon a homework assignment in each session.

At the end of the session, I write down the assignments. I keep one copy for myself and give one to my client. Even when people say they will remember their homework assignments, they often forget. This applies to me to: if I do not write down a client's weekly homework commitment, I too forget. Despite our best intentions, both my clients and I underestimate the lapses of memory that occur as we move on with the rest of our day.

Visualization, Rehearsal of Self-Talk, and Daily Reminders To Reinforce Commitment

At the end of most sessions, have your clients visualize doing their homework assignments and practice sessions. For instance, they might relax with a few deep breaths and imagine repeating their positive, self-affirming statements whenever they are afraid or worried. Further, I might have them imagine, with vivid sensory details, the room they will use for meditation or self-hypnosis, the time of day they select, the fabric of the chair they will sit on, the light coming in the window, sounds, fragrances and any sensory ingredients that will give the image more energy. If you are comfortable using hypnotic techniques, you can incorporate post-hypnotic suggestions at the end of a hypnosis session. Linking suggestions of desired behaviors or thoughts to routinely occurring events in your client's life increases the likelihood that the suggestions will stick. For example, you might say, "As soon as you open your office door, you will automatically take a deep breath and say to yourself, 'I can handle whatever comes up today.'" I also help my clients rehearse self-talk that supports adherence to the assignment. Some clients even put automated reminders in their cell phones or PDAs or a Post-It note in their daily planner.

It is essential to show that I take this commitment to homework assignments seriously. Early in each session, I ask about the client's follow-through and experience while doing the week's homework. If I know a client is having particular difficulty adhering to the agreed-upon practice sessions, I sometimes even give the client a call or send a short e-mail just to check in and see how things are going. Sometimes this added contact, which only takes a few minutes, can make the difference in whether clients keep their commitment to practice. (Before communicating by e-mail, make sure that this form of communication is acceptable and will not pose a risk to the client's confidentiality. It's also best to keep the emails short, and to avoid sensitive issues in e-mail communications.) It is important that clients know that whether I am present with them or not, I am invested in their success, and my investment does not dissipate when they walk out of my office at the end of a session. Likewise, I expect that their commitment to growth won't dissipate when they step out of my office.

For quick reference, here is a summary of the above strategies to enhance transfer:

- Provide psychoeducation on the link between therapeutic homework and successful treatment outcome.
- Make at-home practice part of the therapy contract in the first session.
- Write down the assignments; keep one copy for yourself and give one to your client.
- In the session, direct a guided visualization in which the client sees himself practicing (be specific in seeing place, time, sounds, etc.).
- Use hypnosis to link practice sessions to inevitably occurring cues.
- Ask about compliance with the homework early in the session.
- Provide suggestions for overcoming resistance.
- Brainstorm ways to fit the practice times into their lives.
- Provide in-between-session reminders (by phone or e-mail).
- Provide a model of persistent commitment.

Celebrating Achievements

And now back to you, the client. Just as it is important that I demonstrate my commitment to my clients' growth, it is also important that you and your therapist celebrate each step taken toward recovery, no matter how small. Therapy is a process, and it's easy, at the beginning, to feel overwhelmed by the weight of all your symptoms. Naturally, you will focus on the symptoms of your anxiety disorder in therapy, but it is equally important to acknowledge and celebrate your growth *throughout* this process. Jill Bolte Taylor, a Harvard-trained neuro-anatomist who suffered a debilitating stroke, wrote of the importance of embracing growth and celebration throughout the process of recovery: ". . . for a successful recovery it was important that we focus on my ability, not my disability. I needed people to celebrate the triumphs I made every day because my success, no matter how small, inspired me" (2006, p. 117–118).

I encourage you to take pride in each small step in your recovery. Maybe you made it for two hours instead of one without engaging in a compulsive ritual. Maybe you drove to the parking lot of a shopping center that you have been avoiding for months after having had a panic attack there. Maybe you showed up to your therapy appointment rather than canceling, did 15 minutes of meditation, or listened to your practice CD as you had agreed to do. All of these are steps in the process of recovery and are worthy of your acknowledgement and celebration.

I also encourage you to expand your idea of what progress in therapy is, from just reducing your symptoms to enhancing your entire quality of life. As you are breaking free from your anxiety, what are you gaining? I often ask my clients to recount any novel experiences that might have occurred since our last session. Sara, a mother of two elementary-school-aged children, initially entered treatment with me because her constant worrying was putting a strain on her marriage. One day, a few months into her treatment for generalized anxiety disorder, she remarked that she was enjoying her children more than she ever had before. Her kids apparently noticed a difference too. Sara said, "Last Tuesday after school, Timmy asked me to come out to the backyard with him and play kickball. While we were playing, I told him I didn't think he'd ever asked me to play kickball before. He smiled at me and said, 'Well, you're a lot more fun now. It was really annoying when you used to always say *"be careful."*'" I had no idea my worrying was affecting him. I was always there watching over him. Now that I'm not so worried, we're spending time together in ways we didn't before."

Your treatment will often bring unexpected gifts. As your anxiety becomes less prevalent, there will be more room for other aspects of your life to come front and center. Most clients are delighted by these new changes and shifts.

Empowerment

The other day, my client Christie said something that I've heard throughout my years of practice. She was talking about her first-grader and said, "I'm afraid that Rachel is her mother's daughter. Her teacher told me the other day that Rachel insisted on starting her assignment over on a new sheet of paper when her eraser left a smudge on her paper. And at home she has a fit if I move any of her bathtub toys when I'm cleaning the tub. Even as a toddler, she would cry if we changed her bedtime ritual in the slightest way. She doesn't do the same OCD things that I did when I was a kid, but I can see the same tendencies in her as in me.

"So I've been teaching her some of the same things you've taught me, like how to take a deep breath and refocus when something isn't in the order that I want. Even though I'm sorry that Rachel has anxiety, I feel lucky that we're identifying it early. I even feel relieved to know that therapy is an option for her if she's still having these problems later on down the road, or if they get worse now. When I was younger, I would never have told anybody about all my obsessions and compulsions. I just tried to deal with them the best way I could. It doesn't have to be that way for Rachel. I might have given her my genes, but I don't have to pass on my old ways of coping with my obsessions. I came into therapy for my own OCD, but now, because of the ways I have learned to care for myself, I can be sensitive to Rachel's needs and pass on some of the coping strategies I've learned from you."

As a therapist, it's heartening to know that the change in my clients has a ripple effect on their children as well. Therapy can initiate a process of change that can enhance not only your own life, but the lives of your loved ones.

Many of my clients ask me early in treatment, "Is this ever *really* going to go away? Am I ever going to get my life back?" Each time I hear this question, my heart goes out to the person sitting across from me. I feel the desperation; I sense the urgent desire to lessen their suffering. I look at the person and with absolute honesty and certainty say, "I *know* that you'll get better." Many clients have told me that during the early storms of treatment, they held onto my certainty that they would recover. It helped them stay in treatment, maintain hope, and trust the process without giving up.

Someone once said, "Hope is like a bird that senses the dawn and carefully starts to sing while it is still dark." As uncertain as you may feel at the start of treatment, when it is still dark, I assure you that you will gain far more than you expect. By facing your fears in therapy, you will harness your innate wisdom and strength and tap into inner resources you never knew you had. As ironic as it may sound, some of my clients are actually grateful that they were beset by an anxiety disorder, as it propelled them into a process of change and growth that they otherwise might not have sought. As Ben, the young student with social anxiety disorder, said toward the end of his treatment, "You know, if I hadn't had an anxiety disorder, I probably wouldn't have ever considered going to therapy. But learning to get over my fears has totally changed the way I see myself. I feel more confident now and happier." Whatever challenges anxiety creates in your life, don't resign yourself to them. Be like the little bird singing before dawn and experience your own sunrise. George Patton put his finger on the rewards of your effort when he said, "Accept the challenges, so you may feel the exhilaration of victory."

Resources for Clients and Therapists

Therapeutic Modalities

The associations and institutes below can help people with anxiety disorders find referrals for clinicians with specialized training in different modalities. They also provide professional training in these specialized modalities.

Cognitive Behavioral Therapy

Association for Behavioral and Cognitive Therapies (ABCT)
Tel: 212-647-1890
Fax: 212-647-1865
Web site: http://www.abct.org

National Association of Cognitive Behavioral Therapy (NACBT)
Tel: 800-853-1135
Outside USA: 304-723-3982
Web site: http://www.nacbt.org

Beck Institute for Cognitive Therapy and Research
Tel: 610-664-3020
Fax: 610-664-4437
E-mail: beckinst@gim.net
Web site: http://www.beckinstitute.org

Albert Ellis Institute
Tel: 212-535-0822
Fax: 212-249-3582
Web site: http://www.rebt.org

Relaxation Training

Benson-Henry Institute for Mind Body Medicine
Tel: 617-643-6090
Fax: 617-643-6077
E-mail: mindbody@partners.org
Web site: http://www.mgh.harvard.edu/bhi

Mindfulness

Center for Mindfulness in Medicine, Health Care, and Society
Tel: 508-856-2656
E-mail: mindfulness@umassmed.edu
Web site: http://www.umassmed.edu/cfm/index.aspx

Acceptance and Commitment Therapy (ACT)

Association for Contextual Behavioral Science
Web site: http://contextualpsychology.org/act

Eye Movement Desensitization and Reprocessing (EMDR)

EMDR Institute
Tel: 831-761-1040
Fax: 831-761-1204
E-mail: inst@emdr.com
Web site: http://www.emdr.com

EMDR International Association
Tel: 512-451-5200
Toll Free in the US & Canada: 866-451-5200
Fax: 512-451-5256
E-mail: info@emdria.org
Web site: http://www.emdria.org

Emotional Freedom Technique (EFT)

World Center for EFT
Web site: http://www.eftuniverse.com

Hypnosis

The American Society of Clinical Hypnosis (ASCH)
Web site: http://www.asch.net

The Society of Clinical and Experimental Hypnosis (SCEH)
Web site: http://www.sceh.us

The Milton H. Erickson Foundation
Web site: http://www.erickson-foundation.org

International Society of Hypnosis (ISH)
Web site: http://www.ish-web.org

Biofeedback and Neurofeedback

The Association for Applied Psychophysiology and Biofeedback (AAPB)
Web site: http://www.aapb.org

International Society for Neurofeedback & Research (ISNR)
Web site: http://www.isnr.org

Medicine and Neutraceuticals
Pharmaceuticals

For two reliable sources of in-depth, up-to-date information on medication, I advise consulting the following online resources:

The National Institute of Mental Health
Web site: http://www.nimh.nih.gov/health/publications/mental-health-medications/what-medications-are-used-to-treat-anxiety-disorders.shtml

Anxiety Disorders Association of America
Web site: http://www.adaa.org./finding-help/treatment/medication

Neutraceuticals

American Neutraceutical Association
Web site: www.ana-jana.org

Exercise and Diet

Walter, M.D., Willett, C., Skerrett P. J. (2001). *Eat, drink, and be healthy: The Harvard Medical School guide to healthy eating.* New York, NY: Simon & Schuster.

Harvard Health Publications
Web site: http://www.health.harvard.edu

The Mayo Clinic Web site:
http://www.mayoclinic.com/health/HealthyLivingIndex/HealthyLivingIndex

Associations for Anxiety Disorders

The following associations, organizations, and foundations maintain Web sites that provide a plethora of resources and self-help suggestions.

Anxiety Disorders Association of America
Web site: http://www.adaa.org

Anxieties.com
Web site: http://www.anxieties.com

National Alliance on Mental Illness
Web site: http://www.nami.org

Social Phobia/Social Anxiety Association
Web site: http://www.socialphobia.org

Social Phobia World
Web site: http://www.socialphobiaworld.com

International OCD Foundation
Web site: http://www.ocfoundation.org

National Center for PTSD
Web site: http://www.ncptsd.va.gov

Resources for People with Anxiety Disorders
Workbooks

Antony, M. M., Craske, M. G., & Barlow, D. H., (2006). *Mastering your fears and phobias: Workbook (treatments that work)* (2nd ed.). New York, NY: Oxford.

Bourne, E. J. (1995). *The anxiety & phobia workbook* (2nd ed.). Oakland, CA: New Harbinger.

Davis, M., Eshelman, E. R., & McKay, M. (1982). *The relaxation & stress reduction workbook.* Oakland, CA: New Harbinger.

Forsyth, J. & Eifert, G. (2007). *The mindfulness & acceptance workbook for anxiety.* Oakland, CA: New Harbinger.

Hyman, B. M., & Pedrick, C. (1999). *The OCD workbook: Your guide to breaking free from obsessive-compulsive disorders.* Oakland, CA: New Harbinger.

Martin, A. & Norton, P. (2009). *The anti-anxiety workbook.* New York, NY: The Guilford Press.

Steketee, R.O. (2007). *Compulsive hoarding and acquiring (workbook).* New York, NY: Oxford.

Books

Brach, T. (2003). *Radical acceptance: Embracing your life with the heart of a Buddha.* New York, NY: Bantam Dell.

Chodron, P. (2001). *The places that scare you.* Boston, MA: Shambhala Publications.

Foa, E. B. & Wilson, R. R. (1991). *Stop obsessing!: How to overcome your obsessions and compulsions.* New York, NY: Bantam.

Kabat-Zinn, J. (1991). *Full catastrophe living.* New York, NY: Delta.

Kabat- Zinn, J. (2005). *Coming to our senses: Healing ourselves and the world through mindfulness.* New York, NY: Hyperion.

Nhat Hanh, T. (1975). *Miracle of mindfulness.* Boston, MA: Beacon Press.

Rothschild, B. (2011). *Trauma essentials: The go-to guide.* New York, NY: Norton.

Wehrenberg, M. (2008). *The 10 best-ever anxiety management techniques: Understanding how your brain makes you anxious and what you can do to change it.* New York, NY: Norton.

Wilson, R. R. (1996). *Don't panic revised edition: Taking control of anxiety attacks.* New York, NY: Harper/Perennial Library.

CD Programs

In my CD programs listed below, I use many of the treatment procedures described in this book. They are designed to be an adjunct to psychotherapeutic treatment. They also provide the practitioner with examples of hypnotic phrasing, delivery, and ambient background music.

Daitch, C. (Speaker). (2009). *Alpha/Theta Sailing II* [CD]. Farmington Hills, MI: Center for the Treatment of Anxiety Disorders.

This CD of ambient music is especially useful for clients and clinicians who are using guided imagery, progressive relaxation, or hypnosis. It is designed to assist the client to quickly move into a state conducive to the development of therapist- or self-directed experience. With repeated exposure in therapy sessions, the music becomes a cue for the client to elicit a state of relaxation.

Daitch, C. (Speaker). (2003). *Dialing down anxiety* [CD]. Farmington Hills, MI: Center for the Treatment of Anxiety Disorders.

This audio program utilizes visualization, guided imagery, and established stress and anxiety reduction techniques to counter the overreactivity that accompanies anxiety.

Daitch, C. (Speaker) & Herzog, C. (Contributor). (2010). *Mastering Test Anxiety* [CD]. Farmington Hills, MI: Mindfulness Associates.

This recording is designed to help the listener master fear and anxiety that can interfere with optimal performance on exams. It includes multiple interventions to help the listener remain calm, yet alert and focused during examinations.

Daitch, C. (Speaker) & Herzog, C. (Contributor). (2010). *Overcoming emotional eating: Breaking the cycle of stress and anxiety based eating* [CD]. Farmington Hills, MI: Mindfulness Associates.

This audio program teaches the listener to discern emotionally based cravings from real hunger. The program provides a set of tools to help the listener manage the stress, anxiety and other emotions that lead to overeating.

Daitch, C. (Speaker). (2003). *The insomnia solution* [CD]. Farmington Hills, MI: Mindfulness Associates.

This audio program guides the listener into a relaxed state and the requisite stillness of mind and body necessary for sleep. When used nightly, the listener can train his/her nervous system to elicit the appropriate level of relaxation to foster good sleep habits.

To order the audio programs above, contact:

The Center for the Treatment of Anxiety Disorders
E-mail: canxietydisorders@me.com
Web site: http://www.anxiety-treatment.com
These products can also be found at: http://anxietysolutionsonline.com

Resources for Therapists
Books

Antony, M. M., Craske, M. G., & Barlow, D. H. (2006). *Mastering your fears and phobias: Therapist guide* (2nd ed.). New York, NY: Oxford.

Antony, M. M., & Swinson, R. P. (2000). *Phobic disorders and panic in adults: A guide to assessment and treatment.* Washington, DC: American Psychological Association.

Antony, M. M., & Swinson, R. P. (2008). *The shyness and social anxiety workbook: Proven, step-by-step techniques for overcoming your fear* (2nd ed.). Oakland, CA: New Harbinger.

Barlow, D. H. (2002). *Anxiety and its disorders: The nature and treatment of anxiety and panic.* (2nd ed.). New York, NY: Guilford Press.

Craske, M. G., & Barlow, D. H. (2007). *Mastery of your anxiety and panic: Therapist guide* (4th ed.). New York, NY: Oxford.

Crozier, W. R., & Alden, L. E. (Eds.) (2005). *The essential handbook of social anxiety for clinicians.* Hoboken, NJ: Wiley.

Daitch, C. (2007). *Affect regulation toolbox: Practical and effective hypnotic interventions for the over-reactive client.* New York, NY: Norton.

Davey, G. C. L. & Wells, A. (Eds.). (2006). *Worry and its psychological disorders: Theory, assessment and treatment.* West Sussex, UK: Wiley.

Hammond, D. (1990). *Handbook of hypnotic suggestions and metaphors.* New York, NY: Norton.
(See pp. 40–41 for a list of commonly used hypnotic phrasing and language patterns. See also the audio CD programs listed above for clients. They provide many examples of hypnotic phrasing and use of voice. *Theta*

Sailing II is excellent background music to be played during hypnotic sessions.)

Havens, R. A., & Walters, C. (1989). *Hypnotherapy scripts: A neo-Ericksonian approach to persuasive healing.* New York, NY: Brunner/Mazel.

Hazlett-Stevens, H. (2008). *Psychological approaches to generalized anxiety disorder: A clinician's guide to assessment and treatment.* New York, NY: Springer.

Jongsma, A., (Ed.). (2004). *The complete anxiety treatment and homework planner.* Hoboken, NJ: Wiley.

Nejad, L., & Volny, K. (2008). *Treating stress and anxiety: A practitioner's guide to evidence-based approaches.* Bethel, CT: Crown House Publishing.

Yapko, M. D. (1990). *Trancework: An introduction to the practice of clinical hypnosis.* (2nd ed.). New York, NY: Brunner/Mazel.

Web site

PDR.net: The Physicians' Desk Reference Web site
Web site: http://www.pdr.net

References

Alexander, F., & French, T. M. (1946). *Psychoanalytic therapy: Principles and application*. New York: Ronald Press.

Antony, M. M., & Norton, P. J. (2009). *The anti-anxiety workbook*. New York, NY: Guilford Press.

American Psychiatric Association. (2000). *Diagnostic and statistical manual of mental disorders* (4th ed., text revision). Washington, DC: Author.

Armstrong, J., Meenagh, G. K., Bickle, I., Lee, A. S. H., Curran, E.-S., & Finch, M .B. (2007). Vitamin D deficiency is associated with anxiety and depression in fibromyalgia. *Clinical Rheumatology, 26*(4), 551–554.

Barabasz, A. F., & Watkins, J. G. (2005). *Hypnotherapeutic Techniques* (2nd ed.). New York: Brunner-Routledge.

Barbone, F., McMahon, A. D., Davey, P. G., Morris, A. D., Reid, I. C., McDevitt, D. G., & MacDonald, T. M. (1998). Association of road-traffic accidents with benzodiazepine use. *Lancet, 352*(9137), 1324–1325.

Barlow, D. H. (2002). *Anxiety and its disorders: The nature and treatment of anxiety and panic* (2nd ed.). New York, NY: Guilford Press.

Barlow, D. H., & Cerny, J. A. (1988). *Psychological treatment of panic*. New York, NY: Guilford Press.

Beck, A. T. (2005). The current state of cognitive therapy: A 40-year retrospective. *Archives of General Psychiatry, 62*, 953–959.

Beck, A. T., & Weishaar, M. E. (2008). Cognitive therapy. In R. J. Corsini & D. Wedding (Eds.), *Current psychotherapies* (8th ed.; pp. 263–294). Belmont, CA: Brooks/Cole (Wadsworth).

Blaylock, R. L. (1997). *Excitotoxins: The taste that kills*. Santa Fe, NM: Health Press.

Bolte Taylor, J. (2006). *My stroke of insight: A brain scientist's personal journey*. New York, NY: Penguin Group.

Bourne, E. J., & Garano, L. (2003). *Coping with anxiety: 10 simple ways to relieve anxiety, fear & worry*. Oakland, CA: New Harbinger Publications, Inc.

Broocks, A., Bandelow, B., Pekrun, G., George, A., Meyer, T., Bartmann, U., . . . Rüther, E. (1998). Comparison of aerobic exercise, clomipramine, and placebo in the treatment of panic disorder. *American Journal of Psychiatry, 155*(5), 603–609.

Brown, D. P., & Fromm, E. (1986). *Hypnotherapy and hypnoanalysis*. London: Lawrence Erlbaum Associates.

Burns, D. D., & Spangler, D. L. (2000). Does psychotherapy homework lead to improvements in depression in cognitive-behavioral therapy or does improvement lead to increased homework compliance? *Journal of Consulting and Clinical Psychology, 68*(1), 46–56.

Cameron, O. G., & Hudson, C. J. (1986). Influence of exercise on anxiety level in patients with anxiety disorders. *Psychosomatics, 27*, 720–723.

Charney, D. S., Heninger, G. R., Jatlow, P. I., (1985). Increased anxiogenic effects of caffeine in panic disorders. *Archives of General Psychiatry, 42*(3), 233–243.

Chavira, D., Stein, M., Bailey, K., & Stein, M. (2004). Co-morbidity of generalized social anxiety disorder and depression in a pediatric primary care sample. *Journal of Affective Disorders, 80*(2), 163.

Clark, D. M. (1988). A cognitive model of panic attacks. In S. Rachman & J. D. Maser (Eds.), *Panic: Psychological perspectives* (pp. 71–89). Hillsdale, NJ: Erlbaum.

Coon, D. W., & Thompson, L. W. (2003). The relationship between homework compliance and treatment outcomes among older adult outpatients with mild-to-moderate depression. *American Journal of Geriatric Psychiatry, 11*(1), 53–61.

Corrigan, K. (2008). *The middle place*. New York, NY: Hyperion.

Craske, M. G., & Barlow, D. H. (2007). *Mastery of your anxiety and panic: Therapist guide* (4th ed.). New York, NY: Oxford.

Daitch, C. (2007). *Affect regulation toolbox: Practical and effective hypnotic interventions for the over-reactive client*. New York, NY: Norton.

Daitch, C. (2008). Practice makes perfect: There's no shortcut to lasting change. *Psychotherapy Networker, 32*(5), 48–52.

Davidson, J. R., Potts, N., Richichi, E., Krishnan, R., Ford, S. M., & Smith, R. (1993). Treatment of social phobia with clonazepam and placebo. *Journal of Clinical Psychopharmacology, 13*, 423–428.

Deiker, T. E., & Pollock, D. H. (1975). Integration of hypnotic and systematic desensitization techniques as in the treatment of phobias: A case report. *American Journal of Clinical Hypnosis, 17*, 170–174.

Dunn, A. L., Trivedi, M. H., Kampert, J. B., Clark, C. G., Chambliss, H. O. (2005). Exercise treatment for depression: Efficacy and dose response. *American Journal of Preventive Medicine, 28*(1), 1–8.

Eifert, G. H., & Forsyth, J. P. (2005). *Acceptance & Commitment Therapy for anxiety disorders*. Oakland, CA: New Harbinger.

Eysenck, H. J. (Ed.). (1967). *The biological basis of personality*. Springfield, IL: Charles C. Thomas.

Erickson, M. H. (1958). Further techniques of hypnosis: Utilization techniques. *American Journal of Clinical Hypnosis,1*, 3–8.

Foa, E. B., & Wilson, R. R. (2001). *Stop obsessing!: How to overcome your obsessions and compulsions (revised edition)*. New York, NY: Bantam.

Frederick, C. & McNeal, S. (1993). From strength to strength: Inner strength with immature ego states. *American Journal of Clinical Hypnosis, 35*, 250–256.

Frederick, C., & McNeal, S. (1999). *Inner strengths: Contemporary psychotherapy and hypnosis for ego-strengthening*. Mahwah, NJ: Erlbaum.

Fux, M., Levine, J., Aviv, A., Belmaker, R. H. (1996). Inositol treatment of obsessive–compulsive disorder. *American Journal of Psychiatry 153*(9), 1219–1221.

Golan, H. (1998). Re-alerting: The technique of Harold P. Golan, D.M.D. In Hammond, D. C. (Ed.), *Hypnotic Induction & Suggestion* (p. 55). Chicago American Society of Clinical Hypnosis.

Gray, J., & McNaughton, N. (1996). The neuropsychology of anxiety: Reprise. *Nebraska Symposium on Motivation, 1995: Perspectives on anxiety, panic, and fear* (pp. 61–134). Lincoln, NE: University of Nebraska Press.

Greenberg, P. E., Sisitsky, T., Kessler, R. C., Finkelstein, S. N., Berndt, E. R., Davidson, J. R., . . . Fyer, A. J. (1999). The economic burden of anxiety disorders in the 1990s. *The Journal of Clinical Psychiatry, 60*(7), 427–435.

Greene, R. A., & Feldman, L. (2005). *Dr. Robert Greene's perfect balance: Look younger, stay sexy, and feel great*. New York, NY: Random House.

Hammond, D. (1990). *Handbook of hypnotic suggestions and metaphors*. New York, NY: Norton.

Harris, R. (2009). *ACT made simple: An easy-to-read primer on Acceptance and Commitment Therapy*. Oakland, CA: New Harbinger.

Heimberg, R. G., & Becker, R. E. (2002). *Cognitive-behavioral group therapy for Social Phobia: Basic mechanisms and clinical strategies*. New York, NY: Guilford Press.

Heimberg, R. G., Salzman, D. G., Holt, D. G., & Blendell, K. A. (1993). Cognitive-behavioral group treatment for Social Phobia: Effectiveness at five-year followup. *Cognitive Therapy and Research, 17*(4), 325–339.

Howard, P. J. (2000). *The owner's manual for the brain: Everyday applications from mind-brain research* (2nd ed.). Austin, TX: Bard Press.

Huizink, A., Robles de Medina, P., Mulder, E., Visser, G., & Buitelaar, J. (2002, September). Psychological measures of prenatal stress as predictors of infant temperament. *Journal of the American Academy of Child & Adolescent Psychiatry, 41*(9), 1078–1085.

Hyman, B. M., & Pedrick, C. (1999). *The OCD workbook: Your guide to breaking free from obsessive–compulsive disorders*. Oakland, CA: New Harbinger.

Jackson, M. (2008, April 6). In a rush? Learn to ease 'hurry sickness.' *The Boston Globe*. Retrieved from http://www.boston.com/jobs/news/articles/2008/04/06/in_a_rush_learn_to_ease_hurry_sickness

Jongsma, A., (Ed.). (2004). *The complete anxiety treatment and homework planner*. Hoboken, NJ: Wiley.

Kabat-Zinn, J. (n.d.). *Frequently asked questions*. Retrieved from http://www.mindfulnesscds.com/faq.html

Kagan, J., & Brim, O. G., (Eds.). (1980). *Constancy and change in human development*. Cambridge, MA: Harvard University Press.

Kaitz, M. & Maytal, H. (2005). Interactions between anxious mothers and their infants: An integration of theory and research findings. *Infant Mental Health Journal, 26*(6), 570–597.

Kazantzis, N. & Lampropoulos, G. K. (2002). Reflecting on homework in psychotherapy: What can we conclude from research and experience. *JCLP/In Session: Psychotherapy in Practice, 58*, 577–585.

Kessler, R. C., Chiu, W. T., Demler, O., & Walters, E. E. (2005). Prevalence, severity, and comorbidity of twelve-month DSM-IV disorders in the National Comorbidity Survey Replication (NCS-R). *Archives of General Psychiatry, 62*(6), 617–27.

Kilhstrom, J. (2003). Hypnosis and memory. In J. Byrne (Ed.), *Learning and memory: A comprehensive reference*, (2nd ed.; pp. 240242). Farmington Hills, MI: Macmillan Reference.

Kimura, K., Ozeki, M., Juneja, L. R., & Ohira, H. N. (2007). L-Theanine reduces psychological and physiological stress responses. *Biological Psychology, 74*(1), 39–45.

Kinzler, E., Krömer, J., & Lehmann, E. (1991). Effect of a special kava extract in patients with anxiety, tension, and excitation states of non-psychotic genesis: Double blind study with placebos over 4 weeks. *Arzneimittelforschung, 41*(6), 584–588.

Kirkwood, G., Rampes, R., Tuffrey, V., Richardson, J., & Pilkington, K. (2005). Yoga for anxiety: A systematic review of the research. *British Journal of Sports Medicine, 39*(12), 884–891.

Kirsch, I., Montgomery, G., & Sapirstein, G. (1995). Hypnosis as an adjunct to cognitive-behavioral psychotherapy: A meta-analysis. *Journal of Consulting & Clinical Psychology, 63*, 214–220.

Kotulak, R. (1996). *Inside the brain: Revolutionary discoveries of how the mind works*. Kansas City, MO: Andrews and McMeel.

Lake, J. (2009). Complementary, alternative, and integrative Rx: Safety issues. *Psychiatric Times, 6*(7), 22–29.

Leonardo, E. D., & Hen, R. (2006). Genetics of affective and anxiety disorders. *Annual Review of Physiology, 57*, 117–137.

Leonardo, E. D., & Hen, R. (2008). Anxiety as a developmental disorder. *Neuropsychopharmacology, 33*(1), 134–140.

Linehan, M. M. (1993). *Cognitive behavioral treatment of borderline personality disorder*. New York, NY: Guilford Press.

Middeldorp, C., Cath, D., Van Dyck, R., & Boomsma, D. (2005). The co-morbidity of anxiety and depression in the perspective of genetic epidemiology: A review of twin and family studies. *Psychological Medicine, 35*(5), 611–624.

Miller, J. J., Fletcher, K., & Kabat-Zinn, J. (1995). Three-year follow-up and clinical implications of a mindfulness meditation-based stress reduction intervention in the treatment of anxiety disorders. *General Hospital Psychiatry, 17*(3), 192–200.

Moran, K. (2003). Mindfulness & compassion: The practice of awareness. *Alternatives Magazine, 27*. Retrieved from http://www.alternativesmagazine.com/27/moran.html

Munjack, D. J., Baltazar, P. L., Bohn, P. B., Cabe, D. D., & Appleton, A. A. (1990). Clonazepam in the treatment of social phobia: A pilot study. *Journal of Clinical Psychiatry, 51*, 35–40.

Murray-Jobsis, J. (1996). Hypnosis with a borderline patient. In I. Kirsch, S. Lynn, & J. Rhue (Eds.), *Casebook of clinical hypnosis* (pp. 173–192). Washington, DC: American Psychological Association.

National Center for Health Statistics. (2003). *2002 National Health Interview Survey (NHIS) Public Use Data Release*. Hyattsville, MD: US Dept of Health and Human Services, Centers for Disease Control and Prevention, National Center for Health Statistics.

National Institute of Health. (2009). Dietary supplement fact sheet: Vitamin D. Retrieved from http://ods.od.nih.gov/factsheets/vitamind.asp

Palatnik, A., Frolov, K., Fux, M., & Benjamin J. (2001). Double-blind, controlled, crossover trial of inositol versus fluvoxamine for the treatment of Panic Disorder. *Journal of Clinical Psychopharmacology, 21*(3), 335–339.

Pert, C. B. (1997). *Molecules of emotion: The science behind mind-body medicine*. New York, NY: Touchstone.

Rechtshaffen, S. (1996). *Time shifting: A revolutionary new approach to creating more time for your life*. New York, NY: Doubleday.

Rizzolatti, G. (2005). The mirror neuron system and its function in humans. *Anatomy and embryology, 210*, 419–421.

Roiphe, A. (1999). *1185 Park Avenue: A memoir*. New York, NY: Touchstone.

Ross, B. M. (2009). Omega-3 polyunsaturated fatty acids and anxiety disorders. *Prostaglandins, Leukotrienes, and Essential Fatty Acids, 81*(5–6), 309–312.

Rossi, E. L. (Ed.). (1980). *Collected papers of Milton H. Erickson* (vols. 1–4). New York, NY: Irvington.

Salmon, P. (2001). Effects of physical exercise on anxiety, depression, and sensitivity to stress: A unifying theory. *Clinical Psychology Review February 21*(1), 33–61.

Sanderson, W. C., DiNardo, P. A., Rapee, R. M., & Barlow, D. H. (1990). Syndrome comorbidity in patients diagnosed with a DSM III-R anxiety disorder. *Journal of Abnormal Psychology, 99*, 308–312.

Scheel, M., Hanson, W., & Razzhavaikina, T. (2004). The process of recommending homework in psychotherapy: A review of therapist delivery methods, client acceptability, and factors that affect compliance. *Psychotherapy: Theory, Research, Practice, Training, 41*(1), 38–55.

Schoenberger, N. E. (2000). Research on hypnosis as an adjunct to cognitive behavioral psychotherapy. *International Journal of Clinical and Experimental Hypnosis, 48*, 154–169.

Schore, A. N. (2003). *Affect regulation and the origin of the self: The neurobiology of emotional development.* New York, NY: Norton.

Schwartz, J. M. (with Beyette, B.). (1996). *Brain lock: Free yourself from obsessive–compulsive behavior.* New York, NY: HarperCollins.

Seelig, M. S. (1994). Consequences of magnesium deficiency enhancement of stress reactions; Preventative and therapeutic applications. *Journal of American College of Nutrition, 13*(5), 429–446.

Seger, B. (1980). Against the wind [B. Seger and the Silver Bullet Band]. On *Against the wind* [cassette]. Hollywood, CA: Capitol.

Siegel, D. J. (1999). *The developing mind: Toward a neurobiology of interpersonal experience.* New York, NY: Guilford Press.

Smith, J. C. & O'Connor, P. J. (2003). Physical activity does not disturb the measurement of startle and corrugator responses during affective picture viewing. *Biological Psychology, 63*(3), 293–310.

Spigset, O., Carleborg, L., Hedenmalm, K., & Dahlqvist, R. (1995). Effect of cigarette smoking on fluvoxamine pharmacokinetics in humans. *Clinical Pharmacology & Therapeutics, 58*(4), 399–403.

Thomas, T. R., Hinton, P. S., Donahue, O. M., & Cox, R. H. (2004). Effects of acute 60 and 80% VO$_2$max bouts of aerobic exercise on state anxiety of women of different age groups across time. *Research Quarterly for Exercise and Sport, 75*(2), 165–175.

Veale, D. (2003). Treatment of Social Phobia. *Advances in Psychiatric Treatment, 9*, 258–264.

Wadhwa, P. (2005). Psychoneuroendocrine processes in human pregnancy influence fetal development and health. *Psychoneuroendocrinology, 30*(8), 724–743.

Watkins, J. G. (1992). *Hypnoanalytic techniques: Clinical hypnosis.* New York, NY: Irvington.

Watkins, L. L., Connor, K. M., & Davidson, J. R. T. (2001). Effect of kava extract on vagal cardiac control in generalized anxiety disorder: preliminary findings. *Journal of Psychopharmacology, 15*(4), 283–286.

Wehrenberg, M. (2008). *The 10 best-ever anxiety management techniques: Understanding how your brain makes you anxious and what you can do to change it.* New York, NY: Norton.

Wiederhold, B. K., Jang, D. P., Kim, S. I., & Wiederhold, M. D. (2002). Physiological monitoring as an objective tool in virtual reality therapy. *CyberPsychology & Behavior, 5,* 77–82.

Yoo, S.-S., Gujar, N., Hu, P., Jolesz, F. A., Walker, M. P. (2007). The human emotional brain without sleep: A prefrontal amygdala disconnect. *Current Biology, 17*(20), 877–878.

Yoshimura, R., Ueda, N., Nakamura, J., Eto, S., Matsushita, M. (2002). Interaction between fluvoxamine and cotinine or caffeine. *Neuropsychobiology, 45,* 32–35.

Young, J. (2003). *Schema therapy.* New York, NY: Guilford Press.

Zur, O. (2006). Therapeutic boundaries and dual relationships in rural practice: Ethical, clinical and standard of care considerations. *Journal of Rural Community Psychology, 9*(1). Retrieved from http://www.zurinstitute.com/online/rural14.html

Index

Bourne, E., 204, 205

Brain Lock: Free Yourself from Obsessive-Compulsive Behavior, 166

breath
  attending to, 41–42
  shortness of, 27–28

breathing
  ABCs of, 58–59
  balloon breaths, 60

breathing words
  four square, 59
  mindful, 59

breathing in the light, 62–63

Burke, Edmund, 2

buspirone, 184–85
  in GAD management, 84

caffeine, avoidance of, 203, 206

carbohydrates, in enhancing resilience to anxiety, 205

CBGT. *see* cognitive behavioral group therapy (CBGT)

CBT. *see* cognitive behavioral therapy (CBT)

celebrating achievements, by therapist, 213–14

Center for Applied Cognitive Studies, 198

Cerny, J., 79

checkers, in OCD subtypes, 154

chronic stress, anxiety related to, 28–29

Clark, D., 91–92

cleaners, in OCD subtypes, 154

clomipramine, in OCD management, 175

Clutterers Anonymous, 174

cocaine, anxiety related to, 28

cognitive behavioral group therapy (CBGT), for SAD, 146

cognitive behavioral therapy (CBT)
  in anxiety disorders management, 39–40
  in GAD management, 79–81
  resources for, 217

cognitive statements, strengths and resources reinforced by, 120

cognitive therapy (CT)
  in anxiety disorders management, 34–36
  in GAD management, 76–79
  in PD management, 97–98
  in SAD management, 139
  in SPs management, 118–20

cold sweats, anxiety related to, 28

compliance, with physical exercise, 199–204

compulsions, in OCD, 163

Coping with Anxiety, 204

core beliefs, 76–77

corrective memories
  creating, 129–30
  for trauma-based SPs, 126–30

Corrigan, K., 91–92

countering negative self-appraisal, in SAD management, 146

Craig, G., 46

Craske, M.G., 97–98, 103

CT. *see* cognitive therapy (CT)

daily relaxation regimen, in PD management, 97

daily reminders to reinforce commitment, by therapist, 212–13

deepening phase, in hypnosis, 48

depth/insight-oriented therapy, in anxiety disorders management, 51

desensitization, systematic, 37, 121

desensitization hierarchy, 99

developmental influence, on genetic expression, 20–21

dialing down anxiety, 68–69

Dialing Down Anxiety, 211

diet, healthy. *see* healthy diet

drug(s). *see also specific types and* medication(s)
  anxiety related to, 27–28

dual perspective, in mindfulness, 105

early childhood experience, anxiety and, 22–23

EFT. *see* emotional freedom technique (EFT)

ego state, described, 83

ego state therapy, in GAD management, 83

eicosapentaenoic acid (EPA), 190

Eifert, G.H., 43, 104

1185 Park Avenue, 26–27
EMDR. *see* eye movement desensitization and reprocessing (EMDR)
emotional freedom technique (EFT)
in anxiety disorders management,
46–47
resources for, 218
empowerment, 214–216
environment
in anxiety, 20–21
phobias related to, 109–10
prenatal, 21–22
EPA. *see* eicosapentaenoic acid (EPA)
Erickson, M., 105, 144, 168
ERP. *see* exposure and response prevention (ERP)
escalation, panic attacks and, 90–93
everyday life, mindfulness in, 42–43
evidence-based therapies, in anxiety
disorders management, 56
Excitotoxins: The Taste That Kills, 208
exercise, 197–204
for beginners, 199–201
compliance with, 199–204
described, 197–98
resources for, 219–20
value of, 198–203
yoga, 201–2
exposure, auditory, 171–72
exposure and response prevention
(ERP), in OCD management,
161–65
exposure therapies
in anxiety disorders management,
36
in generalized SAD management,
139–42
graduated exposure in, 99–101
new frontier of, 125–26
in PD management, 99–103
in SP management, 120–26
in specific SAD management,
142–44
virtual reality in, 125–26
external focusing
in OCD management, 167–68
in SAD management, 146–47
eye movement desensitization and
reprocessing (EMDR)

in anxiety disorders management,
44–46
resources for, 218

fatty acids, omega-3, 189–90
FDA. *see* Food and Drug Administration (FDA)
fear, panic attacks and, 90–93
fear hierarchy, in OCD, 164
Feldon, L., 205
fight/flight response, panic attack and,
89–90
fish oil, 189–90
5,4,3,2,1 technique, in OCD management, 168
flooding, in anxiety disorders management, 37–39
Foa, E., 153, 171, 173
focusing, external, 146–47, 167–68
food(s), resilience to anxiety enhanced
by, 205
food allergies, anxiety related to, 28
Food and Drug Administration (FDA)
on kava kava, 193
on neutraceuticals, 195
Forsyth, J.P., 43, 104
four square breathing, 59
Fux, M., 192

GABA. *see* gamma aminobutyric acid
(GABA)
GABHS infection. *see* group A beta-
hemolytic streptococcal (GABHS)
infection
GAD. *see* generalized anxiety disorder
(GAD)
gamma aminobutyric acid (GABA),
191
Garano, L., 204, 205
GE. *see* graduated exposure (GE)
gender
as factor in GAD, 73
as factor in SPs, 116
generalized anxiety disorder (GAD),
70–85
acceptance of symptoms, 81
case example, 84–85
CBT for, 79–81
creation of "safe place" for, 75–76

Moran, K., 171
Mother Theresa, 6
muscle tension, for
    blood/injection/injury phobias,
    124–25

NaSSAs. *see* noradrenergic/specific
    serotonergic antidepressants
    (NaSSAs)
National Institute for Trial Advocacy,
    149
natural environment, phobias related
    to, 109–10
natural food substances. *see* neu-
    traceutical(s)
negative self-appraisal, countering of,
    146
neurofeedback
    in anxiety disorders management,
    53–54
    process of, 54
    resources for, 219
neutraceutical(s), 188–96, 219
    amino acids, 190–91
    cautions and concerns related to,
    194–96
    described, 188–89
    FDA on, 195
    fish oil, 189–90
    GABA, 191
    5-HTP, 190
    magnesium, 192–93
    medicinal plants, 193–94
    minerals, 192–93
    omega-3 fatty acids, 189–90
    theanine, 190–91
    vitamins, 191–92. *see also specific
    types and* vitamins
Nichols, M., 13
Nightmare on Elm Street, 110
non–evidence-based therapies, in anxi-
    ety disorders management, 56
noradrenergic/specific serotonergic
    antidepressants (NaSSAs), 183–84
Norton, P., 118, 185

obsessionals, pure, in OCD subtypes
    156–58
obsessive-compulsive disorder (OCD),

151–77
    ACT for, 169
    anxiety disorders vs., 158–59
    auditory exposure for, 171–72
    avoidance in, 163
    case examples, 175–77
    characteristics of, 153
    checkers, 154
    cleaners, 154
    compulsions in, 163
    described, 151–53
    ERP in, 161–65
    fear hierarchy in, 164
    GABHS infection and, 159
    hoarders, 155
    hoarding issues management in,
    173–75
    major depressive disorder and, 160
    medications for, 175, 186
    mindfulness for, 169–71
    orderers, 154–55
    overview of, 11–12
    postponement for, 172–73
    pure obsessionals, 156–58
    repeaters, 154
    Schwartz's four-step self-treatment
    method for, 166–69
    self-treatment in, 166–67
    SPs vs., 115
    therapeutic techniques and interven-
    tions, 161–75
    thinking ritualizers, 155–56
    Tourette's disorder and, 160
    treatment goals, 161
    treatment of, 161–75
    types of, 154–58
    washers, 154
    who gets it, 159–61
    worriers, 156–58
obsessive–compulsive personality
    disorder, 160
OCD. *see* obsessive–compulsive
    disorder (OCD)
omega-3 fatty acids, 189–90
orderers, in OCD subtypes, 154–55
overprotective parents, anxiety and, 25

palpitation(s), anxiety related to, 28
panic attack(s), 87–88

fear and escalation in, 90–93
fight/flight response in, 89–90
so-what question related to, 98
panic control treatment (PCT), in PD
    management, 101–3
panic disorder (PD), 86–107
    acceptance of, 104
    anticipatory anxiety in, 87, 93
    avoidance in, 87, 93–94
    case example, 107
    components of, 88–89
    CT for, 97–98
    daily relaxation regimen for, 97
    exposure therapies for, 99–103
    graduated exposure for, 99–101
    hallmarks of, 87–88
    major depressive disorder with, 105
    medications for, 106–7, 186
    mindfulness for, 103–6
    overview of, 10
    panic attacks in, 87
    panic control treatment for, 101–3
    psychoeducation for, 96–97
    SPs vs., 114–15
    treatment goals, 95–96
    treatment of, 95–107
    treatment techniques and interven-
        tions, 96–107
    who gets it, 94–95
parasympathetic nervous system, 89
parent(s), overprotective, 25
parenting, anxious, 25
Passiflora incarnata, 194
passionflower, 194
Patton, G., 216
PCT. *see* panic control treatment (PCT)
PD. *see* panic disorder (PD)
Pedrick, C., 174
persistence, of therapist, 212–13
Pert, C., 179
phobia(s)
    animal-related, 110–11
    blood/injection/injury, 111–12, 124–25
    natural environment-related, 109–10
    situational, 109
    specific. *see* specific phobias (SPs)
PMR. *see* progressive muscle relax-
    ation (PMR)
polygenic transmission, 20

post-hypnotic suggestion, in hypnosis,
    49
postponement, in OCD management,
    172–73
post-traumatic stress disorder (PTSD),
    SPs vs., 115
practice, of therapy session material,
    209–16
"Practice Makes Perfect: There's No
    Shortcut to Lasting Change," 209,
    212
prenatal environment, effects on anxi-
    ety, 21–22
progressive muscle relaxation (PMR),
    63–65
    for GAD, 74–75
progressive relaxation, 63–65
pruning, 22
psychoeducation, 211–12
    in anxiety disorders management,
        33–34
    in PD management, 96–97
Psychotherapy Networker, 209
PTSD. *see* post-traumatic stress disor-
    der (PTSD)
pure obsessionals, in OCD subtypes,
    156–58

quetiapine, 186

Razzhavaikina, T., 212
reality, virtual, 125–26
reattribute, in OCD management,
    166–67
Rechtshaffen, S., 29
recovery, hope for, 17
refocus, in OCD management, 167
regression, age-related, 126–29
relabel, in OCD management, 166
relaxation, progressive, 63–65
relaxation techniques, 57–69
    ABCs of breathing, 58–59
    in anxiety disorders management,
        40–41
    autogenics, 65–67
    balloon breaths, 60
    breathing words, 59–60
    dialing down anxiety, 68–69
    four square breathing, 59